I0869072

"Dr. Tony Merida's *Exalting Jesus in Acts* is like having a master preacher/expositor sitting alongside you in the study. This is a commentary by a preacher for preachers. It's exegetically accurate, pastorally keen, and homiletically powerful. In perusing these pages, one not only learns about Acts, but better yet, one is apprenticed into the way of preaching the Scriptures where sermons faithfully and accurately testify about Christ (John 5:39). I can't recommend Merida's offering enough."

Dr. Yancey C. Arrington, teaching pastor, Clear Creek Community Church, Houston, Texas

"Effective pastoral preaching is consistently distinguished by three overarching qualities: (1) accuracy (fidelity to the sacred text, including its Christocentric implications); (2) clarity (pulpit obscurity undermines biblical potency); and (3) simplicity (an extraordinarily difficult task to which very few expositors give necessary attention). *Exalting Jesus in Acts* by Dr. Tony Merida meets these criteria and is a wonderful gift to those called to strengthen the church by the means of preaching and teaching. Without getting entangled in exegetical minutia, Tony wonderfully summarizes, illustrates, and applies what is arguably the most exciting book in the New Testament."

Arturo G. Azurdia III, senior teaching pastor, Trinity Church of Portland and associate professor of pastoral and church ministry, Western Seminary, Portland, Oregon

"Tony Merida has written a learned and eminently practical commentary on Acts for preachers. Tony leads readers through the text like a wise tour guide and then gives preachers tips on how to make the text sing and sting! This is a commentary on Acts by a preacher and for the preacher. Few books on Acts will be as helpful as this one."

Dr. Michael F. Bird, PhD, University of Queensland, lecturer in theology at Ridley College, Melbourne, Australia

"Dr. Tony Merida's commentary on Acts is a perfect mix of exegetical insight and practical application for preachers and laypersons alike. It can, therefore, serve as a valuable source for sermon preparation as well as personal enrichment."

Joseph R. Dodson, PhD, Aberdeen, associate professor of biblical studies, Ouachita Baptist University

"As we seek a church-planting movement in North America and around the world, the church's inspired story of gospel impact in Christianity's early days provides an essential model. Tony Merida's commentary on the book of Acts gives us impressive scholarship and boldly spotlights the text in a way that will help mobilize churches to complete God's mission both locally and around the world. This will be an outstanding resource for pastors as they prepare Jesus-centered sermons on the book of Acts."

Kevin Ezell, president, North American Mission Board, SBC

"The Christ-Centered Exposition series is my preferred commentary for careful exegesis, relevant illustrations, and faithful application. *Exalting Jesus in Acts* by Tony Merida typifies this approach. Merida has done the heavy lifting by subdividing the book into sections that capture the author's intended meaning. It is especially helpful how he spells out the main theme at the beginning of each chapter and then highlights preaching points throughout. I am certain this will be your go-to commentary for the book of Acts in the years to come."

Robby Gallaty, senior pastor, Long Hollow Baptist Church, Hendersonville, Tennessee

"Much has been written on the book of Acts, but this commentary makes its own valuable contribution for the pastor. Tony Merida carefully handles the text of Acts without missing the excitement of Acts. He faithfully expounds the truth of Scripture without forgetting the people to whom we preach. And as he traces the mission of the gospel in Acts, he never loses sight of the glory of the Savior that the gospel announces."

C.J. Mahaney, Senior Pastor, Sovereign Grace Church of Louisville

"One of the challenges people face when studying the book of Acts is trying to figure out what is prescriptive and what is descriptive, especially when it comes to application. What Tony does in this homiletical commentary is provide a healthy understanding of the two while remaining faithful to the author's intent. The book of Acts tells incredible stories of how the gospel moved from region to region as it transformed the hearts and lives of people. Tony brilliantly takes you through each adventure and at the same time shows you the how the golden thread, which is Jesus, runs through the entire book. This is a commentary you want by your side as you navigate through the book of Acts."

One Mokgatle, senior pastor of Rooted Fellowship, Pretoria, South Africa

"Combining vivid, memorable examples and illustrations with careful exegesis, Christ-exalting explanations, and practical application, Tony Merida gives us a sure guide to the book of Acts. If readers will read this commentary reflectively, devoting time in the study questions that follow each chapter to godly introspection and missional resolve, then they will find their lives reflecting their Lord and Savior more fully, and they will find themselves able not only to edify themselves but to edify others."

Philip Moore, European director of Acts 29

"Tony Merida is one of the best preachers of our generation. He knows God's Word, and he knows how to bring God's Word with authority. Merida speaks not just to the mind or the heart or the will, but to the soul. This commentary on Acts will equip you to understand how Jesus worked through his people in the earliest days of our church. This book will also show us how to carry the gospel in an age that looks more and more like the culture of the book of Acts. That means we need the power of the book of Acts. Read and prepare."

Russell Moore, director of the Public Theology Project at *Christianity Today*

"Tony Merida has given us a highly readable and engaging commentary that scores high marks on careful exegesis and Christocentric exposition along with accessible illustrations and relevant applications. These of course are the aims of The Christ Centered Exposition Commentary. He has been careful to respect both the genre of the book and its goal to inspire the church to be a marching missional infantry based on the historic truth of her foundations. I highly recommend it to pastors and studious lay Christians."

Femi Osunnuyi, lead pastor, City Church, Lagos, Nigeria

"An experienced preacher and a lucid thinker, Merida has given us a pastor's dream commentary. It is scholarly without being unwieldy, clear without being reductionistic, and practical without ignoring contextual nuance. In fact, it is because Merida does such a good reading of the text on its own terms that it comes alive in his hands, with Christ as its radiant center. The inclusion of reflection and discussion questions at the end of each section makes this a robust resource for Bible studies as well. This will be a gift not only to preachers but to the congregations they serve."

Glenn Packiam, associate senior pastor, New Life Church, Colorado Springs, Colorado

"As always, Tony delivers fresh biblical insight with compelling conviction and exegetical clarity. This commentary on Acts is a superlative work for all. The consistent application of the text to the local church will be a tremendous resource for God's people."

Kevin Peck, lead pastor, The Austin Stone Community Church, Austin, Texas

"Tony Merida is one of my favorite pastor-scholars. All of his academic work is in service of the church, and his pastoral preaching is plain spoken but undergirded by faithful scholarship. Merida understands the Christian life as spiritual warfare and the book of Acts as a God-inspired field manual for our continuing Great Commission gospel mission. Merida recognizes God as the ultimate author of both history and Scripture. Thus, he gives concentrated attention to the unique contribution of Luke as the author of Acts but never loses sight of the place of Acts in the Christ-centered canonical whole of Scripture."

David E. Prince, pastor of preaching and vision, Ashland Avenue Baptist Church, Lexington, Kentucky

"Luke closes out his Gospel to Theophilus with the believers in the temple praising God. Now he picks up the story and explains what happens next. So does Tony Merida. In a style Bible teachers, pastors, and scholars will want to read, this commentary has the mind of a scholar and the heart of a pastor. I love his outlines, which, in the words of Arthur Golding's translation of The Sermons of J. Calvin in 1583, are 'grist for the preacher's mill.' Read it, study it; but more importantly, let it study you. Tony has mined for gold and found it. You will be richer after you've read it as well."

Dr. Ken Whitten, senior pastor, Idlewild Baptist Church, Lutz, Florida

CHRIST-CENTERED

Exposition

NT / COMMENTARY

FEATURING CSB

AUTHOR Tony Merida

SERIES EDITORS David Platt, Daniel L. Akin, and Tony Merida

CHRIST-CENTERED

Exposition

EXALTING JESUS IN

ACTS

HOLMAN®
REFERENCE
BRENTWOOD, TENNESSEE

B&H Publishing Group
Brentwood, Tennessee

ISBN: 978-1-4336-4709-3

Dewey Decimal Classification: 220.7
Subject Heading: BIBLE. O.T. ACTS—
COMMENTARIES\JESUS CHRIST

Printed in the United States of America

9 10 11 12 13 14 • 28 27 26 25 24

SERIES DEDICATION

Dedicated to Adrian Rogers and John Piper. They have taught us to love the gospel of Jesus Christ, to preach the Bible as the inerrant Word of God, to pastor the church for which our Savior died, and to have a passion to see all nations gladly worship the Lamb.

—David Platt, Tony Merida, and Danny Akin
March 2013

CONTENTS

ACKNOWLEDGMENTS

This commentary is evidence of God's grace. I wouldn't have completed this book apart from the Spirit's strength and the help and encouragement of many people.

My "dear companion," Kimberly, thank you for being my wife! I can't imagine life without you. May the Lord grant us much grace as we seek to magnify him together.

My children—James, Joshua, Angela, Victoria, and Jana—thank you for making my life so adventurous and exciting! I pray you will grow up to make much of Jesus, like the believers in the book of Acts.

To the elders at Imago Dei Church, thank you for your encouragement. I treasure our friendships and partnership in sharing the gospel. May the Lord use us to shepherd the flock faithfully.

Members at Imago Dei, you're a joy to pastor! What an incredible blessing it was to work through the book of Acts with you! May the Lord help us take the gospel to the ends of the earth.

Cody Cunningham, thank you for your hard work in reading through this document and providing editorial improvements. May the Lord bless you as you continue your studies.

Catherine Ridley, thank you for your help with the bibliography. May the Lord make his face to shine upon you.

Ben Palka, thank you for your hard work on parts of this commentary. You're a wonderful brother, a dear friend, and a fine expositor. May the Lord use you mightily in the years ahead.

Joey Dodson, thank you for your encouragement. I thank God that you took your sabbatical in my neighborhood while I was expounding Acts! Your insights and support helped me and ministered to me. May the Lord continue to bless you as you minister the Word in your home, in the academy, and in the church.

To all those cited in this commentary, I also say thank you for your labor in the Word. I couldn't have written this book without standing on the shoulders of so many faithful expositors.

And finally, risen King, Jesus, I thank you. Apart from you, we have no life. Apart from you, we can do nothing. Please use this commentary to build up your blood-bought church and to advance your never-ending kingdom.

SERIES INTRODUCTION

Augustine said, "Where Scripture speaks, God speaks." The editors of the Christ-Centered Exposition Commentary series believe that where God speaks, the pastor must speak. God speaks through His written Word. We must speak from that Word. We believe the Bible is God breathed, authoritative, inerrant, sufficient, understandable, necessary, and timeless. We also affirm that the Bible is a Christ-centered book; that is, it contains a unified story of redemptive history of which Jesus is the hero. Because of this Christ-centered trajectory that runs from Genesis 1 through Revelation 22, we believe the Bible has a corresponding global-missions thrust. From beginning to end, we see God's mission as one of making worshipers of Christ from every tribe and tongue worked out through this redemptive drama in Scripture. To that end we must preach the Word.

In addition to these distinct convictions, the Christ-Centered Exposition Commentary series has some distinguishing characteristics. First, this series seeks to display exegetical accuracy. What the Bible says is what we want to say. While not every volume in the series will be a verse-by-verse commentary, we nevertheless desire to handle the text carefully and explain it rightly. Those who teach and preach bear the heavy responsibility of saying what God has said in His Word and declaring what God has done in Christ. We desire to handle God's Word faithfully, knowing that we must give an account for how we have fulfilled this holy calling (Jas 3:1).

Second, the Christ-Centered Exposition Commentary series has pastors in view. While we hope others will read this series, such as parents, teachers, small-group leaders, and student ministers, we desire to provide a commentary busy pastors will use for weekly preparation of biblically faithful and gospel-saturated sermons. This series is not academic in nature. Our aim is to present a readable and pastoral style of commentary. We believe this aim will serve the church of the Lord Jesus Christ.

Third, we want the Christ-Centered Exposition Commentary series to be known for the inclusion of helpful illustrations and theologically driven applications. Many commentaries offer no help in illustrations, and few offer any kind of help in application. Often those that do offer illustrative material and application unfortunately give little serious attention to the text. While giving ourselves primarily to explanation, we also hope to serve readers by providing inspiring and illuminating illustrations coupled with timely and timeless application.

Finally, as the name suggests, the editors seek to exalt Jesus from every book of the Bible. In saying this, we are not commending wild allegory or fanciful typology. We certainly believe we must be constrained to the meaning intended by the divine Author himself, the Holy Spirit of God. However, we also believe the Bible has a messianic focus, and our hope is that the individual authors will exalt Christ from particular texts. Luke 24:25-27,44-47 and John 5:39,46 inform both our hermeneutics and our homiletics. Not every author will do this the same way or have the same degree of Christ-centered emphasis. That is fine with us. We believe faithful exposition that is Christ centered is not monolithic. We do believe, however, that we must read the whole Bible as Christian Scripture. Therefore, our aim is both to honor the historical particularity of each biblical passage and to highlight its intrinsic connection to the Redeemer.

The editors are indebted to the contributors of each volume. The reader will detect a unique style from each writer, and we celebrate these unique gifts and traits. While distinctive in their approaches, the authors share a common characteristic in that they are pastoral theologians. They love the church, and they regularly preach and teach God's Word to God's people. Further, many of these contributors are younger voices. We think these new, fresh voices can serve the church well, especially among a rising generation that has the task of proclaiming the Word of Christ and the Christ of the Word to the lost world.

We hope and pray this series will serve the body of Christ well in these ways until our Savior returns in glory. If it does, we will have succeeded in our assignment.

David Platt
Daniel L. Akin
Tony Merida
Series Editors
February 2013

Acts

Spirit-Empowered Witnesses

ACTS 1:1-11

Main Idea: Luke begins his second volume by highlighting the ongoing ministry of the ascended Christ that continues through his Spirit-empowered witnesses.

I. How Should We Study Acts?
- A. Not like cold scholars
- B. Not like casual admirers
- C. Like committed soldiers

II. Luke's Message Continues (1:1-2).

III. Jesus's Ministry Continues (1:1-11).

IV. The Church's Witness Continues (1:8).
- A. The people who witness: all believers
- B. The path of a witness: suffering
- C. The power of a witness: the Holy Spirit
- D. The people in need of a witness: the nations
- E. The passion of a witness: Jesus

Multiple times I've been asked, "How old is your church?" Since our congregation is a church plant, people often raise this question, and I have to do the math in my head to answer them. To simplify matters, and to teach a bit of church history, I have started to respond by saying, "We are about two thousand years old!" You see, the account of the early church recorded in the book of Acts is *our* history. The people mentioned in that book are our brothers and sisters.

Of course, the people of God did not originate in the first century. God has always had a people for himself—a people to whom he displays his glory, and a people through whom he displays his glory (to paraphrase my friend, Steve Timmis). Nevertheless, the book of Acts marks a pivotal turning point in redemptive history. Acts describes the history of the mission of the early church, and because we are part of the church's history and mission, the book is of great importance to us.

My children are currently studying United States history, so we are going over the facts and details of the American Revolution, the early presidents, and our founding documents. Learning about these topics is important because we are Americans. American history is our history. But as vital as learning about the founding of our nation is, it is even more important that my children understand church history. It is our spiritual history, a family history.

This history recorded in the book of Acts covers a relatively short period of time. Commentator Michael Green says,

> Three crucial decades in world history. That is all it took. In the years between AD 33 and 64 a new movement was born. In those thirty years it got sufficient growth and credibility to become the largest religion the world has ever seen and to change the lives of hundreds of millions of people. It has spread into every corner of the globe and has more than two billion putative adherents. It has had an indelible impact on civilization, on culture, on education, on medicine, on freedom and of course on the lives of countless people worldwide. And the seedbed for all this, the time when it took decisive root, was in these three decades. It all began with a dozen men and a handful of women: and then the Spirit came. (*Thirty Years That Changed the World,* 7)

So much happened in thirty short years! It makes me ask, What may God do through a modern local group of believers throughout the same period of time?

How Should We Study Acts?

Because Acts involves history, I should clarify what a proper approach to studying history entails. Generally speaking, three types of people study the past: scholars, admirers, and soldiers.

Not like Cold Scholars

While some scholars are no doubt also committed soldiers, anyone who wants to study Acts needs to reject the posture of what I'll call a *cold scholar.* Our purpose in launching into the book of Acts is not merely to analyze dates, places, and people as if we were cramming for a test. Instead, our goal is to allow the message of this book to transform our hearts and lead us to a mission. We must not study the Bible as people scrutinizing a book for insights into the distant past. Rather, we should approach it as people who are desperate to see the God about whom we read move mightily in the present.

Not like Casual Admirers

Some who study history are more hobbyists than scholars; they have a casual interest in historical events that may lead them to read a piece on the Civil War, World War II, or the New York Yankees purely for pleasure. Such people may visit museums and even collect antiques and memorabilia related to their interests, but casual admirers rarely dive deeply into the contents of history. Seldom do they allow the events they read about to change them in the present. We, however, must move beyond merely admiring things about the history of the early church. We must not read the Bible lightly or scan it as if gathering insights to add to a mental museum. We should not be casual admirers but committed soldiers.

Like Committed Soldiers

Good soldiers are known to study history, and they do so to become better soldiers. Good soldiers know there is much to be done. And they see themselves—and we must view ourselves—as continuing a mission. Acts is not merely the history of the early church; it's the history of *the mission* of the early church. And we are to continue that mission. So let us dive into the contents of the book that we may better serve our King.

We need to keep a few principles in mind. First, we should read Acts in light of the entire Bible, with the teachings of both the Old and New Testaments in mind. A failure to allow the whole Bible to help us rightly interpret the book could lead to some serious problems. Second, we should read Acts in light of Luke's Gospel in particular because Dr. Luke wrote both books. Third, we must read Acts in light of its genre. It is a historical book, which means that while in it Luke describes the events of the early church, he does not always commend its practices to us. For instance, I don't think we should read of Paul's "healing handkerchiefs" and assume we need to start a handkerchief ministry! Rather, we must allow the whole of the Bible to help us make interpretations and applications for the modern world. We've got to be sensible soldiers, honoring the dual authorship of this book: it was penned by Luke and inspired by the Holy Spirit.

Since Acts is the second volume by Luke, the book opens as a story already in progress. There is also an abrupt ending to Acts, leaving us with the correct impression that even today the church is living out the mission. As we look at the opening verses of this book, we'll see that three acts are continuing: the message, the ministry, and the witness of

Christ's church. We will look back on the opening section throughout our studies in Acts.

Luke's Message Continues

ACTS 1:1-2

Luke begins his second volume by dedicating it to Theophilus. Luke addresses the same recipient in the prologue to his Gospel. That Theophilus is called "most honorable" (Luke 1:3) implies that he was a Roman official (cf. Acts 24:2; 26:25). And based on Luke's intention of providing more "certainty" to Theophilus (Luke 1:4), he seems to have been a Christian seeker or perhaps a young believer. It is also possible that he gave financial assistance to Luke, allowing his author-friend the means to research and report on the astonishing work God was doing through followers of Jesus Christ.

What do we know about Luke? We know he was a doctor (Col 4:14). As such, he would have been educated and presumably wealthy. He made trips with Paul and was loyal to him, even while the apostle was in prison (Acts 28; 2 Tim 4:11). I can imagine that his medical skills came in handy; Paul regularly needed a doctor after all those beatings he took.

Luke was also a prolific writer. He recorded for us the stories of the prodigal son and the good Samaritan. And his work shows a remarkable depth of precise historical research. Luke traveled and carefully interviewed those with key roles in Christ's life. (In his quest to collect details, he was more like Indiana Jones than a history professor!) He investigated and reported on a vast amount of information. In fact, Luke-Acts is comprised of more material than all of Paul's letters combined, and since Luke was a companion of Paul, it's clear he was involved with writing the majority of the New Testament.

Yet Luke records virtually nothing about his own life. This is a sign of humility. He does not boast about his relationship with Paul, nor does he go into detail about his own story. Instead, in Luke-Acts we read about the man's passion for the life-changing gospel, his sensitivity to the disadvantaged, his heart for prayer, and his concern for the Gentiles. Each of these characteristics reflects the church in Antioch (11:19-30), Luke's hometown according to an ancient second-century document (*Anti-Maricon Prologue to Luke*).

All of this history reminds us that Christianity is not built on man's speculation or on someone's wild imaginings but on historical revelation.

Jesus Christ really did live. He died. He rose bodily. He appeared to hundreds of witnesses. He taught for forty days before ascending. Luke records details about the real life and ministry of Jesus as well as insights into the beginnings of the early church. This is supremely important. While the world wouldn't need a historical Buddha to have Buddhism, it must have a historical Christ to have genuine Christianity. And we do! Further, if Jesus is dead, then Christianity is dead. But he's alive! Historical facts like these serve as wonderful faith builders for Christians and as important apologetic arguments that are useful as we commend the faith to present-day Theophiluses.

Luke says in his Gospel that he wrote about all that Jesus "began to do and teach." In Acts, Luke writes about the same thing: the ministry of Jesus—which continued after his ascension and is still in progress today. The title of the book could be "The Acts of the Lord Jesus through the Apostles and the Church by the Power of the Spirit." After all, the church is continuing the ministry of Jesus. So Luke not only has a *historical* purpose behind his writing efforts but also *ministry* purposes.

Additionally, Luke's second volume appears to have a *political* purpose. He seems concerned about the Roman attitude toward Christianity. Luke, then, plays the peacemaker. He illustrates that Christianity is militarily harmless by showing that some of the Roman officials, such as Cornelius, became Christians; that Christians were legally innocent (the Romans could find no fault in Jesus or in the apostles); and that Christianity was lawful (it was not a new religion but a fulfillment of Judaism).

Finally, Luke clearly has an *evangelistic* emphasis. He not only writes about the good news and Christ's converting power, but he also includes some twenty sermons in Acts, which occupy around one-fourth of the book! Luke surely wanted to win his readers to Christ, and he also underscores the centrality of proclamation in world evangelization. The Christian faith, our faith, is a heraldic faith. Luke shows what led to the explosive growth of Christianity: gospel proclamation.

Jesus's Ministry Continues

ACTS 1:1-11

Luke refers to Jesus in each of the opening eleven verses. This is a fitting opening, for Luke is preparing us to see how Jesus's ministry continues through the church.

Teaching and Doing

Luke reminds us that Jesus's ministry involves both *words* and *deeds*. He refers to all that Jesus began to both "do" and "teach" (1:1). During his earthly lifetime Jesus taught the disciples, and then after his resurrection the risen Christ taught the disciples about the kingdom of God for forty days. What a magnificent forty-day Bible conference that must have been!

In verses 7-8 Jesus responds to a question about whether he will restore Israel. He essentially tells the disciples, "*That's* none of your business" (v. 7), and then proceeds to tell them, "*This* is your business," as he issues to them the mission of bearing witness to him throughout the world (v. 8).

Jesus was all about teaching and doing. Jesus's deeds illustrated his words, and his words explained his deeds. He left the church with the same ministry, intending that we let others see our good deeds that glorify the Father (Matt 5:16) and helping others understand the good news that leads to eternal life.

The words and works of Jesus go together. In the Gospels we see Jesus performing various merciful and miraculous deeds. We also see him teaching with astonishing authority. Similarly, in the book of Acts, we see the church caring for physical needs (e.g., 3:1-10) while also relentlessly preaching the good news (e.g., 3:20) with the Spirit's help. In Romans Paul reflected on his own ministry passion, the Christ-empowered ministry of word and deed among the nations (Rom 15:18-19).

Many things do not belong together. I recently drove by one of those strange places that has two fast-food chains in the same building; they have side-by-side kitchens but divergent menus. The scents wafting from the partnering kitchens combined to form one terrible stink. These two restaurants should never have been joined. The ministry of deeds and words, on the other hand, go together. And when done by the power of the Spirit for the good of others and the glory of the King, they produce a pleasing aroma of worship to God.

The ministry of Jesus is continuing in the book of Acts. But are we faithfully taking part in this mission?

Response to Christ's Resurrection

The ascension of Jesus is in some ways like Elijah passing off the mantle to Elisha. The disciples had been with the greater Elijah, and now Jesus was giving them the privilege and responsibility of doing his work and proclaiming his Word after his home going.

Importantly, this mighty ascension of Jesus was preceded by a transitional period of forty days. We know from the Gospels and from 1 Corinthians 15 that he appeared to more than five hundred people after he rose from the dead. They saw him, touched him, and learned from him; they *knew* he had truly been resurrected. The ministry of Jesus continues, in fact, because Jesus really is alive!

Christ's ascension also included an exaltation. In verses 2 and 11 we read that Jesus was "taken up." Verse 9 says, "A cloud took him out of their sight" (v. 9). This cloud reminds us of Daniel's vision of the Son of Man (Dan 7), of Jesus's transfiguration (Matt 17), and of the exodus cloud (Exod 13). The whole sight is one of magnificent glory. This glorious exaltation demonstrated Jesus's promotion from earth to heaven, and it prefigured the manner of his return—visible, glorious, and climactic.

Some of the early church fathers viewed Psalm 24 as being ultimately fulfilled in the ascension of the totally righteous Lord Jesus and his entrance into heaven. The psalmist says,

> *Lift up your heads, you gates!*
> *Rise up, ancient doors!*
> *Then the King of glory will come in.*
> *Who is this King of glory?*
> *The LORD, strong and mighty,*
> *the LORD, mighty in battle.*
> *Lift up your heads, you gates!*
> *Rise up, ancient doors!*
> *Then the King of glory will come in.*
> *Who is he, this King of glory?*
> *The LORD of Armies,*
> *he is the King of glory.* (Ps 24:7-10)

If this was the heavenly reaction to Jesus's ascension, how did the disciples react to it on earth? With *bewilderment.* Like children watching a floating balloon drifting skyward, the disciples were enamored with the sight. But soon just thinking about the glorious scene filled them with *worship* and *joy* (Luke 24:52), and they returned to Jerusalem in *obedience* to Jesus's words. Our response to the ascended King should mirror theirs: we should joyfully worship and obey him.

The risen King's ministry continues because the King is not dead. It continues because we have his Spirit and his Word. It continues because the kingdom of God is here, and it is still advancing through his Spirit-empowered witnesses.

Acts outlines how Jesus advances his Word among the nations, and the plan is summarized in 1:8. In chapters 1–7 the Lord's Word spreads throughout Jerusalem. In 8–12 the Lord's Word spreads in Judea and Samaria. In 13–20 the Lord's Word spreads to the ends of the earth (in Asia and Greece). And in chapters 21–28 the Lord's Word spreads throughout Rome.

The Church's Witness Continues

ACTS 1:8

In verse 7 the disciples demonstrated a particular interest in and misunderstanding about the restoration of Israel. Jesus directs them to the global nature of his kingdom and to their part in the mission as he calls them to be his witnesses. The disciples were too limited in their thinking. So Jesus rocks their world as he tells them that the plan is for them to cross not just geographical barriers but cultural barriers as well. Jesus blows up any triumphalistic ideas they have as he calls them his witnesses—or more literally, his martyrs. The way of the kingdom is one of suffering before glory.

These believers were to proclaim the person and work of the risen Christ (Luke 24:44-49) as taught by Jesus and foretold in the Old Testament. They were to proclaim how Christ accomplished the ancient prophecy of crushing the head of the serpent, Satan, providing a way for sinners to be reconciled with the Father. Importantly, we as modern disciples of Jesus participate in enjoying this message of life with the first disciples. But they were witnesses in another sense: they actually saw Jesus's death, resurrection, and ascension (Acts 2:32; 3:15; 10:39; 22:15). While we do not enjoy this privilege, we are the recipients of eyewitness testimony that comes to us in the form of the writings of the disciples. Now, like them, we have the privilege of bearing witness about the good news of the Messiah to everyone. Let us consider five aspects of a witness.

The People Who Witness: All Believers

One of the great gifts of Pentecost is that all believers can now speak for God (2:14-21). In a sense all believers are prophets. No believer is a mere fan but a player! The apostles certainly led the church, but the gospel advanced largely through the words and deeds of unordained and uneducated people—informal missionaries. The church today, in fact, desperately needs to recover this practice. The only difference in a believer sitting in his or her American home and a foreign missionary on the field is *location*, not *identity*. Every Christian is a missionary. And so each of us should ask, Where do I serve? To whom do I minister?

The Path of a Witness: Suffering

To follow the Lamb involves suffering. In several places in the Gospels, Jesus told the disciples they would suffer (e.g., Luke 21:10-19; John 15:18-27). In the book of Acts, we find that they indeed did suffer. Crossing cultural barriers and standing up in the face of opposition requires sacrifice. First we see that there was an escalation of persecution in Jerusalem; it moved from threats to floggings to martyrdom. A theme of suffering continues through the rest of the book, and it continues into our day as the evil one rages against the church (Rev 12). Even this, however, is part of God's ordained means of advancing the gospel—dedicated believers share his truth wherever they go, in spite of what they encounter. The gospel never triumphs apart from some measure of sacrifice. Someone has to sacrifice (and sometimes die) so that others may live.

The Power of a Witness: The Holy Spirit

Fortunately, we are not on our own in the mission Jesus assigned us, for Luke reminds us once again of the Spirit's power (cf. Luke 24:49). We must, in fact, be clothed with power to be faithful witnesses. Having received essential teaching, the disciples would eventually be given the essential power required in witnesses of Jesus. The ordinary people of God, equipped with the Word of God, empowered by the Spirit of God, dedicated to the Son of God, can accomplish the mission of God. Sharing the right message is only half the matter. We must also be personally reliant on the Spirit of God.

We see two marks of the Spirit's work in the disciples: *boldness* and *the magnification of Jesus*. References to Spirit-empowered boldness appear through the book (e.g., 4:29; 28:31). This is how Peter could stand at Pentecost and preach so courageously after cowering in the presence of a little girl just weeks earlier. Further, we are reminded that the Spirit purposes to glorify Christ (John 16:14). Peter has a spotlight ministry that always focuses attention on Jesus. This is a great reminder that when people are living a Spirit-empowered life, their thoughts and words will be centered on Christ, not self (see Acts 4:20).

The Peoples in Need of a Witness: The Nations

Christians have no tribal deity. We have a Savior who loves and died for the nations! That means that we must relinquish any prejudices that keep us from sharing him faithfully. We must repent of any ethnocentrism or unconcern for unreached peoples. Jesus sent ordinary people *to the nations,* just as he sends us.

The Passion of a Witness: Jesus

A zeal for the kingdom comes only when we have a passion for the King. As these disciples gazed into heaven in astonishment of Jesus's glory, and as they later received Jesus's promise of the Spirit's power, they were enamored with Jesus. And we should have a similar attitude toward him. Because to phrase things negatively, little love for the King produces little zeal for the King's mission.

May the Spirit deepen our love for this global Savior as we seek to understand and apply the message of Acts. Let us pray for Spirit-empowered boldness, for a love for all the diverse people groups around the world, and ultimately for hearts enthralled with the King of kings.

Reflect and Discuss

1. What are some ways people react to the idea of studying history? How should we study Acts?
2. What do you find most striking about the life of Luke?
3. Of what significance is Theophilus?
4. What were some of Luke's purposes for writing Acts?
5. Why do you think so many sermons/speeches appear in Acts?
6. How does Jesus's ministry continue in the church today?
7. How does the ascension of Jesus encourage believers?
8. Who should bear witness to Jesus? Why should they?
9. What does Acts 1:8 suggest about ethnic diversity and the value of people groups around the world?
10. What about Acts 1:8 encourages you most? Why?

How to Discern the Will of God

ACTS 1:12-26

Main Idea: The first major event after the ascension of Jesus, when the apostles and disciples convened to choose a replacement for Judas, teaches much about discerning God's will for our lives.

I. Choosing Judas's Replacement (1:12-26)

II. Make Decisions in View of God's Plan of Redemption.

A. What are the immediate ramifications for the gospel?

B. What are the eternal ramifications for the gospel?

III. Distinguish between God's Revealed Will and God's Concealed Will.

IV. Start with God's Revealed Will.

A. Trust the Bible as your authority.

B. Let the Bible interpret your life.

C. Do what the Bible says.

V. Look for God's Concealed Will through the Lens of God's Revealed Will.

A. Gather all the information.

B. Seek God in prayer.

C. As you trust in God's sovereignty, make a decision and go with it.

Do you have any important decisions to make? If so, do you want to know what God's will is regarding those decisions? Chances are you will answer both questions with an emphatic *yes!* You probably know other people who are faced with decisions as well. Some will consider adopting children. Some will consider changing jobs this year or relocating to another city, state, or country. Some will decide where to go to college or graduate school. Some will consider making major purchases like a home or a car or a business. Some face the prospect of getting married. Others will need to determine whether God wants them to pull up roots and go to a mission field overseas. And the list of possible decisions people face continues.[1]

---

[1] Jim Shaddix originally delivered this exposition at our local church.

Most of us make discovering God's will more complicated than it really is! The Father wants you to know his will about important decisions in your life, so he provides guidance in his Word. After Jesus ascended to heaven, his followers needed to know who was supposed to fill the apostolic office vacated by Judas, who committed suicide after he betrayed Jesus. The way they approached that decision is significant for two reasons: it had huge ramifications for the future of Christ's kingdom, and it provided a helpful model for the way his followers approach weighty decisions. Those two things must go together—finding God's will in decision making and doing so in view of advancing Christ's kingdom.

Choosing Judas's Replacement

ACTS 1:12-26

Luke has purposed in Luke and Acts to record details about the real life and ministry of Jesus as well as the beginnings of the early church. While Luke shows that Christianity is founded on the historical resurrection, he also demonstrates that those who proclaimed the resurrection were trustworthy. After his crucifixion and death, the Lord Jesus "presented himself alive to [his disciples] by many convincing proofs, appearing to them over a period of forty days and speaking about the kingdom of God" (v. 3). Jesus commanded them "not to leave Jerusalem, but to wait for the Father's promise" (v. 4). The disciples and apostles, along with Jesus's mother and half brothers, obediently returned to Jerusalem to wait and pray (vv. 12-14). The lives of these individuals had been changed by an encounter with Jesus, and they were committed to him and his mission.

Luke lists the eleven apostles by name (v. 13), helping readers understand Peter's imminent speech (vv. 16-22). Jesus previously appointed twelve apostles, corresponding to the twelve sons of Jacob, the tribal leaders of Israel. For Peter, the apostolic number of twelve had to be restored, as the true Israel needed to be complete. Israel was suddenly entering a new era in redemptive history. The eleven apostles thus went into the upper room and were in consensus with Mary and the brothers of Jesus as they "united in prayer" (v. 14). Luke will develop the importance of prayer throughout Acts.

Luke highlights a moment in which Peter stood up and spoke from the Psalms about God's providence over Judas's betrayal and God's command for Judas to be replaced (vv. 15-16). After the resurrection of Jesus, Peter realized that all of the Scriptures testify about Jesus. Here is another example of how the apostles were clearly Christ centered in their interpretation of the Scriptures. Citing Psalms 69:25 and 109:8, Peter applied the psalmist's judgment on a wicked man as being repeated in his own day—having happened even more literally regarding the fate of Judas than in the case of David's adversaries. As the treasonous men in Psalms 69 and 109 rejected the friendship and blessing of King David, even more so had Judas rejected the friendship and blessing of King Jesus.

Peter defines qualifications for the replacement apostle. The individual who would take Judas's place as the twelfth must be an eyewitness of Jesus's life and resurrection (vv. 21-22). Christianity is founded on the historical resurrection, and those who first proclaimed the resurrection had to be trustworthy and informed.

Two men, Joseph and Matthias, were put forward as meeting the criteria set forth by Peter. The apostles and disciples turned to the Lord in prayer to seek his will on the decision (vv. 24-25). Lots were cast and "the lot fell to Matthias," so he was numbered with the eleven apostles (v. 26).

Make Decisions in View of God's Plan of Redemption

The primary reason this story is in the Bible is not to help us learn how to find God's will. It informs us about how God sovereignly worked to advance his mission. However, that must reveal to us *something* about finding his will. And I think the obvious lesson is that we must make our decisions in view of God's unfolding plan of redemption. If the reason we're still on the planet is to advance his mission of redeeming people, then it just makes sense that every decision we face must be approached in view of that purpose. In filling Judas's spot, these early Christians were answering some questions that are important for us to ask any time we're trying to discern God's will.

What Are the Immediate Ramifications for the Gospel?

The word *apostle* means "one who is sent." Jesus had instituted the formal office in order to appoint some men who could be sent out to proclaim his gospel with supernatural power. Their role was crucial for the immediate advancement of the gospel after the Lord left the earth. The apostles were eyewitnesses who had observed Jesus's life and could confirm his resurrection (cf. 1:21-22). And they were firsthand learners—or disciples—who could accurately pass on his teaching. His words would thus become the solid foundation on which his church would be built (cf. Eph 2:19-22).

By filling Judas's office, the church was acknowledging and valuing the need for such eyewitness testimony to the gospel in the days following Jesus's departure. The formal apostolic office in view here obviously was a unique, irreplaceable role limited to these twelve men. They would have no formal successors since no further eyewitnesses could arise after they died. But these early Christians were rightly concerned about the immediate advancement of the gospel, and a similar concern should underlie every decision we make. We should approach every decision by weighing how each choice will either enhance or hinder gospel advancement.

What Are the Eternal Ramifications for the Gospel?

It was imperative to fill Judas's office also for a broader kingdom purpose. Jesus had told the twelve apostles they would have a unique role in the coming kingdom of God. They would judge the twelve tribes of Israel (Matt 19:28; Luke 22:28-30). By filling Judas's office, the church was acknowledging and valuing the special role of the apostles. These men had important work to do.

Every decision we make matters. Our choices can have eternal impact.

Distinguish between God's Revealed Will and God's Concealed Will

ACTS 1:12-26

Part of God's will is written in black-and-white. The believers about whom we read in chapter 1 knew part of God's will because they knew the Scriptures. They knew there was an apostolic office, and they knew they were to fill the office vacated by Judas because God said so.

The primary place we can find God's will is in the pages of the Bible. In his Word he has revealed everything necessary for our redemption. That means we don't have to wonder whether we should be making disciples, praying, living holy lives, bearing fruit, loving people who aren't lovable, being faithful in our marriages, or caring for orphans. Those things and more are part of his revealed will, the Bible. We can be confident that pursuing those things is always the right course of action.

Not all the specific outworkings of God's will for specific individuals, however, are recorded in the Bible. While the early Christians knew

pelea sobre alcohol/drogas que tuvo con su ser querido. ¿Qué dijo/hizo la otra persona? ¿Qué dijo/hizo usted? ¿Quién dijo qué primero, segundo, tercero, etc.? Escríbalo como si se tratara del guion de una película. Trate de capturar todas las sutilezas. Luego, vuelva al escenario que describimos antes (la persona que bebe llega tarde a cenar, el cónyuge se molesta, se produce una pelea). Note que el cónyuge sobrio pudo cambiar el curso de la pelea al cambiar su forma de responder a la situación. Específicamente, el cónyuge dejó de atacar y, en vez de ello, le dijo a su ser querido cómo su conducta lo(a) hacía sentirse. También se aseguró de que supiera que lo(a) ama pero a su consumo de alcohol no.

Ahora, busque puntos en el escenario de su pelea en los que pueda ejercer el control. Pregúntese si está alimentando las llamas de la pelea o, posiblemente, reforzando la conducta que lo(a) hizo enojar. Escriba en su historia una respuesta más controlada (suave) de su parte que le dificulte a su ser querido seguir peleando. Recuerde: empiece con sus sentimientos, muestre comprensión y amor, y tenga claras las circunstancias bajo las cuales estaría abierto(a) a estar juntos o hablar del problema. Ensaye este nuevo guion en su cabeza tan frecuentemente como pueda. Cuando vuelva a surgir una situación similar, estará mejor preparado(a) para evitar los fuegos artificiales.

Si tiene dificultades para proponer alternativas a su rutina estándar, no se preocupe. Cuando termine este programa, será todo(a) un(a) experto(a).

Base del programa

Este programa lo(a) ayuda a asumir su parte de la relación. No coloca la responsabilidad de la persona que bebe en usted. *Las Alternativas* se basan en años de investigación científica y han comprobado un alto nivel de eficiencia para muchas personas en su misma situación. La abrumadora mayoría de los seres queridos que beben de nuestros clientes se ponen en tratamiento y lo siguen en una proporción de seis o siete veces más que la mayoría de otros adictos. Además, la gente que usa las *Alternativas* nos dice que le brindan un sentido de esperanza, comprensión y oportunidad. Pueden ayudarlo(a) a mejorar su calidad de vida, su relación y la vida de su ser querido.

Las Alternativas se basan en el hecho de que los miembros de la familia y otras personas que son importantes para la persona que consume alcohol son quienes tienen mayor influencia en su vida. Ya sea en una dirección positiva o negativa, la persona que bebe reacciona de manera más fuerte a quienes le son más cercanos. Usted es una de esas personas, por lo que está en posición de conducir esas reacciones en una dirección positiva. Puede tener un enorme impacto favorable en su ser querido. (Piense en sí mismo/a como navegante y conductor/a; usted tiene el mapa que muestra cuáles caminos puede seguir *y* tiene el control del volante).

Al convivir con alguien muchos años, usted tiene una perspectiva de sus hábitos que muy pocos tienen. De hecho, usted podría conocer a la persona que bebe tan bien, o incluso mejor, de lo que se conoce ella misma. Debido a que usted está motivado(a) y quiere trabajar por lo que desea, usted puede hacer cambios poderosos. La combinación de su conocimiento y su determinación es lo que lo(a) coloca en el asiento del conductor. Nosotros apoyaremos sus esfuerzos ofreciéndole *Alternativas* a las estrategias que ha usado y han fallado antes. Aunque, evidentemente, la vida no tiene garantías, estamos seguros de que podrá aprender un estilo más eficiente para relacionarse con su ser querido, de modo que mejore su calidad de vida y aumente la probabilidad de que esa persona vea la sobriedad bajo una nueva óptica.

Lo que puede esperar

A diferencia de algunos enfoques, *no* le enseñamos a separarse de la persona que ama. Por el contrario, tratamos de todas las formas de ayudarlo(a) a hacer que la relación funcione. Enfatizamos la educación, el empoderamiento y la esperanza. Usted aprenderá a asumir el control de su vida y a desarrollar una mejor relación con su ser querido. No obstante, también aprenderá a garantizar una mejor calidad de vida para usted incluso si, al final, la otra persona elige seguir bebiendo. En ese punto, usted habrá hecho todo lo posible por ayudarla y estará listo(a) para dejar la relación con la conciencia tranquila.

Las personas que adoptan las *Alternativas* experimentan diversos resultados. Algunas de hecho llegan al punto en el que saben que la única forma de seguir adelante es dejar la relación. Sin embargo, muchas más descubren que aplicar sistemáticamente las *Alternativas* produce resultados más saludables. Es bastante común que el camino lleve al tratamiento del alcolismo y a la terapia de parejas o familiar para ayudar a trabajar en las diferencias de la relación. Asimismo, hemos visto a mucha gente hacer cambios positivos en su vida laboral y social y hablamos tanto de quienes beben como de la gente que los ama. Nos concentramos en el panorama general, en vez de "apenas" en las conductas asociadas con la bebida. Usted aprende a aumentar los placeres de su vida y a cuidarse. Como resultado, son posibles cambios en todas las áreas de su vida. Todo depende de los cambios que quiera y por los qué esté dispuesto(a) a trabajar. De la misma forma en que Dorothy siempre tuvo los medios para volver a casa desde Oz (¿recuerda las zapatillas rojas?), usted siempre tiene el poder de cambiar. Ahora aprenderá a aprovechar ese poder y hacer que ocurran los cambios.

Al final de la jornada, se verá de una forma diferente. Usted no será ni la víctima ni el(la) culpable de su relación. Habrá asumido el control de su vida, habrá hecho cambios positivos y estará en la posición de decidir racionalmente adónde quiere ir a partir de allí.

Clarisse, cuya historia conocerá a continuación, aprendió las *Alternativas* y decidió que quería que su matrimonio funcionara. A pesar de lo que algunos pensarían que era una situación imposible, ella hizo cambios pequeños y cuidadosamente pensados y transformó una pesadilla en una relación con futuro.

Clarisse y Manuel

Cuando Clarisse llegó al programa para aprender las *Alternativas,* llevaba más de trece años en una relación agresiva. Su esposo, Manuel, ganaba mucho dinero y ella se hacía cargo de los niños y la casa. Para el resto del mundo parecía un hogar feliz. Sin embargo, Manuel se emborrachaba casi todas las noches y agredía verbalmente a Clarisse y a los niños. Él esperaba que ella satisficiera los deseos sexuales de él sin importarle los sentimientos de ella y, si se resistía, la forzaba físicamente a tener sexo con él.

A ella le tomó unos cuantos meses armarse de valor y decirle a su esposo que estaba en terapia. Se lo dijo después de que él comentó que últimamente ella parecía "menos reclamona". A él no le hizo gracia la idea de que ella le contara a un extraño sobre su vida, pero "la dejó ir" y no interfirió. Clarisse siguió asistiendo a las sesiones y aplicando las técnicas del programa. Tras varios meses, a Manuel le dio curiosidad el programa y quiso conocer al terapeuta. La primera reunión fue difícil pero, eventualmente, entró voluntariamente a terapia marital con ella.

Más de un año después de que Clarisse empezó a aprender las *Alternativas* ella *y* Manuel seguían en terapia marital. Él había dejado la bebida y estaba trabajando en su relación con ella y los niños. Ella estudiaba en la universidad comunitaria y se sentía extremadamente orgullosa de sus logros. Clarisse le dejó claro a su esposo que nunca más toleraría una relación que no respondiera a sus necesidades y las de sus hijos. Aunque Clarisse y Manuel tardaron un poco más de lo normal en empezar a hacer cambios positivos, su historia ilustra cómo se pueden cambiar incluso las situaciones que parecen imposibles, con trabajo, valor y paciencia.

Cientos de padres también han descubierto que la implementación de las *Alternativas,* en vez de los reclamos y las amenazas, ha hecho una enorme diferencia en su capacidad de orientar a sus adolescentes en una dirección positiva. Rita y Jorge llegaron terriblemente preocupados por su hijo de dieciséis años, Manny, quien parecía que estaba consumiendo marihuana y rumbo a un camino que ellos sabían que no le trarería nada bueno.

Rita, Jorge y Manny

A Rita y a Jorge les preocupaba particularmente la tendencia creciente de Manny de volver a casa después de la hora en que debía hacerlo y no escuchar la alarma para despertarse los días de clase. Preocupada, Rita revisó la habitación de Manny y, en efecto, encontró una pipa de marihuana y unas semillas que parecían sospechosas en la gaveta de su armario. En vez de hacerle un escándalo (lo primero que quisieron hacer), Jorge y ella primero pensaron con calma en todas las cualidades y conductas de Manny de las que se sentían orgullosos. Llegaron a la conclusión de que, si le iban a exigir cambios, también debían ser capaces de decirle todo lo que lo volvía un chico maravilloso. Luego, identificaron las actividades y privilegios que sabían que lo recompensaban. En particular, a Manny le encantaba usar el auto de la familia para salir con su novia. Además, la novia de Manny era una chica encantadora con quien Rita comentó el problema y le respondió que a ella no le gustaba que Manny consumiera drogas y ya le había pedido que las dejara. Juntas, acordaron que la novia limitaría su contacto con Manny a las veces en que no hubiera consumido drogas. Si aparecía en su casa con la mínima impresión de que había fumado, ella le decía que realmente disfrutaba su compañía cuando no se drogaba y que volviera después. Por su parte, los padres de Manny le dejaron claras sus expectativas con respecto a respetar la hora de volver a casa y consumir drogas y le prometieron que, si respetaba el toque de queda, se deshacía de los accesorios para consumir drogas y les mostraba una prueba de orina "limpia" los viernes, le prestarían el auto la noche del sábado. Al principio, Manny se enojó por la situación, pero sus padres y su novia no cedieron en el plan y, eventualmente, él se dio cuenta de que la vida era mucho más divertida si cumplía con su parte. A medida que su conducta mejoraba y sus padres tenían más oportunidades de reforzárselo, sus conversaciones se volvieron más cómodas y productivas.

La estructura del libro

Uno de los aspectos más difíciles al escribir este libro ha sido tomar el proceso dinámico e interactivo que ocurre en la terapia y trasladarlo al papel plano y silencioso. Fue algo que discutimos mucho para encontrar la mejor forma de hacerlo. ¿Debíamos presentarlo en una secuencia de 1-2-3 y guiarlo(a) a usted en todo el proceso típico de un cliente promedio? ¿O solo incluirlo todo sin ninguna secuencia particular y pedirle que eligiera lo que le pareciera interesante, como si fueran bocadillos en una bandeja de comida? Ninguno de estos abordajes nos gustaba. Rechazamos la estrategia del 1-2-3 porque sabemos que usted no es un(a) cliente(a) promedio que necesita la secuencia típica. Usted es único(a). Usted le aporta a la tarea su personalidad y sus gustos y preferencias, habilidades y talentos personales. Súmemosle la singularidad de su ser querido y la idea de lo "típico" deja de tener sentido. Esto nos dejaba la opción de ofrecerle un montón de consejos y técnicas sin instrucciones claras sobre cuándo hacer qué. Esto parecía un poco más interesante pero nos quedaba un problema: si usted ya tuviera todas las destrezas desarrolladas para reunir estrategias y crear alternativas productivas a los reclamos, las súplicas y las amenazas, no estaría leyendo este libro. Por eso, sentimos que le debíamos mucho más que una bandeja de bocadillos.

Concluimos que la mejor forma posible de presentar las *Alternativas* era una combinación de los enfoques de 1-2-3 y el montón de opciones. De esta forma, en los tres primeros capítulos, incluimos los componentes esenciales que todos deben entender antes de que puedan lograr un verdadero progreso. Los capítulos restantes, le brindan todas las habilidades y el conocimiento para los que la secuencia es menos importante. Al determinar sus próximos pasos, puede aplicar el material de los capítulos que le resulten más relevantes en ese momento. No obstante, recomendamos enfáticamente que lea todo antes de empezar a elegir qué prácticar. Es probable que el título de un capítulo o el encabezado de una sección lo(a) hagan pensar que ya sabe o no necesita ese material y, en realidad, el capítulo ofrece un nuevo abordaje de un tema antiguo y podría facilitarle mucho las cosas sobre la marcha. Así que tómese su tiempo y asegúrese de haber empacado todo lo que necesita, de que sus mapas de carretera estén actualizados y que tenga el tanque del auto lleno de gasolina. No se salte nada.

La decisión más fácil con respecto a la estructura del libro fue incluir ejemplos de gente real con la que hemos trabajado. Para parafrasear un dicho antiguo: creemos que una imagen en palabras vale más que mil instrucciones. En otras palabras, en cada capítulo ilustramos las técnicas con ejemplos de cómo las han utilizado otras personas. Esto lo(a) ayudará a ver las diversas formas en que puede usar las *Alternativas* en su vida.

Además, hay actividades distribuidas en cada uno de los siguientes capítulos para que las realice. Para ayudarlo(a) a usar cada actividad y mejorar sus destrezas, le mostraremos cómo los personajes de los diversos estudios de caso las completaron. Si usted es como la mayoría de las personas, se verá en la tentación de leer los ejemplos completados y pensará que basta saber qué hacer. Atención: ¡el saber no sustituye el hacer! Si no trabaja en las actividades por su cuenta, la probabilidad de que sea capaz de aplicar las destrezas será muy baja. Le recomendamos que tenga un cuaderno para completar las actividades. Con algunas tardará apenas unos momentos, otras realmente lo(a) pondrán a pensar. Se le pedirá que medite en el material que acaba de leer, en las situaciones y los problemas de su vida, en sus sueños, sus decepciones... Todo tipo de cosas. *El objetivo de las actividades es ayudarlo(a) a procesar verdaderamente el material de cada capítulo y apropiárselo.*

Al seguir su jornada, analizará las situaciones y hará planes. Verá que lo más práctico es mantener un cuaderno para registrar sus pensamientos y planes, además de organizar sus hojas de actividades. Un "hecho" primordial en el mundo del cambio en la conducta es que la gente que registra la información importante de su vida es la que suele tener más probabilidades de éxito a la hora de hacer estos cambios. Prepárese para el éxito. Trabaje en el programa trabajando en las actividades.

Cada capítulo empezará con un estudio de caso diferente donde se describen los personajes cuyas hojas de actividad ilustran los puntos que enseñamos. Al final de cada capítulo, encontrará la historia continua de Kathy y Jim. Se trata de una pareja ficticia cuya historia es una combinación de las historias de muchas personas reales que han pasado por este programa. Su historia ilustra puntos importantes y lo(a) ayudarán a hacerse una idea de cómo se aplican las *Alternativas* en la vida real. Aunque Jim y Kathy son ficticios, sus experiencias son las experiencias reales de gente que ha tenido éxito con este programa.

Kathy y Jim: la necesidad de una Alternativa

Kathy y Jim eran novios desde la adolescencia y se casaron poco después de graduarse de la secundaria. Tras ocho años de matrimonio, Kathy entró al programa. Su historia podría resultarle familiar.

Después de la secundaria, Kathy aceptó la propuesta matrimonial de Jim en vez de ir a la universidad. Jim muy pronto consiguió un buen empleo, con un salario estable en una fábrica local y, como la mayoría de los amigos de la secundaria de Jim también se quedaron en la ciudad, siguió frecuentando al mismo grupo. En la secundaria, solían beber cerveza regularmente, así que mantuvieron la tradición de encontrarse para "tomar unas cuantas". Lamentablemente, la cantidad de Jim fue aumentando hasta que llegó al punto de ponerle más atención a la bebida que a Kathy.

Al principio de su matrimonio, Jim y Kathy pasaban mucho tiempo juntos: pescaban y acampaban todo el año y disfrutaban a su familia que iba en aumento. No obstante, con el paso del tiempo, dejaron de hacer las actividades que los habían aproximado en primer lugar. Cuando Kathy llegó al tratamiento, nos contó que hacía cinco años que no iban a pescar ni acampar y que Jim había perdido completamente el interés en sus tres hijos. Lo único que le interesaba era beber y pasar tiempo en el bar.

Kathy dijo que había tratado de hablar con Jim para que la ayudara con los niños o la casa, pero él decía que como era quien pagaba las cuentas, cuidar la casa y los niños era deber de ella. También nos dijo que le daba miedo hablarle a Jim de la bebida porque la última vez que lo había hecho, él la había golpeado. Después de ese incidente, ella se encerró en la casa dos semanas para que los vecinos no vieran los moretones. A los niños les dijo que se había caído por la escalera.

Kathy estaba asustada y se sentía paralizada. Había perdido la oportunidad de ir a la universidad, nunca había trabajado y no veía cómo podría mantenerse a ella y a los niños. Hablar con Jim era impensable porque le daba miedo que se enojara. Cocinaba, limpiaba y hacía lo que se supone que debía hacer una "buena esposa", pero cada vez se deprimía más. Kathy subió de peso y se avergonzaba de su apariencia, dejó de visitar a sus amigas y raramente invitaba a sus familiares para que la visitaran. Las fiestas se volvieron una pesadilla porque tenía que ver a otra gente y nunca sabía qué tan borracho estaría Jim o cómo podría portarse. En sus propias palabras: "Mi vida es un desastre completo. Siento que me estoy muriendo. Si no fuera por los niños, simplemente me iría".

capítulo 2

El mapa de carretera

Holly y Dan

Holly llegó a nuestra clínica tras siete años de vivir, como ella misma lo dijo: "al borde". Cuando se casó, su esposo Dan era lo que se llama un "bebedor social", pero a medida que fue ascendiendo en su trabajo, empezó a beber para desestresarse al final del día. "La publicidad es un negocio despiadado", decía, y necesitaba un trago para "relajarse" después del trabajo. A pesar de las repetidas sugerencias de Holly de que pensara en buscar otro empleo que fuera menos estresante y más satisfactorio, Dan se apegaba a su puesto, sus aspiraciones profesionales y a la botella que necesitaba para tolerarlo todo. A medida que Dan subía en la compañía, su consumo de alcohol también amentaba. Todos los días, llegaba del trabajo, se ponía ropa cómoda, cenaba con Holly y luego se preparaba el primero de muchos whiskys con agua del resto de la velada. Era cuando empezaban las discusiones interminables. Sin hijos (a Holly le daba miedo tener un bebé en estas circunstancias) ni amigos, que habían desaparecido por la intensidad de Dan, no había nada que hacer que no fuera seguir peleando.

En este capítulo, trabajará en tres objetivos. Primero, hará un esbozo de todo lo que sabe de los patrones de consumo de bebida de su ser querido. (Probablemente le sorprenderá todo lo que sabe).

Luego, usará esa información para obtener lo que llamamos una "base de referencia" de los hábitos de beber. En otras palabras, lo(a) ayudaremos a descubrir cuánto su ser querido bebe en realidad y en qué circunstancias. Finalmente, con esa información a mano, usted elaborará planes de acción específicos para cambiar su conducta y, de esta forma, cambiar la conducta de su ser querido que consume alcohol.

Hacer un mapa de la bebida

La vida con su ser querido le ha brindado una enorme cantidad de experiencia y conocimiento sobre sus patrones de consumo de alcohol. Cada vez que piensa "Sabía que haría eso" o "Aquí vamos *de nuevo*", lo comprueba. Usted reconoce el camino que suele seguir la conducta de su ser querido. De hecho, es probable que haya veces que le da la impresión de tener premoniciones de lo que hará la persona. Este conocimiento lo(a) coloca a usted en una posición única para orientar la conducta de la persona que bebe en la dirección que usted desea. Sin embargo, primero necesita un mapa. Use su experiencia para descurbrir qué es lo que dispara el consumo de alcohol, lo que lo aumenta y lo que lo reduce, qué lugar ocupa usted en medio de todo y dónde están las trampas. En otras palabras, si desea llegar a su destino, ¡use un mapa!

El mapa de la bebida tiene tres partes principales. La primera describe los disparadores de la bebida. Puede compararlos con las señales de la carretera que le avisan que se aproxima una salida. La segunda, describe los primeros signos de intoxicación; que puede comparar con las indicaciones para reducir la velocidad que encuentra en las salidas de la carretera. A veces, los signos de intoxicación son obvios, como cuando la persona tiene el trago en la mano y una sonrisa boba. En otras oportunidades, debe ser más perspicaz para saber si la persona que bebe solo está de mal humor o si fue la bebida que se tomó en el camino a casa la causante de ese estado. En otras palabras, debe reconocer las pistas que le indican si su ser querido sigue tranquilamente la ruta de la sobriedad o ya tomó una salida rumbo al alcohol. Finalmente, el mapa muestra las consecuencias de beber. Una vez que su ser querido toma la salida hacia la bebida, le aparecen una serie de caminos posteriores. A veces, lo que usted hace con el fin de que la persona deje de beber en realidad la inclina más a la bebida. Por eso es tan importante no solo identificar los disparadores y las señales, sino también hacer el mapa de lo que sucede entre ustedes dos cuando la persona bebe. Su mapa lo(a) ayudará a descubrir lo que la conduce a más bebida y lo que la devuelve a la ruta de la sobriedad y la conducción tranquila.

Disparadores de la bebida

Los disparadores de la bebida son los eventos, estados de ánimo, personas, horas, días, pensamientos, lugares u olores que llevan a su ser querido a beber o le indican a usted que está a punto de hacerlo. En el momento en que ocurre un disparador, la persona aún no se ha tomado nada, pero no hay duda de que lo hará. Puede comparar estos disparadores con las señales de la carretera que le informan que su salida se aproxima. Recuerde: no es porque hay una señal en la carretera indicando que se aproxima una salida que usted tenga que tomarla. De la misma forma, algo puede ser un disparador de la bebida para su ser querido aunque no *siempre* lo haga beber. Para nuestros fines, la definición de un disparador de la bebida implica que *con frecuencia* conduce al consumo de alcohol.

Aunque todas las personas son singulares, algunos disparadores son bastante comunes, así que los enumeramos en la Actividad 1. Lea la lista y marque los que se aplican a su ser querido. Esto lo(a) ayudará a ver el tipo de señales que buscamos. Al final de la lista, agregue los que no hayamos incluido y correspondan a su ser querido. Trate de recordar todas las circunstancias que frecuentemente lo llevan a la bebida. A continuación, le mostramos los disparadores que Holly ve en el mapa de la bebida de Dan. Holly primero marcó los elementos en la Actividad 1 que le resultaron familiares. Luego los revisó, pensó a fondo y los resumió e individualizó según el patrón típico de Dan. Estudie el trabajo de Holly y luego haga el suyo en su cuaderno.

Actividad 1. Disparadores de la bebida

¿Cuáles de ellos suelen disparar la bebida en su ser querido?

	Aburrimiento
X	Un mal día en el trabajo
	Un buen día en el trabajo
X	Un día común en el trabajo
X	Sentimientos de intranquilidad
	Depresión
	Tomar un aventón a la casa después del trabajo con amigos
	Ver deportes con amigos
	Ver deportes solo(a)
	Que los niños lo(a) irriten o incomoden
	Pelear con usted
	Sentirse bien y querer celebrar
	Recibir amigos en casa
	Buscar un tema para pelear
	Tensión premenstrual (TPM)
X	Se queja de su jefe
X	Reclama de los compañeros
	Anda deprimido(a) por la casa
X	Una agenda demasiado llena
	Habla de la falta de sentido de la vida
	Los chicos hacen mucho ruido (o, al menos, la persona que bebe reclama de que lo hacen)

¿Cuáles disparadores no hemos incluido y suelen llevar a su ser querido a la bebida? Agréguelos a la lista y luego resuma todo de forma que refleje el patrón típico de la persona que bebe con la que usted convive. Holly resumió el patrón de Dan de esta forma.

Patrón de bebida de Dan

Dan tiene un empleo muy estresante, lo que para la mayoría de la gente no es una causa automática para beber pero, para él, no hay duda de que es un disparador de la bebida. A menudo se siente inadecuado en el trabajo y le preocupa que un día "descubran" su "falsedad". Por eso, cuando se acercan los plazos de entrega de los proyectos (que suelen ser muy cortos en publicidad), o Dan debe hacer una presentación en la que siente que será evaluado, su nivel de estrés aumenta muchísimo.

A lo largo de los años escuchando a Dan hablar de su trabajo y viendo su consumo de licor por las noches, Holly identificó los siguientes disparadores de la bebida. Tome en cuenta que, en el caso de Dan, todos giran en torno del estrés de que lo evalúen.

Disparadores de la bebida de Dan

- *Entrega de un proyecto en tres semanas*
- *Dan tiene que hacerle una presentación a un cliente en presencia de su jefe*
- *Funciones de la compañía (picnics, torneos de golf, fiestas, etc.) en las que Dan socializa con personas de niveles jerárquicos más altos*
- *Comentarios de los colegas que hacen que Dan crea que le darán a otra persona una asignación que él quiere*
- *Todas las veces en que Dan vuelve a casa y dice que fue un día de "matar"*

(Sabemos que mucha gente que consume alcohol no necesita un "disparador" específico para empezar a beber; no obstante, por lo general, es posible encontrar un patrón que suele anteceder las borracheras).

Señales de bebida

Ahora que tiene una imagen general de lo que lleva a su ser querido a buscar la bebida, piense en cómo usted nota que ya lo encontró. Entre el primer trago y la borrachera, suele haber señales que le indican que alguien está dejando la sobriedad y acercándose a la bebida. Una vez que el alcohol llega al cerebro, se acabaron los razonamientos y las negociaciones. El licor y otras drogas interfieren casi de inmediato en la capacidad de la persona de pensar con claridad. En ese momento, usted solo tiene dos objetivos. El primero y el más importante es estar a salvo. Si su ser querido muestra cualquier señal de violencia, usted debe implementar su plan de seguridad (consulte el Capítulo 3). Si la seguridad no es un problema, su segundo objetivo se vuelve el más importante: no hacer nada que estimule un mayor consumo de alcohol. Los mapas conductuales que desarrolle le mostrarán cómo lograr esta segunda meta.

¿Qué es lo que cambia cuando su ser querido empieza a beber? ¿Empieza a caminar de un lado para otro? ¿Le pesan los párpados? ¿Empieza a buscar un tema para pelear? Revise la lista de la Actividad 2 y agregue cualquier señal que falte y que indique que empezó el episodio de bebida. Si este ejercicio le resulta diifícil, trate de recordar la última vez que la persona se emborrachó y vaya enumerando en retrospectiva lo que sucedió antes o cómo se veía su ser querido en cada momento.

Holly describió las señales de bebida de Dan de la siguiente forma. Estudie las respuestas de Holly y luego complete la Actividad 2 en su cuaderno, con respecto a su ser querido.

Actividad 2. Señales de bebida

Sé que mi ser querido empezó a beber cuando él o ella ...	
	Llega a casa con varias cervezas
X	Aprieta la quijada o los puños
	Se le ponen los ojos vidriosos
	Le pesan los párpados
X	Empieza a levantar o bajar la voz
X	Dice que trabaja mucho y se merece al menos un trago
	Se pone de mal humor
	Empieza a arrastrar el habla
	Se pone sentimental
X	Camina de un lado a otro por la casa
	Se pone menos sentimental
	Se aísla de mí o de la familia
	Insiste en que los niños tengan "tiempo de calidad" con él o ella aunque estén ocupados con otra cosa
	Quiere que lo(a) dejen solo(a)
	Tiene cambios de humor radicales
	Se rehúsa a comer

Piense en otras señales que indiquen que su ser querido va rumbo a emborracharse. Enumérelos y luego resúmalos para reflejar el patrón típico de su ser querido que bebe. Holly resumió el patrón de Dan de la siguiente forma.

Señales de bebida de Dan

Dan pasa por periodos en los que intenta que yo no vea que empezó a beber porque sabe que me voy a enojar mucho. Cuando hace eso, a menudo se toma un trago en algún lugar antes de llegar a casa o se ofrece a hacer algún mandado después de la cena y pasa al bar de Joe. Incluso si no le huele el aliento a alcohol, sé que bebió por las siguientes señales:

- *Sube el tono de voz.*
- *Aprieta la quijada.*
- *Se afloja la corbata (cuando está sobrio nunca se la afloja antes de llegar a casa porque dice que afecta su imagen).*
- *Se le olvida quitarse los zapatos al llegar, y siempre se los quita si está sobrio.*
- *Abre a cada rato la refrigeradora buscando algo para comer pero nada se le antoja.*
- *Se queja de que en su trabajo nadie valora su talento.*

Buen trabajo. Ahora usted tiene una buena idea de cuáles situaciones son de alto riesgo para que su ser querido consuma alcohol (es decir, los disparadores de la bebida) y cuáles son las señales de que va rumbo a la bebida. Esto completa la primera y la segunda parte del mapa.

Consecuencias de la bebida

La parte final del mapa ilustra las consecuencias de la bebida. Cuanto más específicamente pueda identificar una secuencia paso a paso que termine en bebida o en problemas relacionados con ella, más fácil será descubrir cómo cambiar ese patrón.

¿Cuáles son los resultados de la bebida de su ser querido? Aunque este ejercicio resulte deprimente, sin él, su mapa estará incompleto, así como su capacidad de cambiar su situación.

Deténgase un momento y piense en todas las consecuencias causadas por la bebida de su ser querido. Asegúrese de considerar no solo las consecuencias inmediatas, como las peleas y las resacas, sino también, las consecuencias negativas de largo plazo, como las deudas financieras, los problemas médicos, las oportunidades perdidas y los amigos alejados. Piense también en cualquier consecuencia positiva que usted experimente de la bebida de esa persona. Puede sonar extraño pero es posible que la bebida de su ser querido tenga alguna función útil en su vida. Tal vez le permita evitar una relación sexual insatisfactoria o mantiene a ser querido dependiente de usted. No estamos diciendo que *tiene que* haber una consecuencia positiva. Apenas que usted necesita considerar honestamente la posibilidad de no pasarlo por alto al empezar a hacer cambios. Recuerde que el conocimiento es poder.

Holly pudo identificar consecuencias de la bebida de Dan en las que no había pensado antes. Ser consciente de ellas la ayudó a descubrir qué debía cambiar y cómo hacerlo.

Use la Actividad 3 para empezar su propia lista de consecuencias de la bebida. Recuerde pensar a largo y a corto plazo, así como en los costos para su ser querido y para usted. Este es el trabajo de Holly con la actividad. Haga su propia actividad en su cuaderno.

Actividad 3. Consecuencias de la bebida

La bebida ha hecho que mi ser querido o yo ...	
	Nos sintamos enfermos
X	Tengamos resacas terribles
	Nos sintamos culpables o avergonzados
X	Faltemos al trabajo
	Seamos más extrovertidos en las fiestas

	Nos despidan del trabajo
X	Perdamos el placer en nuestra relación
	Tengamos dificultades para criar a los niños
	Tengamos accidentes de auto
	Nos arresten por conducción en estado de ebriedad
	Tengamos dificultades financieras
	Experimentemos problemas físicos
	Experimentemos o temamos la violencia
	Nos avergoncemos de la conducta alcohólica
X	No podamos relajarnos
	Tengamos una conducta insegura (por ejemplo, conducir demasiado rápido o conducir tras haber bebido)
	Perdamos amigos
	Nos hayamos vuelto físicamente menos atractivos
	Tengamos una vida social dañada o perdida
	Desarrollemos una mala reputación en la comunidad
	Tengamos problemas de peso
X	No podamos tener sexo
X	Tengamos una relación sexual inhibida
	Tengamos una relación sexual menos inhibida
X	Terminamos con mis o nuestras cosas rotas
	Temor de que nunca nos separemos porque la persona que bebe me necesita
X	Evitemos lidiar con otros problemas porque siempre estamos lidiando con la bebida
X	Evitemos una relación sexual insatisfactoria

Piense en otras consecuencias de la bebida que sean importantes para usted. Enumérelas y luego resúmalas para que reflejen su situación. Holly resumió su situación de esta forma.

Consecuencias de la bebida de Dan

Siempre pensé que la bebida de Dan básicamente causaba nuestras peleas y punto. Claro que me preocupaban los problemas que podría causar en el futuro pero en realidad no pensaba que estuviera haciendo tanto daño en este momento. Cuando me detuve a pensar al respecto, me di cuenta de que había muchas consecuencias más de lo que creía.

- *Peleas (obvias)*
- *Mis migrañas (más frecuentes y fuertes cuando él bebe)*
- *Faltas ocasionales al trabajo: Dan por su resaca, yo por la migraña*
- *Dan no ayuda a recoger la cocina o lavar los platos tras la cena ni colabora con las tareas domésticas como pagar las cuentas y sacar la basura*
- *Nos permite evitar hablar sobre tener hijos (Dan realmente quiere, pero yo no estoy segura de querer interrumpir mi carrera)*
- *Nuestra vida sexual es casi inexistente*
- *Dan se vuelve torpe y rompe sus anteojos*

Veamos cómo Holly y Dan reúnen todo lo que hemos abordado hasta ahora.

Holly identificó los disparadores de la bebida de Dan como situaciones relacionadas con el trabajo que lo hacen sentirse evaluado y no dar la talla. Estos son los días "despiadados" de los que habla Dan. Holly también identificó las señales de que Dan bebió y se va a emborrachar. Cuando Dan llega a casa con la corbata floja y la quijada apretada, ella sabe que salió del trabajo más temprano y se detuvo en el bar local para tomarse un trago. La quijada también le dice que de nada le sirve hablarle de la bebida (no se puede tratar de tener una conversación racional con alguien cuyo cerebro está bajo la influencia de una droga). Las consecuencias para Dan y Holly probablemente a usted también le resultan familiares: peleas, enojo, resentimiento, pérdida de la intimidad, palabras groseras que duelen aún después de que se instala el silencio, vidrios rotos cuando Dan se vuelve torpe y días de trabajo perdidos para ambos (Dan por la resaca y Holly por la migraña y la tristeza).

Su tarea más importante en este momento es asegurarse que poder identificar los disparadores de la bebida de su ser querido, de saber cuándo empezó a beber y cuáles son las consecuencias más probables. Con esa información a mano, puede empezar a hacer cambios. De la misma forma que Holly sabe cuándo Dan llega a casa buscando bebida y peleas, usted sabe cuándo su ser querido va por ese camino. Sabiendo esto, usted puede elegir no tomar esa ruta. En vez de participar en el mismo ciclo de siempre de peleas y lágrimas, póngales atención a los disparadores y las señales y cambie las consecuencias que están dentro de su control. Usted puede salir de la situación, cambiar lo que dice, cómo se ve y lo que hace. Conforme avancemos, verá que realmente puede cambiar muchas cosas.

Tenga una base de referencia

"Base de referencia" simplemente se refiere a un punto de partida. Tener una base de referencia de la persona que consume alcohol significa calcular de la mejor forma posible cuánto y con qué frecuencia bebe. En otras palabras, describir sus patrones de bebida actuales. Hay dos razones para establecer una base de referencia. Una es completar el mapa que describe todo lo que sabe sobre el consumo de alcohol de su ser querido, y la otra es ayudarlo(a) a reconocer el progreso conforme ocurra.

¿Cuánto bebe su ser querido?

El primer paso para obtener una base de referencia es descubrir con qué frecuencia y cuánto bebe su ser querido. Use la Actividad 4 para ello. Piense con detenimiento y trate de responder todas las preguntas. Si le resulta difícil tener una idea clara del consumo de alcohol de la persona, use un calendario y piense en cada día. ¿La persona bebió ayer? Si la respuesta es sí, ¿cuánto bebió? ¿Y el día anterior y el día antes de ese? ¿Su ser querido tiende a beber menos/más durante la semana o el fin de semana, o el patrón cambia cada semana? Si tiene un patrón estándar de beber, este ejercicio resultará más fácil pero, de cualquier forma, es importante.

Casi toda la gente que bebe tiene "días especiales para beber" en los que tiende realmente a exagerar. Según la persona, los días especiales para beber pueden ser los feriados, los días de pago, el domingo del Super Bowl (o cualquier domingo), las finales de la Stanley Cup, los cumpleaños, los viernes por la noche o cualquier otro día que funcione como excusa para abrir la botella.

Si cree que su ser querido bebe más de lo que usted puede observar o bebe más de lo que usted sabe, siga sus instintos. Mucha gente que consume alcohol en exceso esconde bebidas, así que es probable que usted tenga razón. De cualquier forma, no puede monitorear sus actividades las veinticuatro horas del día así que calcule lo mejor que pueda.

Al responder las preguntas de la Actividad 4, use la siguiente definición de bebida como guía. Cada una de las siguientes opciones cuenta como una bebida:

12 onzas (355 ml) de cerveza
4 onzas (118 ml) de vino
1-¼ onzas (37 ml) de licor con 40 % de alcohol
1 onza (29 ml) de licor con 57,1 % de alcohol

Cada una de estas cantidades contiene ½ onza (14,8 ml) de etanol, que es el químico en el alcohol que lo vuelve una droga.

Actividad 4. Calcule la bebida durante una semana común

Nota: Si su ser querido no trabaja en semana estándar, de lunes a viernes, ajuste la actividad como corresponda.

1. *¿Cuántas bebidas consume usualmente un lunes, martes, miércoles y jueves típicos? Multiplique el consumo diario común por 4.* ________
2. *¿Cuántas bebidas consume generalmente un viernes típico?* ________
3. *¿Cuántas bebidas consume usualmente un sábado típico?* ________

4. ¿Cuántas bebidas consume generalmente un domingo típico? ________

5. Sume sus respuestas a las preguntas 1, 2, 3 y 4. ________

El total de la línea 5 refleja la cantidad de bebidas de su ser querido durante una semana típica. Compare este número a su cálculo de su consumo de alcohol típico hace un año, hace tres años o cuando se conocieron. ¿Esta cifra ha aumentado con el paso de los años? ¿La cantidad de bebidas aumenta o disminuye en días especiales (feriados, vacaciones u otros momentos especiales?

También puede calcular cuántas horas al día se gastan bebiendo o en actividades relacionadas con el alcohol. El tiempo que se gasta en las tiendas que venden alcohol, los bares, de resaca y en prisión o en el hospital forman parte de los costos y el patrón de la bebida. Súmele también a su base de referencia cualquier otra droga que consuma su ser querido. Una imagen detallada de dónde está usted actualmente es conocimiento que lo(a) ayudará a llegar adonde quiere estar mañana. Repita este ejercicio de forma periódica a medida que implementa las *Alternativas.* Los cambios en estos números serán una forma de medir el impacto de sus esfuerzos con su ser querido que bebe. No obstante, recuerde que, aun si esa persona no avanza a la sobriedad, la medida más importante de éxito será una mejor calidad de vida para usted y para quienes dependen de usted.

¿Cuánto es demasiado?

Incluso sin el ejercicio detallado que acaba de realizar, estamos seguros de que ya ha discutido con su ser querido sobre cuánto bebe. Usted ha argumentado que es demasiado y, muy probablemente, la otra persona, ha dicho que no es tanto. Por mucho que la mayoría de las veces usted esté seguro(a) de que bebe en exceso, es posible que también haya veces en qué se pregunte quién es el que está loco aquí. Después de todo, usted conoce a otra gente que bebe tanto como su ser querido. Además, es probable que a veces beba menos y usted se pregunte si usted está exagerando. Al fin y al cabo, ¿qué es un consumo de alcohol normal?

Hay muchas definiciones de consumo de alcohol normal y consumo de alcohol problemático. De hecho, ¡reúna a un grupo de expertos en consumo de drogas en un salón y estará en mitad de un manicomio! A nosotros en realidad no nos preocupa mucho cuántas onzas de alcohol son "oficialmente" demasiadas. La definición que nos parece más útil con la gente real es: *si el consumo de alcohol de una persona está causando problemas, esa persona bebe demasiado.*

Tampoco tendemos a no etiquetar a nadie como alcohólico. Además de la incapacidad de los expertos en ponerse de acuerdo en exactamente quien amerita este título, "alcohólico" es una etiqueta estigmatizada que ha alejado a mucha gente que bebe del tratamiento. Si su ser querido tiene la intención de hacer el esfuerzo de parar, ¿es necesario etiquetarlo?

Respire profundamente

Resaltar la extensión del problema como usted acaba de hacer pueder ser muy desagradable. Esta podría haber sido la primera vez que usted realmente identificó todo el impacto del alcohol en su vida... y es posible que sea peor de lo que había notado. Así que, deténgase, respire profundamente y recuerde que documentar el problema no ha cambiado nada. Su ser querido no bebe ni más ni menos que antes. Usted ahora simplemente es consciente de ello y está preparado(a) para asumir las riendas. Con un mapa completo de la bebida, usted puede empezar a pensar en cómo agregar caminos planos y más saludables al terreno.

Rediseñar el mapa

Rediseñar el mapa de la bebida significa reorganizar su forma de interactuar con la persona que bebe para eliminar o minimizar los disparadores que conducen al alcohol. En vez de mirar a su ser querido ir de una borrachera a otra, usted desarrollará nuevos caminos que vayan de los antiguos disparadores de la bebida a nuevas actividades sin alcohol. Para ilustrar a qué nos referimos, hablemos de Ed y Lydia.

Ed y Lydia

Ed llevaba años tratando de que Lydia redujera la bebida, pero nada había funcionado. Reclamos, súplicas, amenazas, pequeñas trampas... todo topaba con un muro. Lydia no "se caía de borracha", como ella misma decía, y no estaba dispuesta a renunciar a algo que la hacía sentirse tan bien rápidamente cuando se estresaba. Ed, por su parte, veía la bebida de Lydia como un problema serio porque la hacía faltar al trabajo, olvidarse de buscar a los niños en la guardería e incluso conducir ebria con los niños en el auto (una vez). Finalmente, Ed probó un abordaje diferente. Abandonó la batalla y elaboró el mapa de la bebida de su esposa y sus propias respuestas (tal y como usted acaba de hacerlo). Luego, pensó en nuevos comportamientos para sí mismo que, por su parte, generaran diferentes comportamientos en Lydia. Por ejemplo, cuando Lydia llegaba a casa reclamando del trato injusto que recibía de su jefe (un disparador conocido de la bebida para ella), Ed le masajeaba los hombros y le decía cuánto él y los niños la valoraban, incluso si el jefe era un idiota. Luego, le decía que tomara una ducha caliente mientras él preparaba la cena y le dejaba claro que realmente disfrutaba su compañía cuando ella estaba sobria. Sabiendo que una ducha caliente era una de las formas favoritas de Lydia para desestresarse (además del licor), Ed podía alejarla lo suficiente de la botella de vino para mejorarle el ánimo, servir la cena y orientar la atención de su esposa a temas más agradables. Ed empezó a hacer esto con frecuencia y él y Lydia aumentaron las experiencias positivas que compartían después del trabajo, lo que incrementó la probabilidad de que Lydia saliera del trabajo con la expectativa de sentirse bien al llegar a casa. Por su parte, esta expectativa positiva la ayudaba a bajar los niveles de estrés del trabajo y facilitaba que no bebiera.

Usted puede redefinir el mapa de la conducta de su ser querido, como Ed, usando la información que recopiló en este capítulo. Para ello, examine los disparadores de la bebida de su ser querido y concéntrese primero en los dos o tres más comunes. En cada caso, describa todo lo que sepa: todos los detalles del propio disparador (quién, qué, dónde, cuándo, por qué, cómo) y todas las consecuencias, incluso cómo reaccionan usted y los demás. Además, describa los patrones de la bebida: ¿empieza con "solo un" trago y lentamente continúa hasta la borrachera o la persona bebe con rabia, pesado y rápidamente?

La forma más fácil de rehacer el mapa de la conducta de su ser querido es dibujarlo en un papel, como hizo Ed con Lydia en el siguiente ejemplo. Use flechas para mostrar cómo un evento lleva al próximo.

> Lydia llega a casa reclamando. ➔ Ed le dice que él también tuvo un día complicado y los niños piden atención. ➔ Lydia se sirve un trago mientras empieza a organizar la cena. ➔ Ed le pregunta si se va a emborrachar de nuevo. ➔ Lydia le responde que la deje en paz y se toma el primer trago mientras sigue preparando la cena. ➔ Ed le dice que es un pésimo ejemplo para los niños. ➔ Lydia se sirve otro trago. ➔ Ed sale de la cocina echando chispas. ➔ Los niños empiezan a llorar. ➔ Lydia pone algo a calentar en el horno, se sirve otro trago y se va a la habitación a cambiarse la ropa del trabajo. ➔ Ed la sigue y se disculpa. ➔ Ella acepa la disculpa pero ahora está un poco "alegre". ➔ Lydia vuelve a la cocina y vuelve a llenar su copa dos o tres veces más. ➔ Cuando la cena está lista y la familia se sienta a la mesa, Lydia está ebria, Ed está furioso y la velada es un desastre.

Una vez que Ed hizo el mapa con la secuencia que viene después del disparador de Lydia (la interacción desagradable con su jefe), pudo pensar en cómo interrumpirla. En este caso, él sabía que el disparador era más que apenas un mal día en el trabajo. El verdadero disparador era el estrés que Lydia sentía. Así que él decidió interrumpir la secuencia introduciendo cierta reducción del estrés desde el principio. Cuando Lydia llegaba a casa molesta, en vez de señalar que "todos tienen días malos en el trabajo" (así que "deja de lamentarte"), Ed se concentraba en ayudarla a relajarse. Claro que eso significó un poco más de trabajo porque le tocó asumir la cena y evitar que los niños corrieran a concentrar la atención de su madre, pero el esfuerzo valió la pena. Lydia se mantuvo sobria y pudieron empezar a disfrutar las noches juntos.

Antes de que veamos el mapa revisado de Ed, es importante destacar que no le estamos sugiriendo que asuma permanentemente todo el trabajo de la relación. De hecho, las metas de largo plazo son que usted tenga menos trabajo asumiendo solo(a) a su familia y que su ser querido se vuelva un miembro involucrado y responsable. No obstante, desde este momento y hasta que eso suceda, usted tendrá que hacer un esfuerzo adicional. De todos modos, es muy probable que usted ya esté asumiendo la mayor parte del trabajo. Esta es una continuación de esa situación, pero con un resultado de largo plazo mucho mejor.

Muy bien, este es el mapa revisado de Ed. Las rutas anteriores están en *(itálica y entre paréntesis)* y las nuevas conductas en **negrita.**

> Lydia llega a casa quejándose. ➔ *(Ed dice que él también tuvo un día complicado y los niños piden atención.)* **Le masajeo los hombros y le digo cuánto los niños y yo la valoramos. Le digo que tome una ducha mientras resuelvo la cena. Además, le digo que el baño la ayudará a relajarse sin necesidad de un trago, de forma que nuestra noche sea más agradable.** ➔ *(Lydia se sirve un trago mientras empieza a organizar la cena).* **Lydia se ducha mientras preparo la cena.** ➔ *(Ed le pregunta si se va a emborrachar de nuevo.* ➔ *Lydia le dice que la deje en paz y se toma el primer trago mientras sigue preparando la cena.* ➔ *Ed le dice que es un mal ejemplo para los*

niños. ➔ *Lydia se sirve otro trago.* ➔ *Ed sale de la cocina reclamando.* ➔ *Los niños empiezan a llorar.* ➔ *Lydia, después de poner algo a calentar en el horno, se sirve otro trago y se va a la habitación a cambiarse la ropa del trabajo.* ➔ *Ed la sigue y se disculpa.* ➔ *Ella acepta la disculpa pero ya está un poco pasada de alcohol.* ➔ *Lydia vuelve a la cocina y se sirve dos o tres tragos más.* ➔ *Cuando la cena está lista y la familia se sienta a comer, Lydia ya está ebria, Ed está furioso y la noche es un desastre).* **Lydia baja relajada y disfrutamos la cena.**

Examine el mapa de su ser querido que bebe para detectar el disparador más común o más complicado y pregúntese si podría estar encubriendo el verdadero disparador, como pasaba en el caso de Lydia. No obstante, no profundice demasiado aquí. A menudo, las cosas realmente son lo que parecen. Si dividir el auto después del trabajo con sus amigos de bebida los días de pago es un disparador para la persona que bebe, es probable que ese sea verdaderamente el disparador, y usted necesita concentrarse en encontrar otra forma de que su ser querido vuelva a casa después del trabajo. Podría ofrecerle recogerlo usted mismo(a) y llevarlo a cenar (a un restaurante que no venda licor). De esta forma, usted no solo lo ayuda a evitar un disparador fuerte, sino también sustituye la conducta de beber por una alternativa saludable y grata.

Revise el mapa de los disparadores que haya seleccionado, con cuidado de trazar el mapa actual completo y, luego, agregue desvíos en cada punto en el que pueda cambiar algo. También, tenga en cuenta que si su primer desvío no funciona, es útil tener un segundo desvío planeado para los siguientes puntos en la secuencia. En el caso de Ed, si el masaje en los hombros y el baño no hubieran funcionado, podría haber planeado una respuesta comprensiva (consulte el capítulo 9) a las quejas de Lydia y tener un plan de respaldo sugiriendo salir todos a cenar, tras haber seleccionado cuidadosamente un restaurante con un menú infantil y sin permiso para vender licor. De esta forma, Lydia pasaría rápidamente a una actividad relajante y sin alcohol.

Mientras conversan durante la cena, también sería útil que Ed ayudara a Lydia a concentrarse en otra cosa. En vez de lamentarse porque su jefe es un idiota o de menospreciarse por pensar que merece sus comentarios desagradables, Ed podría ayudarla a pensar en algo positivo que tenga que ver con los niños o en unas vacaciones que estén planeando. La idea es simplemente bajarle las revoluciones a la situación al pasar de un tema negativo a uno positivo.

Al hacer su plan, asegúrese de no seguir las mismas vías de siempre. Si los métodos que ha venido probando no han funcionado, es poco probable que lo hagan ahora. Busque nuevas formas sin enfrentamientos de lograr sus metas (consulte el capítulo 9). Recuerde también que la meta no es probar que la persona que bebe está equivocada y usted tiene la razón (por muy satisfactorio que sea). Su meta es lidiar con este problema con el alcohol y construir una vida mejor. No pelee con su *ser querido que bebe*. Pelee con el *problema*.

Cambiar el patrón a partir de la primera bebida require un cuidado adicional. Como siempre, el objetivo más importante es mantenerse a salvo. Si su ser querido tiene la tendencia de ponerse violento, asegúrese de trabajar con el capítulo 3 antes de hacer cualquier cambio. No sea mártir. Si su ser querido muestra señales de agresión, cambie el tema, evítelo y, si es necesario, salga del lugar. Recuerde que el alcohol cambia el funcionamiento del cerebro, así que cualquier cosa que usted haga después de que empieza la bebida debe concentrarse en su comportamiento y en alejarse de una situación no deseada. No pierda el tiempo discutiendo, negociando o debatiendo con una mente infectada por el alcohol.

Usted conoce las señales de que viene una borrachera desde el principio, así como de que la persona ya está ebria. A los borrachos es mejor dejarlos solos porque el funcionamiento cerebral restante es demasiado poco para que usted trate de hacerlos entrar en razón. Sin embargo, si la persona acaba de empezar a beber, la situación podría ser, de alguna forma, manejable. Por ejemplo, si usted llega a casa después del trabajo y su ser querido llego primero y ya tiene la mirada típica de "Me tomé algo", usted tiene dos opciones. Puede seguir el mapa tradicional de preguntarle si ha estado bebiendo (lo que es obvio) y decirle cuán decepcionado(a), molesto(a) y herido(a) usted se siente. A partir de ahí, pueden tener la pelea tradicional, la persona seguirá bebiendo y el día terminará con el desastre tradicional. Por otra parte, usted puede tener un nuevo mapa como guía y mejorar las probabilidades de que la velada termine bien. Considere el siguiente escenario.

Mamá:	Hola, mi amor. ¿Qué tal tu día?
Eric:	Horrible. Tuve un día pésimo. Por dicha se acabó.
Mamá:	Lamento que hayas tenido un día tan pesado. ¿Qué tal si vamos a cenar afuera?
Eric:	No. Solo quiero relajarme. Necesito otro trago.
Mamá:	¿Y si te hago un café y un omelet [su comida favorita]? ¿Quieres que le ponga algo especial?
Eric:	Sí, quiero un poco de jamón y de pimientos. Me muero del hambre.

En este caso, las cosas salieron bien para Eric y su mamá. Ella reconoció que él estaba de mal humor y le ofreció una forma sin alcohol de mejorarlo. No se puso a discutir si él debía evitar la bebida, entonces no formó parte del problema. La mamá ofreció una solución. No obstante, no siempre las cosas salen bien. Veamos cómo podrían haberse complicado, aunque no de una forma horrible, para Eric y su mamá.

Mamá:	¡Hola! ¿Qué tal tu día?
Eric:	Fue largo e insoportable, por dicha se acabó.

Mamá:	Lamento que haya sido tan pesado. ¿Qué tal si salimos a comer algo?
Eric:	No, gracias. Nada más quiero estar solo y tomarme un trago.
Mamá:	Puedo cocinar algo, lo que se te antoje. Nada más dime que quieres.
Eric:	Ya te lo dije: estar solo. Quiero tomarme mi trago en paz.
Mamá:	Por lo visto no me quieres por aquí, y prefiero no verte beber. Me voy a duchar y a dormir temprano. Espero que te sientas mejor. Nos vemos por la mañana.

Note cómo, en esta versión, la mamá le da a Eric su espacio. Empieza tratando de ser empática y le ofrece una solución sin alcohol, pero él está decidido a seguir la vía de la bebida. Así que, en vez de ponerse a discutir con él y volverse parte del problema, la mamá sabiamente optó por retirarse de la situación y hacer algo agradable para ella: una ducha y una buena noche de sueño. Si se hubiera mantenido en la situación, la tensión habría aumentado y, no solo nada se hubiera resuelto esa noche, sino también se habrían peleado y estarían molestos para hablar en la mañana siguiente. De esta forma, Eric se salió con la suya, la mamá tuvo una noche mejor que si se hubiera quedado con él y podrían tratar de tener una conversación razonable al día siguiente.

No se sobrecargue rehaciendo el mapa de todos los patrones de conducta de la persona que bebe. Usted ha vivido con el problema todo este tiempo; no necesita solucionarlo todo en un día. De hecho, tratar de hacerlo solo lo(a) dejará agotado(a). Esta es una nueva forma de vivir, así que tómese su tiempo para incorporarla poco a poco. El cambio es una jornada, no un evento. No se produce de la noche a la mañana. Ocurre con el paso del tiempo.

Seleccionar los mapas de carretera con los que quiere empezar puede ser difícil. Puede haber muchas áreas de su vida lastimadas. No obstante, nuestra recomendación es empezar con una interacción típica específica a que le incomode. Por ejemplo, usted y su ser querido tienen una pelea todas las noches sobre beber delante de los niños o la hora en que suelta la Internet y la bebida. Elija algo que sea bastante concreto, no una situación continua como ser groseros entre ustedes. Además, asegúrese de seleccionar una interacción que esté, al menos parcialmente, dentro de su control. Usted no puede resolver las peleas de su ser querido con otra gente. Pero sí puede resolver las peleas entre ustedes.

Ahora que ha identificado los disparadores, las señales y las consecuencias de la bebida de su ser querido, está listo(a) para empezar a trazar su mapa. Las actividades 5 y 6 le muestran cómo Holly tomó toda la información que tenía de la bebida de Dan y creó dos versiones de su mapa de carretera: una describe dónde suelen terminar ella y Dan y la otra adónde ella quiere llegar.

Los siguientes capítulos le brindarán muchas técnicas que puede usar en sus nuevos mapas de conducta. Por ahora, planee los cambios que pueda y luego lea cuáles enfoques pueden ayudarlo(a) a diseñar mapas de carretera más poderosos.

Actividad 5. El mapa antiguo

Dan llega a casa con señales claras de que se tomó algunos tragos. → Holly le dice que llega dos horas tarde para cenar y empieza a golpear las ollas al servirle la comida. → Dan le dice que pare. Que tuvo un mal día. → Holly se pone furiosa y le responde: "Yo también trabajo, ¿sabes? Mi día no fue fantástico y tú podías haberme llamado". → Dan le grita: "Te dije que pararas. Me largo". Se devuelve al bar. → Holly pasa el resto de la noche lavando platos y llorando.

Actividad 6. El mapa nuevo

La ruta anterior está en *(itálica y entre paréntesis)* y las nuevas conductas en **negrita**.

Dan llega a casa con señales claras de que se tomó algunos tragos. → *(Holly le dice que llega dos horas tarde para la cena y empieza a golpear las ollas mientras le sirve la comida).* **Holly le dice: "Qué dicha que llegaste. Estaba preocupada. ¿Quieres comer?"** → *(Dan le dice que pare. Que tuvo un mal día).* **"No", responde, "Solo quiero ver el juego".** → *(Holly se pone furiosa y le responde: "Yo también trabajo, ¿sabes? Mi día no fue fantástico y tú podías haberme llamado").* **Holly empieza a guardar la cena y le dice a Dan que puede comer después si le da hambre. "Ahora", agrega, "me voy a la habitación a leer".** → *(Dan le grita: "Te dije que pararas. Me largo". Se devuelve al bar).* **"¿No quieres ver el juego conmigo?" le pregunta él.** → **"No", responde ella, "No me gusta estar contigo cuando has bebido".** → *(Holly pasa el resto de la noche lavando platos y llorando).* **Dan mira el juego solo y Holly se mete a la cama a leer una novela.**

Recuerde que lograr su meta final significa sacrificarse un poco por ahora. Holly realmente no quería irse a la habitación. Lo que en verdad quería era que Dan volviera a casa sobrio. Y, como no fue así, quería gritarle y que él se sintiera tan mal como ella. No obstante, sabía que eso no ayudaría en lo más mínimo a que llegara el día en que pudiera contar con que él volviera a casa sobrio. Meterse sola a la cama con una novela no era exactamente lo que quería, pero fue considerablemente mejor que llorar sobre el lavaplatos. La otra parte fundamental de este "nuevo mapa" es que Holly le dejó claro a Dan que ella solo disfruta estar con él cuando está sobrio. Este es un punto importante. Sin acusaciones ni peleas, usted debe buscar la honestidad con su ser querido. El hecho de que la bebida lo(a) haga a usted infeliz no es algo que deba ocultarse. Apenas debe expresarse mediante una forma de hablar directa y sin confrontación y, especialmente, a través de su conducta. Holly *le dijo* a Dan cómo se sentía y *se lo mostró* saliendo de la habitación. Esto es parte del proceso de llevar a su ser querido en dirección a la preparación para el cambio. Si Dan, en este caso, hubiera quedado curioso, o incluso incómodo, por la conducta de Holly y la hubiera seguido a la habitación para preguntarle qué le pasaba, habría sido una buena oportunidad para que ella le hablara de sus esperanzas y sueños con respecto a la relación.

Resumen de la acción

Este capítulo presenta el componente central del programa de *Alternativas.* Al identificar los disparadores y las consecuencias de la bebida de su ser querido y al aprender a trazar el mapa de su conducta, usted pasó a la posición de ver el panorama general. Ya no tiene que sentirse victimizado(a) por los eventos que siempre parecen fuera de control. Puede aclarar qué dispara y mantiene estos eventos, cambiar su reacción y, de esta forma, cambiar el resultado. Pase algún tiempo trazando los patrones de bebida más problemáticos y resuélvalos paso a paso. Si puede pedirle a un amigo, familiar o terapeuta que lo(a) ayude a hacer una lluvia de ideas sobre las soluciones, mucho mejor. A veces, las ideas de otra persona pueden ser reveladoras y en otras ocasiones apenas pueden hacerlo(a) sentirse mucho más inteligente.

Repaso

- Identifique los disparadores y las consecuencias de la bebida de su ser querido para diseñar un mapa rumbo a la sobriedad.

- Disparadores = razones para beber (eventos, pensamientos y sentimientos, por ejemplo).
- Señales de bebida = señales de que su ser querido ya se tomó un trago (o dos).
- Consecuencias = resultados de la bebida (buenos y malos).
- Mapa de carretera = la herramienta que usted usa para descubrir cómo los disparadores y las consecuencias funcionan juntos y cómo puede cambiarlas.

Kathy y Jim: Mapeo de nuevos patrones

Una de las cosas que a Kathy más le preocupaban era la tendencia de Jim de parar a tomarse algo con sus amigos en el camino a casa después del trabajo. Pasó años peleando con él por eso y, en el proceso, se insultaban mucho. Llegó al punto en que el tema se volvió tan sensible que Kathy no sentía que podía mencionarlo sin generar una pelea violenta.

Kathy trazó el mapa de los eventos que solían hacer que Jim pasara a tomarse un trago y llegara a casa tarde y borracho. Se dio cuenta de que esto por lo general ocurría los días en que Jim llamaba para avisar que iba a llevar a Charles, su amigo, a casa porque su auto estaba en el taller (de nuevo). Cuando los dos se subían al auto, parecía que iban en piloto automático directo al bar. Al llegar, según Jim, él invitaba a Charles a un trago y luego Charles le devolvía el favor. Después de dos tragos, por lo general decidían que tenían tiempo para una partida rápida de billar, pedían unas cuantas bebidas más y luego se les olvidaba para dónde iban originalmente. Cuando Jim se acordaba de su familia, ambos estaban borrachos, Jim estaba atrasado, Kathy estaba enojada, y la noche se había arruinado.

Kathy trazó el mapa de esta situación, marcó cada evento entre el problema en el auto de Charles hasta la pelea de ella con Jim al llegar a casa. El simple hecho de verlo todo tan claro hizo que Kathy se sintiera menos impotente. Luego, se sentó y escribió afirmaciones claras del problema para cada punto del mapa (consulte el capítulo 8). Anotó una afirmación sobre el auto de Charles, la oferta de Jim de llevarlo, la decisión de ir a beber, etc. Sobre el auto de Charles, se dio cuenta de que no había nada que ella pudiera hacer. Ella y Jim no tenían condiciones de prestarle dinero a Charles para que comprara un auto nuevo ni tenían un auto adicional para regalárselo (¡cómo le habría gustado que así fuera!). Entonces pasó al momento en que Jim la llamaba para decirle que iba a llevar a Charles a casa. Kathy hizo una lluvia de ideas con una lista larga de soluciones. Iban desde amenazar a Jim con dejarlo si él no le decía a Charles que le pidiera a otra persona que lo llevara, hasta ofrecerse a llevar ella misma a Charles a su casa. La solución que eligió finalmente fue decirle a Jim que estaba preparando su cena favorita e invitar a Charles a acompañarlos. Esto cambió la "situación de Charles" de algo negativo a algo, potencialmente, positivo. Luego, le dijo a Jim que la cena estaría lista exactamente a las 5:30 (la hora a la que llegarían a casa si no pasaban a beber a ningún lado) y que fueran puntuales.

La primera vez que Kathy usó esta estrategia, Jim y Charles llegaron a las 6:30. A esa hora, la cena estaba fría y Kathy se había ido con los niños a la casa de una amiga a pasar la noche. Le dejó una nota en la mesa diciendo que había esperado hasta las 6:00. La siguiente vez que Jim llamó para avisar que iba a llevar a Charles, Kathy usó la misma estrategia, pero le recordó que no lo esperaría si pasaba a tomarse algo. Él prometió venir directo a casa y así lo hizo. Cuando llegó, Kathy tuvo el cuidado de hacerlo sentirse bien por llegar a casa y no echarle en cara que la vez anterior él había metido la pata. Solo se aseguró de que tuvieran una cena agradable y le dijo a Jim cuánto disfrutaba su compañía. (Es importante tomar en cuenta que Kathy eligió esta estrategia particular porque sabía cuánto Jim valoraba las cenas familiares; si no fueran importantes para él, este plan no habría funcionado).

Aunque Kathy sentía que era injusto tener que ser quien trataba de que todo saliera bien, recordó que era un precio bajo a pagar por trazar una vida mejor para ella y su familia. Su meta definitiva valía el esfuerzo actual.

capítulo 3

Ir a lo seguro

Beth y su papá

Beth sabía que su papá tenía un carácter terrible. A pesar de eso, cuando era más chica, por lo general podía calmarlo con un abrazo o una disculpa. No obstante, cuando la madre de Beth falleció, las cosas empeoraron. Lo mismo sucedió con la bebida y con su carácter. Los abrazos y las súplicas de Beth ya no eran capaces de tranquilizarlo. Una noche, la situación llegó a su punto más bajo cuando su padre golpeó la mesa con el puño y la amenazó mientras discutían. Después de ello, en un par de ocasiones, incluso la empujó contra la pared al salir de la habitación tirando la puerta. Por primera vez en su vida, Beth realmente le temía a su padre. Ella sabía que, antes de que pudiera hacer cualquier cosa para "arreglar" la relación, tenía que lidiar con el hecho de que él se había vuelto una amenaza para ella.

Es común que el alcohol y la violencia vayan de la mano. Junto con la habilidad de transformar al más tímido en el alma de la fiesta y al más alegre en un objeto inanimado, el alcohol también puede transformar a la persona más ecuánime en un huracán de furia... o en algo mucho peor. El paso más importante de su esfuerzo por mejorar su vida es asegurarse de que usted y los otros miembros de su hogar estén a salvo.

Independientemente de que su ser querido que bebe haya sido violento (física o verbalmente) alguna vez, le recomendamos que se tome su tiempo para leer este capítulo y se prepare para lo peor. Si la violencia no ha sido un problema para usted antes, sinceramente esperamos que esto no cambie. Si lo "peor" nunca llega a ocurrir, usted habrá pagado un precio bajo por el privilegio de decir que nunca necesitó usar su "plan para el peor de los casos". Por otra parte, si las cosas se ponen violentas, usted sabrá qué hacer para protegerlos a usted y a quienes están bajo su responsabilidad. También es importante considerar que las técnicas para reconocer las alertas de la violencia son útiles para reconocer alertas de un aumento en el enojo, el aburrimiento, las ganas de beber, etc.

Empezaremos hablando de lo que realmente significa la violencia y seguiremos con instrucciones paso a paso para desarollar un plan de escape, reconocer y responder a las señales de advertencia y pensar en una estrategia para responder si hay violencia.

Debido a que es imposible cubrir todas las situaciones peligrosas, usted deberá pensar detenidamente en sus experiencias. Si las situaciones que mencionamos no describen exactamente las suyas pero se sienten ligeramente familiares, deténgase y explórelas. Podrían hacerlo(a) pensar en una experiencia que se ajusta al concepto que comentamos aunque no necesariamente a las palabras.

Si ha habido violencia en su hogar y usted tiene miedo, actúe con cuidado. Esto no es una carrera. Evalúe con calma si cualquier cambio que considere implica riesgo de disparar violencia. Coméntelo con un terapeuta, si tiene acceso a uno. Haga sus planes con cuidado y calcule los plazos pensando en la seguridad.

¿Qué es la violencia?

Antes de que decida que esta es una pregunta tonta, responda estas preguntas. Decida si cada una de las siguientes situaciones es violenta o no.

1. Su ser querido llega oliendo a alcohol a la fiesta trimestral de su compañía. Cuando usted le cuestiona la situación, lo(a) hace a un lado y se va directo al buffet.
2. Usted le pregunta a su esposo por qué llega tarde a cenar. Él empieza a gritarle que usted es una bruja majadera y que él debería callarla de una vez por todas. Sigue vociferando e insultándola hasta que usted sale de la casa.
3. Usted y su conyuge están en medio de una discusión, cuando su hija pequeña entra a la habitación reclamando del hermano. Su cónyuge le grita a su hijita que se le ha dicho cientos de veces que no interrumpa y que ahora va a tener motivos para llorar. Su cónyuge le da una nalgada a la niña muy fuerte para que usted escuche.
4. Mientras usted sacude la chequera, le pregunta a su pareja sobre esos saques de dinero en el cajero automático. Su pareja se pone furiosa y empieza a gritar por su falta de confianza y a decir que aporta tanto dinero como usted, así que no es problema suyo en qué lo gasta. A medida que la pelea aumenta de intensidad, su pareja lanza la taza de café contra la pared y sale gritando de la cocina.
5. Mientras cenan con amigos, su esposo bebe más de la cuenta. Cuando ustedes dos están solos en casa, usted está furioso(a) y se lo dice. Él responde que trabaja duro para mantener a la familia y que usted no tiene derecho de cuestionarlo. Le dice que se calle o él lo(a) va a callar.
6. Usted va al bar donde su esposa está bebiendo para llevarla a casa. Ella se burla de usted por ser un(a) aguafiestas y lo(a) avergüenza públicamente. Cuando usted la toma del brazo para llevársela, ella le da una bofetada.

Si marcó cualquiera de las situaciones anteriores como no violentas, es hora de repensar su definición. (También tome en cuenta que esta lista no describe todas las formas de violencia). Esto es lo que dice el *Diccionario Webster* al respecto:

> Violencia *n* **1 a:** uso de la fuerza física para lastimar o agredir **b:** un caso de trato o procedimiento violento **2:** lesión causada por distorsión, infracción o profanación: ULTRAJE **3 a:** acción o fuerza intensa, turbulenta o furiosa y, con frecuencia, destructiva **b:** sentimiento o expresión vehemente: FERVOR **c:** atributo contrario o discordante: DISCORDANCIA **4:** alteración excesiva

Note que la violencia es más que golpes o empujones. También es una lesión por distorsión (como tergiversar sus palabras y transformarlas en algo lleno de odio) y vulgaridad (decirle groserías). Violencia es cualquier fuerza furibunda, destructiva (como lanzar cosas), así como una discordancia vehemente (como amenazar con callarlo/a de una vez por todas). En otras palabras, cada una de las situaciones anteriores es violenta.

Contrario a lo que algunos programas de televisión muestran y algunas películas podrían sugerir, la violencia *no* es una parte natural del amor o la sexualidad. Ni es un "derecho" de los padres sobre los hijos, o de los hijos sobre los padres. Nadie lo(a) golpea, amenaza con golpearlo(a) o agrede verbalmente porque lo(a) ama. De hecho, la violencia no tiene absolutamente nada que ver con usted. Solo tiene que ver con la persona que la ejerce. La violencia le indica que esa persona está frustrada y molesta, que perdió el control de sus sentimientos y acciones y que está cien por ciento concentrada en sí misma. Más allá de ser el blanco, usted no es importante. Es verdad que usted podría haber sido parte de la escena que disparó la violencia, pero usted no es la causa de ella.

Usted no necesita cambiar (volverse un/a mejor cónyuge, pareja, hijo/a o padre) para volverse merecedor(a) de un tratamiento no violento. Es su derecho. Ahora. Si la persona que bebe ha sido violenta con usted o las personas que le importan, ella es la única que se ha pasado de la raya, independientemente de lo que usted haya hecho y haya formado parte de la escena que disparó la crisis.

Ni siquiera si usted hizo o dijo algo hiriente, no hay justificación para el uso de la violencia como expresión de ese dolor. Le garantizamos que otras personas han hecho lo mismo que usted en situaciones similares y no han sido agredidas. Usted tampoco tiene que aceptar la violencia. Piense en las conductas que usted aceptará o no de su ser querido. La elección es suya.

Plan de seguridad

Antes de que hablemos de la respuesta a la violencia, elaboremos un buen plan con una salida de emergencia.

El primer paso al hacer una salida de emergencia es estar seguro(a) de tener sus maletas empacadas. Literalmente. Prepare una maleta o una bolsa pequeña con las cosas que usted necesitaría para pasar dos o tres noches fuera de casa. Asegúrese de incluir un cambio de ropa, artículos de higiene personal (aspirina, pasta de dientes, etc.), dinero, números de teléfono, documentos importantes y un juego de llaves adicional. Si tiene hijos u otras personas bajo su responsabilidad, empaque las cosas de ellos también.

Una vez que tenga esta maleta preparada, puede mantenerla en su auto o en una casa segura. Una casa segura es cualquier lugar donde pueda quedarse y no se le permita entrar a su ser querido que bebe. Además de los hogares de amigos de confianza o familiares, las buenas casas seguras incluyen abrigos para casos de violencia doméstica o habitaciones de hoteles de paso. Si está involucrado(a) en un programa de los Doce Pasos, otros miembros o su padrino/madrina podrían ayudarlo(a). Si tiene hijos que viven con usted, es importante tomar en cuenta su seguridad y necesidades al elegir una casa segura.

Podría ser difícil para usted identificar a un amigo o familiar en quien confiar. Todos los meses y años de proteger, sobrevivir y ser avergonzado (a) por la persona que bebe podrían haberlo(a) aislado. Hablaremos más sobre cómo combatir este aislamiento en un capítulo posterior, pero ahora pensemos en quién podría confiar. ¿Se le ocurre algún amigo o familiar que esté dispuesto a volver su hogar en una casa segura para usted? Si es así, hable con esa persona, hoy mismo. Si no, hay organizaciones locales capaces y dispuestas a ayudarlo(a). Busque el directorio telefónico y busque abrigos para casos de violencia doméstica, centros de salud mental, abrigos para mujeres, centros para atención de casos de abuso de alcohol y drogas, grupos de apoyo, organizaciones cívicas, departamentos de policía y grupos de la iglesia que brindan ayuda a las personas involucradas en disputas de violencia doméstica. Si en el directorio no encuentra ninguna organización que parezca capaz de ayudarlo(a), llame al departamento de policía local o a la agencia de servicios sociales del estado y pida recomendaciones de casas seguras en su comunidad. Sí existen. Simplemente podría requerir un pequeño esfuerzo encontrarlas. Y, con respecto a la vergüenza de pedir ayuda, usted no es quien está cometiendo la conducta socialmente inaceptable. Usted es quien está siendo prudente.

Si es posible, anote más de una casa segura. En circunstancias ideales, usted tendría varias casas seguras pendientes, en caso de que una no esté disponible cuando usted la necesite o si la persona que bebe logra ingresar.

Con su bolsa de escape empacada y una casa segura disponible, está listo(a) para salir de una situación peligrosa si se presenta. Al trabajar con los siguientes ejercicios de este capítulo, usted deberá ser capaz de bajar la tensión de la mayoría de las situaciones antes de que lleguen a ese punto, pero si no puede hacerlo, puede cruzar la puerta y tiene adónde ir.

Si se encuentra en una situación violenta o potencialmente violenta, sin escape posible, llame al 911. La policía tiene experiencia en abordaje de violencia doméstica y, por lo general, podrá sacarlo(a) a usted de la situación de forma segura y ayudarlo(a) a encontrar un lugar seguro.

Si sale de su casa pero necesita volver por sus pertenencias, asegúrese de obtener la asistencia de la policía. No tiene sentido pasar por todo el trabajo de salir con seguridad para dar la vuelta y regresar al caos.

En muchos estados, las víctimas de violencia pueden solicitar una orden de alejamiento del sistema judicial local. Una orden de alejamiento temporal no es una solución permanente pero su objetivo es mantener a la persona violenta alejada hasta que las cosas se calmen.

Evaluar el potencial de violencia

La probalidad de que su ser querido que bebe se volverá violento está muy relacionada con su conducta anterior. Si ha sido violento en el pasado, hay una buena posibilidad de que esa violencia sea parte del futuro. Note que dijimos "posibilidad". Un pasado violento no garantiza un futuro violento de la misma forma que un pasado no violento no garantiza un futuro no violento. En ambos casos, la responsabilidad de protegerse es suya. Solo la *acción* puede mantenerlo(a) a salvo.

Evaluar el riesgo de violencia empieza con revisar el pasado. Deténgase un momento y piense en su vida al lado de su ser querido que bebe a lo largo de los años y complete la siguiente actividad. Puede ver cómo Beth la completó a continuación.

Actividad 7. Seguimiento de la violencia

Anote cualquier episodio violento que recuerde. Esto incluye gritos, empujones, amenazas verbales, amenazas físicas, golpes, patadas, sacudidas, golpes con objetos, cosas quebradas, amenazas de usar armas, o cualquier acto de agresión sexual. Una vez que haya hecho una lista que sienta que está completa, anote cuántas veces recuerda que hayan ocurrido estos actos violentos. Estas son las notas de Beth.

Episodios violentos	Cantidad de veces
Groserías e insultos; culparme de todos sus problemas	¡Docenas! 3 a 4 veces por semana durante varios meses
Hacerme a un lado	0 a 12 (casi 1 por semana durante los últimos 3 meses)
Lanzarme contra el sofá	1
Lanzar objetos	1

Ahora, revise su lista y haga un círculo alrededor de los episodios que ocurrieron dentro de los últimos seis meses. Estos son los comportamientos en los que más necesita reconocer señales de advertencia iniciales. Independientemente de que su lista sea larga o solo contenga un incidente, usted corre riesgo.

Reconocer las alertas

Los actos violentos no ocurren de la nada. Se van concentrando como si fuera una tetera donde pusimos a hervir agua. La tetera no está haciendo burbujas ni silbando cuando la enciende. Empieza fría y poco a poco se va calentando hasta que, eventualmente, se acumula el vapor y empieza a silbar... O la tapa explota. De forma similar, casi siempre hay una secuencia de eventos que se van acumulando en intensidad hasta que resultan en una explosión física o verbal.

Desde su punto de vista, probablemente parezca que la violencia de su ser querido que bebe surge de la nada. Eso se debe a que usted está tan cerca que es difícil ver claramente. Un poco como estar de pie en su patio y tratar de ver la redondez de la tierra. Usted necesita cierta distancia para apreciar la forma de nuestro planeta. Podemos empezar a darle la perspectiva de la violencia que necesita mirando las situaciones de otras personas. Empecemos mirando la interacción de Carla y Jack la última vez que él llegó a casa tarde del trabajo, después de haber estado bebiendo. Mire la progresión de eventos paso a paso que llevaron de una situación no violenta a una violenta.

Paso 1: Jack llega dos horas tarde a cenar. Estuvo en el "happy hour" del bar local y está un poco ebrio.

Paso 2: Carla le dice: "Muy bien, lo hiciste de nuevo. Arruinaste nuestra cena y demostraste que eres un padre irresponsable".

Paso 3: Jack dice: "Lo siento" y se dispone a abrazar a Carla que se pone tensa. Jack empieza a enojarse y agrega: "Tuve que reunirme con unos tipos de la planta para hablar de negocios. Era un asunto de trabajo".

Paso 4: Carla responde: "Estoy harta de estas idas al bar por asuntos de trabajo. Por lo menos podías haber llamado. Estaba preocupada".

Paso 5: Jack le dice: "Déjame en paz. Te estás poniendo insoportable. Te dije que era un asunto de trabajo. Estoy cansado y no quiero hablar al respecto".

Paso 6: Carla le dice: "Nunca quieres hablar al respecto, pero nunca me avisas dónde estás. Me asusto".

Paso 7: Jack responde: "Si escucho una palabra más me voy a devolver al bar y vas a ver lo que es estar borracho. Ahora déjame en paz antes de que te acabe a golpes. ¿Dónde está mi cena?".

Esta interacción completa tardó un minuto y, para Carla y para Jack, la sensación es que fue un solo evento. Para Carla, el evento fue que Jack llegara tarde a casa. Para Jack, el evento fue que Carla le reclamara. No obstante, como puede ver, ocurrió una serie de cosas además de que Jack llegara tarde o Carla le reclamara. Jack trató de disculparse y ella lo rechazó. Él se enojó y ella también. Carla le pidió que tuviera consideración por sus sentimientos y él la ignoró. Carla mencionó problemas pasados ("nunca quieres hablar al respecto"), y él amenazó golpearla. Fue una secuencia rápida pero poderosa que terminó en una amenaza y la probabilidad de violencia física.

A partir del ejemplo, puede ver cómo se desarrolla la violencia. Al dividir la interacción en pasos, resulta más fácil identificar los puntos donde se podría haber detenido la tensión que llevó a la violencia. Carla podía haber detenido la progresión en el paso 4 o el paso 6 suspendiendo la conversación u ofreciendo una afirmación positiva o comprensiva (consulte el capítulo 9). Recuerde que Jack estaba ebrio así que realmente no era razonable pensar que se podía razonar con él. No obstante, el dolor y el enojo de Carla fueron más fuertes y ella siguió discutiendo aunque fuera inútil y, en última instancia, se volviera peligroso. ***Carla no es el problema,*** *pero ella puede empezar la solución.* Para defender su posición, debe aprender nuevas formas de interactuar con Jack, incluso si esto significa retroceder aunque sepa que tiene razón. Hacer este cambio le dará a Carla mayor control de la situación y le permitirá llevar las cosas hacia una dirección saludable. Una vez que haya pasado el peligro, Carla tendrá una amplia oportunidad de expresarse y garantizar que se satisfagan sus necesidades. Sin embargo, en ese momento, la seguridad es la necesidad principal.

Aprenda a detectar las señales de alerta de la violencia potencial. Las señales de alerta son afirmaciones, expresiones o conductas que suelen preceder un acto violento. Una mirada penetrante o caminar de un lugar a otro son ejemplos de posibles señales de alerta. En nuestro ejemplo, la frase de Jack, "Estoy cansado y no quiero hablar al respecto", podría haber sido la alerta que Carla no percibió. También podía haberse alertado a la posibilidad de violencia cuando las palabras de Jack se pusieron más agresivas ("déjame en paz" e "insoportable").

Sabemos que, al calor del momento, no se puede analizar cada frase y acción. Sin embargo, pensar en las alertas antes de que ocurran aumentará su sensibilidad a ellas.

Volvamos a Jack y Carla a ver si usted nota cualquier alerta que Carla pasó por alto. Carla y Jack están preparando una cena para celebrar el aniversario de los padres de Carla. Jack no está muy de acuerdo en recibirlos porque cree que a los padres de Carla él no les cae bien. Es domingo por la tarde y Jack ha estado bebiendo.

Carla: Sabes que mis padres te aprecian. Solo no entienden por qué bebes tanto.

Jack: No quiero oír nada al respecto. Tus padres me detestan y siempre ha sido así. Creo que están celosos porque me llevé a su preciosa hijita. No los quiero aquí. Llévatelos a cualquier restaurante de comida rápida.

Carla: Sé que es difícil para ti convivir a veces con mis padres, pero ellos te aprecian. Hace casi un año que no nos visitan y esta es una ocasión especial.

Jack: Esta es mi casa, yo soy quien paga la maldita hipoteca y ya dije que nada vienen a hacer. Punto final.

Carla: Por favor, Jack. Esto es importante para mí. Solo esta vez, ¿no podemos hacer algo bonito para ellos?

En este punto, Jack lanza su cerveza contra la pared y vuelca la mesa.

Jack: Si te escucho decir una palabra más sobre esta estúpida cena, lo vas a lamentar. Ahora, limpia todo esto. Me largo de aquí. ... ¿Vas a decir algo más?

¿Pudo ver las señales de alerta? Sin duda, usted pudo ver con qué rapidez la furia puede asumir el control de una situación. En un minuto Carla está suplicando para tener una cena agradable con su familia y al siguiente hay vidrios rotos y cerveza por toda la sala. Pero, ¿que pasó entre una cosa y otra?

Si se fija con atención en esta interacción, puede ver varias señales de alerta que Jack lanza, aunque haya sido sin intención. Tal y como lo hizo en la última pelea, Jack le dejó claro a Carla rápidamente que con ese tema estaba pisando en terreno minado, que él "no quería oír nada al respecto". En ese momento, Carla podía haber evitado los resultados al dejar de insistir. Tras la primera señal de alerta, las palabras de Jack se volvieron más groseras al referirse a la "maldita hipoteca". Carla podía aprender a detectar este patrón en las palabras de Jack y ver las groserías como una señal de alerta clara de que está a punto de explotar. Tras ver la señal de alerta, Carla podía haber evitado el desastre que ocurrió cambiando de planes o diciéndole algo que lo tranquilizara.

Planificar respuestas seguras a las señales de alerta

En este punto, usted podría sentirse hasta cierto punto molesto(a) porque parece que le estamos sugiriendo que ceda ante la conducta irracional de la persona que bebe. No es así. Por el contrario, lo(a) estamos ayudando a aprender a manejar su propia conducta para protegerlo(a) y seguir trabajando para mejorar su vida y su relación. Defender su punto de vista no vale una nariz quebrada. Esta es una de esas situaciones en las que "perder la batalla para ganar la guerra" es apropiado.

Sepa cuándo ceder para mantenerse a salvo. Además, recuerde su meta de largo plazo. Si quiere pasar más tiempo sin alcohol con su ser querido o influir en cuánto bebe, podría tener que renunciar a ciertas cosas al principio para disfrutar de mayores beneficios después. Y usted ya ha invertido suficiente dolor emocional en esta relación. No necesita tener también el dolor físico. Nada vale moretones o huesos rotos.

El siguiente ejercicio podría ser un poco difícil pero es necesario para brindarle la perspectiva que necesita para reconocer las señales de alerta de su ser querido. Lea cómo Beth completó la actividad y luego complete la suya en su cuaderno.

Actividad 8. Identificar las señales de alerta

Recuerde la situación violenta o casi violenta que ocurrió. Descríbala con la mayor cantidad de detalles que pueda. Piense en lo que usted estaba haciendo, dónde estaba, qué sentía y en qué estaba pensando. Trate de recordar qué generó el problema. ¿Cómo subió la intensidad? Anote quién dijo e hizo qué. También trate de recordar el tono emocional durante la interacción. Estos antecedentes, o disparadores, que llevaron a la dificultad son hechos importantes que se deben revisar.

Una vez que haya recreado la situación de la mejor forma posible, examine cada parte para determinar qué podría haber hecho diferente para evitar la violencia. En otras palabras, de la misma forma que examinamos las señales de alerta en los escenarios de Jack y Carla, examine las señales de alerta en los suyos. Vuelva a sus notas y haga un círculo en las señales de alerta que vea. Vea cómo Beth (del ejemplo al principio del capítulo) trazó el mapa de lo que sucedió después de que su padre llegó a casa borracho, se acostó a dormir, no se levantó cuando sonó la alarma del reloj por la mañana y se rehusó a alistarse para ir a trabajar. Las alertas de Beth se muestran en **negrita**.

Quién	Dijo	Hizo	Emoción
Beth	"Papá, estás atrasado. Levántate".	Le toqué el hombro para despertarlo.	Molesta
Papá	**"Déjame en paz".**	Se volvió hacia el otro lado.	
Beth	"Tienes que levantarte o perderás este empleo, como te pasó con el último".	Le sacudí el hombro.	Enojada, preocupada
Papá	"Te dije que me **dejes en paz**".	**Me miró** con rabia.	**Irritado**
Beth	(levantando la voz) "Vas a hacer que perdamos la casa".	Le empujé el hombro.	Furiosa
Papá	(gritando) "Ya te dije que me **dejaras en paz**".	Saltó de la cama y me pegó.	Furioso

Una vez que haya identificado sus señales de alerta, debe pensar en cómo usarlas para protegerse. La Actividad 9 lo(a) ayuda con eso.

Actividad 9. Respuestas más seguras a las señales de alerta

Registre aquí cada una de las señales de alerta de la Actividad 8 y piense en qué podría haber hecho de forma diferente para interrumpir el aumento de la presión y evitar la violencia. Al lado de cada señal de alerta, escriba qué podría haber dicho o hecho para evitar la explosión. En otras palabras, planee sus respuestas seguras a las señales de alerta. Vea cómo Beth completó la actividad a continuación.

Alerta	Respuesta más segura
Decirme que lo dejara en paz	Decir "Te voy a dejar tranquilo. Solo quería garantizar que supieras qué hora es". (Y ¡salir de la habitación!)
Mirarme con rabia	Decir "Ya veo que no quieres oír esto. Entonces, me voy".

El siguiente ejemplo también le muestra cómo Carla podría haber completado las Actividades 8 y 9 con otra situación con Jack.

Notas de Carla en la Actividad 8

Quién	Dijo	Hizo	Emoción
Carla	"Otra vez has estado bebiendo y llegas tarde a cenar".	Me quedé de pie contra el fregadero	Tristeza
Jack	"Pues ya llegué, así que **déjame en paz**".	Se sentó a la mesa y **me miró fijamente**	¿?
Carla	"La cena está arruinada y volviste a decepcionar a los niños".	Me quedé de pie contra el fregadero	Tristeza, enojo
Jack	**"¡No quiero oír nada al respecto!"**	**Dio un puñetazo** en la mesa	Enojo
Carla	"Nunca quieres oír nada al respecto!.	Lloré	Tristeza, enojo
Jack	**Insultos**	Lanzó al suelo los platos que estaban en la mesa y me agarró del brazo	Enojo

Notas de Carla en la Actividad 9	
Alerta	**Respuesta más segura**
"Déjame en paz" mientras me veía con furia	Cambiar el tema
"No quiero oír nada al respecto" y dio un puñetazo en la mesa	Decir "Okay" y cambiar el tema

Carla optó simplemente por dejar las cosas así debido a la señal de alerta, lo que funciona y resuelve el peligro inmediato. No obstante, aún tendrá que resolver su propia frustración y dolor por la situación. Aunque no sea una buena idea tratar de hacerlo cuando Jack esté enviando señales de alerta, sería útil tener un plan para sentirse mejor. Por ejemplo, podría llamar a su hermana para contarle lo bien que manejó la situación (se siente bien jactarse un poco), salir a cenar, llamar a una madrina de un programa de Doce Pasos, o desahogarse de otra forma la frustración... pero de manera segura. Luego, cuando Jack y ella estén tranquilos, puede expresarle sus necesidades y deseos. Al planear sus respuestas más seguras, piense también en cómo se desahogará de la frustración con seguridad. Además, tenga en mente que, en última instancia, mejorar la relación y dejar atrás el problema de la bebida será más satisfactorio que cualquier gratificación inmediata que pueda obtener al gritarle a la otra persona.

Ahora que ha empezado a identificar las alertas de su ser querido que bebe, está más sensible a la hora de verlas. La próxima vez que usted y él se peleen, esté atento(a) a estas señales y, cuando las vea, *¡no las ignore!* Claro que la pregunta difícil es ¿cómo cambiar la ruta cuando ve esas señales de alerta, está enojado(a) y en medio de la discusión? Siga leyendo.

Practicar las respuestas seguras

Las señales de alerta le advierten del peligro. También hacen otra cosa. Le calientan la sangre. Cuanto más furiosa y beligerante se pone la persona que bebió, más se molesta usted. Por eso, su desafío es doble: reconocer las señales de alerta y controlar sus propias emociones para responder de forma segura.

La mejor forma de dominar sus emociones en estas situaciones es estar preparado(a) para ellas. Usted ya se ha preparado bastante en las Actividades 8 y 9. Ahora, decida una señal que pueda brindarse cuando surja una alerta y le recuerde que la pelea del momento no es tan importante como su seguridad y sus metas de largo plazo para esta relación. Por ejemplo, podría decirse: "¡Alerta! ¡La seguridad ante todo!" u otra afirmación que le resulte natural.

Ahora que ha identificado algunas de las señales de alerta más importantes, además de pensar en formas seguras de responder a ellas, puede ayudarse a practicarlas. Saque un tiempo todos los días para imaginar las situaciones horribles que describió en la Actividad 8 y visualícese reviviéndolas pero, esta vez, respondiendo con su lenguaje interno de alerta y las conductas que escribió en la Actividad 9. Cuanto más practique esto mentalmente, más fácil será hacerlo en la vida real.

Cuando es demasiado tarde

Si las señales de alerta se han presentado y usted se encuentra en medio de una explosión de violencia, hay algunas acciones que puede seguir para ayudarse. Primero, reconozca que la explosión es una señal de alerta incuestionable de que es hora de terminar la discusión. Los huesos rotos no ayudan a defender su argumento.

Si puede, salga de la casa o el apartamento y vaya a un lugar donde otras personas puedan ver lo que está sucediendo. En el mejor de los casos, responderán y vendrán a ayudarlo(a) o evitarán que los niños corran riesgo. En el peor de los casos, pueden ser llamados como testigos.

Recuerde siempre que la policía está apenas a tres dígitos de distancia. Marque el 911 o, mejor aún, téngalo en su memoria de marcación rápida para que necesite presionar menos botones para obtener ayuda. Incluso si no puede quedarse al teléfono para brindarle información a la policía, el sistema de emergencias puede rastrear su llamada hasta su dirección y la ayuda va a llegar.

Diga lo que sea necesario para calmar a quien lo(a) esté agrediendo. Si quiere escuchar que usted estaba equivocado(a) y él(ella) tiene razón, dígaselo. Si le exige una disculpa o dinero, déselos. Haga lo que sea necesario para detener el ataque. Cuando termine y usted esté a salvo, puede seguir los pasos para recuperar su dinero o su ego. Durante el ataque, la única meta importante es terminarlo.

Si la experiencia le ha enseñado que cuando trata de ser gentil, la persona que bebe lo interpreta como que está siendo condescendiente y eso aumenta su furia, use el sentido común al responder. Simplemente podría planear salir de la casa cuando vea la mínima alerta, con el fin de evitar la situación potencialmente peligrosa. Haga lo que sea necesario. Póngase a salvo.

Resumen de la acción

Si completó todos los ejercicios de este capítulo, ha dado un paso importante para avanzar. Al garantizar su seguridad y la de quienes dependen de usted, liberará su energía para concentrarse en lograr los cambios que desea.

En este punto, debería tener una bolsa de escape lista y guardada donde pueda refugiarse si la violencia se vuelve un riesgo. Si ya tiene una casa segura disponible, podría guardar su bolsa de escape allí. Si no, manténgala en su auto o en la casa de un vecino. *¡Priorice encontrar una casa segura!* No espere hasta que sus hijos estén aterrorizados y su nariz esté sangrando para pensar adónde ir. Sépalo de antemano y salga con la tranquilidad de que realmente estará a salvo.

Revise el trabajo que hizo en las Actividades 8 y 9 ensaye mentalmente sus nuevas respuestas seguras a las señales de alerta.

Esté atento(a) a las señales de alerta y use sus nuevas destrezas para cambiar los resultados. Usted tiene el mismo derecho que los demás a ser tratado(a) con dignidad y a sentirse seguro(a) en su propia casa. Si la situación llega a un punto donde ya no puede cambiar el curso, váyase con sus dependientes a la casa segura. Cuando las cosas se calmen, puede decidir cuál es el mejor paso a seguir. Sin embargo, lo primero y lo más importante es estar a salvo.

Repaso

- Bolsa de escape lista para salir.
- Respuestas seguras preparadas ante las señales de alerta de violencia.
- Casa segura preparada y esperando en caso de que la necesite.

Kathy y Jim: fuera de la oscuridad

La única vez que Jim golpeó a Kathy, la asustó lo suficiente para evitar cualquier confrontación adicional. Aunque esto cumpía el propósito de evitar otro encuentro con los puños de su marido, también significaba que no podía hablar con él sobre sus problemas. Vivía en un agujero negro de miedo.

Cuando Kathy decidió que las cosas habían ido demasiado lejos y que quería una vida diferente, una de sus primeras acciones tenía que ser superar el miedo a Jim que la paralizaba. Al hacer un análisis detenido de la situación violenta que la había asustado, así como de las otras de violencia verbal, pudo identificar un par de señales de alerta de Jim cuando pierde el control. La primera es decir: “No puedo con esto”. Aunque Kathy lo había oído decirlo muchas veces, siempre lo interpretó como que él no quería molestarse en lidiar con el tema. Cuando escribió sus interacciones con él y las analizó, tal como le hemos mostrado en este capítulo, Kathy se dio cuenta de que Jim realmente no podía lidiar con la conversación y que lo que decía era la primera señal de que estaba perdiendo el control. Otra alerta que identificó fue que justo antes de golpearla, había empezado a cerrar y abrir los puños (como si tuviera una tensión de la que no podía deshacerse) y a caminar de un lado a otro, cada vez más rápido.

Además de identificar las señales de alerta, Kathy preparó bolsas con sus cosas y las de los niños y las dejó en casa de su hermana. Su hermana y su cuñado habían aceptado brindarle una casa segura si la necesitaba.

Una vez que se había asegurado de tener un lugar de escape y de sentirse segura de que sabría cuando parar la conversación si fuera necesario, Kathy por fin pudo relajarse un poco cuando Jim estaba presente. No se sintió lista inmediatamente para enfrentarlo o incluso para tratar de cambiarlo, pero tampoco sentía que era un felpudo en su casa. Ahora tenía destrezas para mantenerse a salvo. La situación no era tan oscura como había creído. Aunque no había habido ningún cambio relevante, ella sabía que había dado un paso importante para recuperar el control de su vida.

capítulo 4

Elegir un destino

María y Mark

Cuando Mark nos pidió ayuda, estaba tan molesto por la bebida de María que casi no recordaba incluso por qué se había casado con ella. Cuanto más él se esforzaba porque ella dejara el alcohol, ella más bebía. Las peleas y los gritos eran constantes. Por las noches, se emborrachaba a pesar de las súplicas de él pero en la mañana se consumía de remordimiento y prometía no volver a beber. Y, a pesar de la cantidad de veces que rompía la promesa, Mark no perdía las esperanzas de que la próxima vez la cumpliera... hasta la siguiente noche en que ella llegaba a casa y se embriagaba de nuevo. Mark hacía todo lo que estaba en su poder para mostrarle cuánto la amaba: le daba un baño y la metía en la cama con sábanas limpias cuando ella se sentía mal, llamaba al empleo de María para excusarla cuando la resaca le impedía ir a trabajar, y generalmente le facilitaba al máximo concentrarse apenas en mejorar. Pero nada mejoraba. Por el contrario, todo estaba peor.

Este es un buen momento para detenerse y pensar en lo que quiere lograr con este programa. ¿Quiere que su vida sea como era antes de que el alcohol se volviera el centro de su relación? ¿O desea otras cosas en las que no pensaba en ese momento? Si pudiera hacer una película de su "vida mejor", ¿cómo sería? ¿Quién estaría en ella? ¿Qué harían los personajes? ¿Cómo se tratarían entre ellos?

Cambiar su vida de forma exitosa es más fácil si tiene una visión de cómo quiere que sea. Piense en lo que extraña de los buenos tiempos y cómo quisiera vivir en el futuro. Antes de seguir leyendo, tome unos minutos para explorar sus recuerdos y sus sentimientos. Luego, complete la Actividad 10. Échele un vistazo a la forma en que Mark completó esta actividad y anote sus propias respuestas en su cuaderno.

Actividad 10. Una vida mejor

Complete con calma los pasos A a D. Asegúrese de brindar tres ejemplos en cada paso.

A Describa tres actividades que solía disfrutar con su ser querido que bebe y que ya no hacen juntos.

1. *Hacer caminatas nocturnas*
2. *Visitar a la familia juntos*
3. *Ir a la iglesia*

B Describa tres actividades que la persona que bebe hace actualmente y que a usted le gustaría que dejara de hacer.

1. *Servirse un trago al llegar a la casa por las noches*
2. *Mentir sobre dónde ha estado cuando llega tarde a casa*
3. *Reírse de mí cuando le pido que no beba*

C Describa tres actividades que la persona que bebe hace actualmente y que le gustaría que hiciera con más frecuencia.

1. *Mirar la TV conmigo cuando está sobria*
2. *Ayudarme con el trabajo del jardín*
3. *Pasar más tiempo con Nancy, una vecina que no bebe*

D Describa tres actividades que usted y su ser querido que bebe no han hecho antes y le gustaría que hicieran juntos.

1. *Ir a la sinfónica*
2. *Practicar un deporte como tenis o racquetbol*
3. *Plantar una huerta de vegetales*

Dentro de poco, volveremos a las actividades que anotó en este ejercicio. Mientras tanto, esperamos que haya notado algo muy importante de lo que le pedimos que escribiera. Le pedimos que describa actividades, *conductas específicas,* que le gustaría que su ser querido que bebe haga o no. No le dimos la oportunidad de escribir cosas como: "Debería ser más agradable" o "No debería ser tan molesto(a)". Ese tipo de afirmaciones son deseos y, aunque los deseos funcionan muy bien a la hora de soplar las velas del cumpleaños o de ver una estrella fugaz, no ayudan mucho en la vida real. Usted necesita concentrarse en conductas específicas si quiere ver alguna mejora. Si lo que escribió en la Actividad 10 no describe conductas específicas, vuelva y hágala de nuevo hasta que así sea.

Detalles, detalles, detalles

Claramente, su meta final es que su ser querido pase menos tiempo bebiendo y más tiempo siendo una pareja o un familiar amoroso. Esa es una meta espectacular, pero un poco imprecisa. Por ejemplo, ¿cuánto es "menos" tiempo? ¿Usted se refiere a ningún tiempo? Exactamente, ¿qué hace o no una "pareja amorosa"?

Uno de los errores más comunes que comete la gente cuando se propone hacer cambios es que no saca el tiempo para desarrollar una imagen detallada de los cambios. Dice cosas como "Quiero ser más feliz" o "Quiero que mi matrimonio mejore", pero no piensa detenidamente en qué significan exactamente esas afirmaciones. Por ejemplo, ¿ser "más feliz" significa ganar más dinero o tener una mejor vida sexual o tener más amigos o tener el mejor jardín del barrio? ¿En un "mejor matrimonio" la pareja pasa más o menos tiempo junta? Afirmaciones como "más feliz" y "mejor" funcionan con deseos, no con metas. Las metas son descripciones precisas de adónde quiere llegar. Sin la afirmación de una meta específica, es difícil saber qué hacer para avanzar hacia la meta, y es difícil decir cuándo quiere llegar a ella. La gente que no se fija metas claras, con frecuencia trabaja como loca y no llega a ningún lugar. No queremos que eso le pase a usted.

Traducir los deseos en metas

Hemos descubierto que la mayoría de los cambios deseados por la gente que ama a personas que beben se pueden agrupar en varias categorías generales, que encontrará a continuación. Piense en las metas puntuales que quiere lograr y las categorías a las que corresponden. Al leer cada descripción, ponga mucha atención a los ejemplos que brindamos. Verá que, aunque los títulos de las categorías parecen metas al principio, son en realidad direcciones a las que quiere ir. Sus afirmaciones sobre las metas tendrán que ser mucho más específicas para llegar a alguna parte. Puede comparar el deseo al vecindario al que quiere mudarse y la meta al mapa detallado que lo llevará al frente de su nueva casa.

"Ayudar a mi ser querido a alcanzar la sobriedad"

Hay una enorme variedad en el tipo de metas que provienen de este deseo. Hay diferentes formas de definir "ayuda", así como diferentes formas de definir la "sobriedad".

Según su punto de vista, "ayuda" puede ser aprender a modificar la conducta de la persona que bebe al manejar la suya (nuestra definición), o puede significar asumir la pesada tarea de castigar la conducta no deseada. Incluso puede significar desapegarse por completo y dejar a la persona resolverlo por su cuenta. Piense en cómo quiere ayudar a su ser querido y escriba sus metas de forma que lo reflejen. Obviamente, nuestra esperanza es que usted vea el mérito de aprender a manejar su propia conducta, de modo que pueda influir en su ser querido de forma positiva. Recuerde que: siempre que usted cambia su conducta hacia otra persona, cambia toda la interacción (o reacción).

Llegar a una definición de "sobriedad" puede ser tan difícil como definir "ayuda". Para algunas personas, la "sobriedad" significa nunca más tocar el alcohol, mientras que para otras significa ser capaz de beber sin embriagarse ni afectar sus sentidos o capacidades. No podemos decirle cuál es la definición correcta para su ser querido. Hay estudios que han mostrado que algunas personas con problemas de consumo excesivo de alcohol pueden aprender a beber con moderación, pero nosotros también conocemos a otras que no lo logran. Solo su ser querido puede llegar a esta conclusión y, lamentablemente, podría ser una cuestión de prueba y error hasta descubrirlo. Si la persona ha tratado varias veces de beber con moderación y ha fallado, podría ser señal de que esta no sea una opción para ella. Por otro lado, también podría significar que estaba usando las técnicas incorrectas. Piense en lo que cree que sea posible para su ser querido y con qué nivel de alcohol usted está dispuesto(a) a vivir. Luego, prepárese para ajustar su forma de pensar a medida que su ser querido aborda el problema. Sus metas tendrán que adecuarse. No obstante, mientras tanto, aclare en su mente lo que significa para usted la "sobriedad". Asegúrese de considerar sus propios patrones de consumo de alcohol (si usted bebe). Por ejemplo, podría no ser razonable esperar que su ser querido renuncie completamente al alcohol si usted pretende seguir tomando una copa de vino por las noches, mientras prepara la cena.

Antes de definir sus propias metas en esta categoría, pruebe su capacidad de reconocer afirmaciones de metas claras en el siguiente test.

Test

Decida si cada afirmación es una meta clara o apenas un deseo.

1. Haré que mi estilo de comunicación sea más PIUS (consulte el capítulo 9) para minimizar las peleas con mi ser querido, de modo que tengamos la oportunidad de conversar con calma sobre las opciones para reducir su consumo de bebida.
2. Haré todo lo que pueda para ayudar a mi ser querido a abstenerse de consumir alcohol.
3. Aprenderé a usar mi conducta para cambiar la conducta de mi ser querido y que logre mejorar.

4. Aprenderé a usar estrategias científicas para cambiar la conducta, como las que se enseñan en las *Alternativas,* con el fin de hacer que para mi ser querido sea más interesante reducir la bebida que seguir bebiendo.
5. Dejaré de facilitarle las cosas a mi ser querido con respecto a la bebida (encubriéndolo y limpiando su desorden), de modo que le resulte más trabajoso beber que mantenerse sobrio y, por lo tanto, reduzca su consumo de alcohol.

Si reconoció las afirmaciones 1, 4 y 5 como afirmaciones de metas claras, está en lo correcto. Cada una de esas afirmaciones dice claramente qué hará el Ser Querido Preocupado (SQP) y qué espera lograr. Por otra parte, las afirmaciones 2 y 3 son menos precisas. En la afirmación 2, la dedicación de quien manifiesta el deseo es clara ("haré todo lo que pueda"), pero no está claro exactamente qué significa hacer eso. La afirmación 3 empieza bien al describir lo que hará la persona pero termina mal con el deseo mal definido de que el ser querido que bebe "mejore". ¿Qué significa eso? ¿Cómo sabrá el SQP cuándo logró la meta o incluso si las estrategias que está usando son las correctas?

"Reducir el riesgo de violencia en mi familia"

Usted ya ha dado pasos positivos en esta área, pero hablemos un poco sobre las diferencias entre los deseos y las metas en esta categoría.

Aunque "reducir el riesgo de violencia en mi familia" podría parecer una afirmación clara de una meta, si empieza con esta única dirección, tendrá dificultades en hacer que suceda. Ya lo(a) ayudamos a avanzar en este tema al guiarlo(a), en el capítulo 3, a la meta de "reducir el riesgo de violencia mediante un plan de salida de emergencia, aprender a identificar las primeras señales de violencia y cambiar la conducta para interrumpir el aumento de la tensión que genera la violencia". Si solo le hubiéramos dicho que hiciera su mejor esfuerzo para reducir el riesgo de violencia en su familia, habríamos sido de poca ayuda. Al escribir el capítulo 3 de acuerdo con la meta específica que acabamos de describir, pudimos mostrarle claramente qué hacer.

"Reducir el estrés emocional en mi vida"

Esta categoría genera una amplia gama de metas posibles, de modo que tendrá que pensar cuidadosamente en qué debe cambiar para reducir su estrés. Tal vez piense que lo que incluye en esta categoría se logrará mediante las metas de las otras categorías. Por ejemplo, la libertad del miedo a la violencia, que se aborda mediante las metas de la categoría "reducir la violencia", eliminará cierto estrés. De forma similar, si ser capaz de confiar en que su ser querido vuelva a casa después del trabajo sobrio y a tiempo para la cena es un alivio para el estrés, es posible que ya haya abordado este punto con otras metas que se ha fijado. Sin duda, algunos cambios para reducir el estrés no se han abordado en otras categorías de metas. Los ejemplos incluyen metas como "incorporar una socialización más agradable en mi estilo de vida al regresar a mi club de tejido" o "reducir los dolores de cabeza por tensión al aprender una técnica de relajamiento práctica".

Antes de que trate de generar una meta para reducir el estrés emocional en su vida, revise los factores de estrés en las diferentes áreas de su vida. Piense en su relación con la persona que bebe, con otros miembros de la familia, en su trabajo, su vida social y los comportamientos asociados con la salud. Una vez que tenga una imagen razonablemente completa de lo que causa su estrés, puede pensar en cuál sería la más eficaz para concentrarse en ella y qué puede cambiar.

"Hacer que mi ser querido se ponga en tratamiento"

Si ha venido luchando con esta situación hace mucho tiempo, probablemente ha deseado hasta el cansancio que el problema simplemente desaparezca. Incluso podría haber hecho esfuerzos sobrehumanos para tratar de "curar" a su ser querido por su cuenta.

No obstante, el hecho de que esté leyendo este libro nos dice que el problema sigue allí. También nos dice que está listo(a) para dar el siguiente paso. En nuestra opinión, ese paso es el tratamiento.

Hablaremos detenidamente sobre el tratamiento en el capítulo 11. Por ahora, solo nos concentraremos en la idea de hacer que su ser querido que bebe se ponga en tratamiento. Y hay casi tantas formas de intentarlo como personas que beben. Usted puede tratar (o puede haber tratado) con reclamos, súplicas, amenazas, artimañas, coerción, chantaje, seducción, ruegos y simples pedidos. Usted también puede tratar de usar la relación que tiene con su ser querido para hacer que quiera cambiar porque hay más beneficios en el cambio que en seguir borracho. Este último método es el que enseñamos y el que la investigación científica ha mostrado que es el más eficaz. Por eso, al definir la meta que ayudará a que se cumpla su deseo de que su ser querido se ponga en tratamiento, considere esta afirmación: "Al cambiar mi forma de interactuar con mi ser querido que bebe, lo ayudaré a tomar la decisión de que ponerse en tratamiento mejorará su vida". Lo que aprende al trabajar con este libro está diseñado para ayudarlo(a) a lograr esa meta.

"Aprender a apoyar la sobriedad y el tratamiento de mi ser querido"

Esto podría ser un nuevo concepto para usted. No mucha gente ha pensando en lo que significa apoyar el tratamiento o la sobriedad. Aunque usted no es la causa de los problemas de su ser querido, la relación que han desarrollado con el paso del tiempo podría ayudar a perpetuar la bebida. Por eso, si la persona que bebe se pone en tratamiento o logra la sobriedad pero la relación no cambia, mantenerse sobria podría ser más difícil de lo necesario. Por ahora, comprométase a lograrlo, pero deje la definición de este objetivo para cuando haya leído el capítulo 11. Cuando hablamos de ayudar a su ser querido a ponerse en tratamiento, también hablamos de las formas en que puede mover las cartas para que se mantenga en el tratamiento lo suficiente con el fin de alcanzar la sobriedad.

Las categorías de deseos y metas que hemos comentado son las que vemos con más frecuencia en el trabajo clínico. No obstante, usted podría querer lograr otros objetivos. Que no los hayamos mencionado no significa que no sean importantes. Por el contrario, las metas que le importan a usted son las *únicas* que cuentan. Use la Actividad 11 para trazar las metas que quiere lograr durante los próximos meses.

Actividad 11. Metas

Anote en su cuaderno las metas que quiere lograr en cada una de las categorías que se enumeran. Puede ver en los ejemplos que se brindan cómo Mark fue muy específico con respecto a lo que quería que pasara. Sea tan específico(a) como pueda y no se preocupe si las metas se sobreponen entre las categorías. Nadie está evaluando esto. Mientras usted entienda por qué está trabajando y qué es lo que le importa, está perfecto.

Ayudar a mi ser querido a alcanzar la sobriedad

Quiero aprender a hablar con María sobre su bebida sin pelear. Quiero identificar si es un buen momento para hacerlo y exactamente cómo empezar la conversación. Quiero ser capaz de disfrutar con ella de nuevo.

Reducir el riesgo de violencia en mi familia

Quiero aprender a detener las explosiones de furia de María antes de que se salgan de control y empiece a lanzar cosas. Quiero aprender a mantener mi enojo bajo control para no empeorar las cosas.

Reducir el estrés emocional en mi vida

Quiero irme al trabajo sin preocuparme por María. También quiero tener tiempo solo para hacer las cosas que disfruto, ya sea con ella, con otros amigos o solo. Hace mucho que no hago otra cosa que preocuparme y estar pendiente de ella.

Hacer que mi ser querido se ponga en tratamiento

Quiero descubrir cómo puedo hablar con María sobre la necesidad de que se ponga en tratamiento sin que se transforme en una pelea (creo que estoy siendo repetitivo pero esto es realmente importante). Quiero aprender más sobre los problemas del alcohol para poder ayudarla. Quiero descubrir qué he hecho mal hasta ahora.

Aprender a apoyar la sobriedad y el tratamiento de mi ser querido

Necesito aprender a hacer que el tratamiento y dejar de beber le resulten tan fáciles como sea posible. Debe haber algo que yo pueda hacer para ayudarla cuando acepte parar. Además, necesito garantizar que no haga nada que pueda afectar sus posibilidades.

Otras...

Quiero que nuestra relación tenga más actividades agradables compartidas y menos peleas cuando deje de beber. No quiero que alcance la sobriedad y luego me odie por forzarla a esto. Creo que esta meta tiene que ver con todo. Quiero que tengamos una buena vida. Por eso, necesito aprender lo más que pueda sobre el proceso de dejar de beber y la prevención de recaídas de modo que esté seguro de que mis acciones le faciliten la sobriedad.

Un punto importante

Antes de que continuemos nuestra jornada, necesitamos reforzar un punto importante. Después de la intensidad de pensar en todo lo que quiere cambiar, probablemente se esté sintiendo un poco abrumado(a). Tiene mucho trabajo por delante. El punto importante que queremos reforzar es: *relájese. Usted está en el camino correcto.* Ya ha tomado algunas decisiones difíciles. Es importante que recuerde su progreso y que valore cuánto esfuerzo implica. Incluso el ejercicio de fijarse metas que acabamos de hacer es difícil. No todos tienen las capacidad de hacer un inventario de su vida y trazar una ruta para cambiar. Usted es especial en su intención de aventurarse y tratar de mejorar su vida. Lo va a lograr. El camino es difícil, pero usted tiene un buen mapa de carreteras y el compromiso de usarlo. Dé un paso a la vez y las cosas se alinearán, poco a poco, pero de forma segura.

Prioridades

Este programa tiene que ver con usted. De la misma forma en que ayudar a su ser querido que bebe es una prioridad, es esencial tener en cuenta que *usted* está en en centro de todo. Usted es quien sufre por la bebida. Usted es quien mantiene a la familia unida. Usted es quien encubre, recoge y da la cara por la persona que bebe. Usted es quien ya aguantó demasiado. Usted es quien más quiere el cambio y quien está haciendo que ocurra. Esto significa, en toda esta confusión, *que usted es el personaje más importante.*

Al pensar en sus metas, tenga en cuenta que para lograrlas, necesita tener la energía y el corazón para seguir adelante. *Para tener la seguridad de poder hacerlo, tiene que cuidarse.* En la mayoría de los casos, eso significa poner las metas relacionadas con su salud y bienestar personales en lo más alto de la lista. *De hecho, la experiencia nos ha enseñado que las personas más eficientes a la hora de ayudar a otras son quienes se ayudan primero.*

Vea las metas que definió en la Actividad 11 y ponga una estrella grande al lado de las que se orientan a satisfacer sus necesidades. Tal vez haya fijado metas para aumentar su bienestar al unirse a un equipo de boliche o planee salir con un primo o haya decidido que hace mucho no incluye el ejercicio en su vida y quiere volver a caminar. En medio de la convivencia con su ser querido que bebe, esté atento(a) a sus prioridades; cuídese para que pueda ayudarlos a ambos. No se pierda al tratar de ayudar a su ser querido con problemas de bebida.

¡Sueñe!

Al fijar todas las metas y hacer los planes asociados con este programa, a veces es fácil perder de vista el panorama general de cómo quiere sentirse. Es decir, todas las conductas que quiere que su ser querido aumente o reduzca, todos los cambios que quiere que ocurran: todos forman parte de su sueño. Usted quiere que el dolor se vaya. Y quiere más que eso. Quiere sentirse bien, conocer el amor y disfrutar la vida. Es importante mantener el contacto con ese sueño.

Después de leer esta sección, cierre los ojos y piense en su relación con su ser querido en otros tiempos... cuando la vida era agradable. Si el ser querido es su cónyuge, podría pensar en la época en que empezaban a salir y trataban de impresionarse. Usted recuerda esos momentos: se compraban regalos, hacían felices lo que el otro quería hacer, tenían cenas románticas o caminatas en el parque, el sexo era apasionado. ¿Recuerda la emoción de una nueva relación? Piense en cómo se sentía. ¿Recuerda los sentimientos cálidos? ¿La sensación de esperanza y de futuro? ¿Recuerda cuando no podían esperar para verse, para pasar tiempo juntos, sin importar cuándo o dónde? Piense también en los planes para el futuro que tenía. ¿Puede visualizar cómo iba a ser su relación? Recuerde estas expectativas y cómo todo parecía posible.

Si usted es el padre de una persona que bebe, recuerde los sueños que tenía para su hijo(a), las aspiraciones, la vida que aún desea para él o ella. Tal vez tenga otros hijos a los que les va muy bien, o un sobrino o el hijo de un amigo cercano que tiene el tipo de vida que usted quería para su hijo(a) que bebe. Use estos pensamientos para ayudarse a recordar las esperanzas que tenía. Sabemos que, como padre, usted quiere lo mejor para sus hijos. ¿Cuáles son esos sueños?

En la Actividad 12, usted va a anotar esos pensamientos. Escríbalos uno por uno y sea tan específico y positivo como pueda. Por ejemplo, tal vez esperaba pasar tiempo de calidad con su ser querido, salir a cenar, socializar con amigos o ir al cine.

Actividad 12. Mi vida perfecta

Describa su visión de una relación perfecta. Al escribir, sea claro(a) y positivo(a). Por ejemplo, "Quiero divertirme más con él o ella; ya no nos divertimos nunca" es impreciso y negativo. No define la diversión y hace una afirmación negativa al describir lo que no sucede, en vez de lo que quiere que suceda. Usted puede volver a escribir este ejemplo para hacerlo optimista y específico. "Me gustaría que una vez por semana Sal me llevara al cine y una vez por semana pudiéramos salir a comer a un lugar bonito". Otro ejemplo específico y positivo podería ser "También me gustaría que Sal y yo pasáramos tiempo sin los niños para relajarnos más y distraernos menos". Lea cómo Mark completó la actividad. Note que no es superespecífico en este momento. Está definiendo una visión de adónde quiere llegar. A medida que avance, su visión se volverá más específica, de modo que lo que él necesita hacer resulte más claro y tenga una sensación fuerte de su progreso. Escriba en su cuaderno su descripción de una relación perfecta.

Me gustaría que María dejara de beber por completo. Me gustaría que ella y yo fuéramos al cine y a cenar al menos un par de veces al mes como solíamos hacer. Me gustaría hacer caminatas en el parque y tener una vida social saludable como antes. Quiero que visitemos a la familia y los amigos y vayamos a las actividades sociales de la iglesia. Quiero poder hablarle a María de mis sentimientos y que ella me hable de los suyos. Me gustaría que trabajáramos juntos en nuestro plan financiero. Quiero que hablemos de tener a nuestra propia familia y de lo que eso significa para ella. Quiero que los dos trabajemos en empleos que sean satisfactorios.

Al trabajar en la Actividad 12, recuerde que esta es la situación "perfecta", así que no se limite con respecto a lo que quiere. Usted está describiendo su sueño y ninguna regla dice que los sueños deban ser prácticos. Anote todos los pensamientos, deseos, actividades y comportamientos que se le ocurran y que a usted le gustaría cambiar en su relación. La única exigencia es que sus frases sean específicas y positivas. Cada uno de nosotros crea su propia realidad, pero primero tenemos que visualizarla. Así que sueñe.

Resumen de la acción

Usted sentó bases importantes en este capítulo. Después de que haga a un lado este libro durante un tiempo, vuelva a examinar sus metas y revise dos cosas. Primero, asegúrese de que realmente le importen y, segundo, de que sean específicas. Vuelva a trabajar en ellas si la idea de lograrlas no lo(a) estimula verdaderamente. Será especialmente importante tener metas muy ansiadas conforme avanza porque habrá momentos en que deba morderse la lengua o ser muy valiente para lograrlas.

Repaso

- Defina metas específicas y significativas para su relación.
- Asegúrese de que el destino por el que está trabajando sea lo suficientemente atractivo para seguir adelante en todos los altibajos de la jornada de cambio.

Kathy y Jim: crear el futuro

Cuando Kathy y Jim se casaron, eran la pareja "perfecta". A ella le encantaba el sentido de aventura y el espíritu lúdico de él y a él le encantaba la agilidad mental y la naturaleza compasiva de ella. Casi no había nada que no disfrutaran hacer juntos. Iban al cine o salían con sus amigos prácticamente todos los fines de semana y a menudo pasaban las noches abrazados en el sofá viendo televisión u oyendo música. Acampar, pescar y el simple hecho de reírse a carcajadas eran una parte importante de su vida.

Sin embargo, a medida que aumentó el consumo de alcohol de Jim, su tiempo juntos se fue deteriorando y Kathy se vio cada vez más sola. También empezó a gastar muchísimo tiempo tratando de encontrar formas de que Jim redujera la bebida. Botaba el licor que él llevaba a la casa, "se olvidaba" de darle los mensajes de teléfono de sus amigos de tragos, le escondía las llaves del auto para que no pudiera salir y gastaba toda su saliva suplicándole a Jim que volvieran a tener la vida juntos que tenían antes. Obviamente, no logró nada. De hecho, Jim se quejaba de que ella no lo dejaba en paz y él ni siquiera sabía qué era lo que ella quería. Todos sus esfuerzos lo empujaban aún más hacia la bebida.

Solo cuando Kathy vio con detenimiento lo que ella estaba haciendo y aclaró sus metas, las cosas empezaron a cambiar. En vez de suplicarle a Jim que volviera a ser como antes, Kathy aclaró en su mente exactamente qué era lo que extrañaba. Hizo una lista de las cosas que solían hacer juntos y quería que él hiciera ahora y las cosas que él hacía ahora y ella quería que dejara de hacer. Tuvo el cuidado de describir cada una de forma clara y muy positiva. En vez de decirle a Jim que quería que fuera cariñoso como antes, le dijo que quería que él "pasara una noche o dos por semana viendo televisión u oyendo música con ella". De manera similar, en vez de decirle que criticara menos a los niños, le pidió que le hiciera un elogio o le dijera una palabra cariñosa a cada niño todos los días "porque ellos te imitan y eso hace que quieran portarse mejor".

(Note cómo Kathy se las ingenió para elogiar a Jim al mismo tiempo en que le pidió que halagara a los niños).

Cuando Kathy supo exactamente qué quería que Jim hiciera, fue mucho más fácil encontrar formas efectivas y positivas de comunicárselo a él. Al soñar con el futuro que quería con Jim, Kathy pudo seleccionar y modificar sus metas específicas para ayudar a crear ese futuro. Cada vez que Kathy evitaba una pelea o dejaba de resolver las cosas para Jim, sabía que estaba avanzando en la dirección correcta. Aunque Jim no asumió de inmediato el cambio, notó que Kathy había dejado de reclamar y que su tiempo juntos era más agradable que antes. Poco después de que Kathy cambió su estilo de hacer las cosas, Jim incluso comentó que parecía ser "menos insoportable esos días". Tal vez no era el tipo de elogio que solía hacerle pero, sin duda, era mejor que lo que le decía unas cuantas semanas atás. En ese momento, Kathy supo que tenían futuro.

capítulo 5

El asiento del conductor

John y su mamá

A pesar de sus reservas sobre cuán preparado estaba John para vivir solo, su madre aceptó ayudarlo a alquilar su propio apartamento durante su primer año de universidad. Se sentía orgullosa de las notas de su hijo y de su personalidad extrovertida, pero le preocupaba su afición por las fiestas y el alcohol. Durante el año escolar, quedó cada vez más claro que la tendencia de John por la fiesta estaba interfiriendo con su capacidad de mantener sus notas y el empleo de medio tiempo con el que pagaba parte de sus gastos. En el receso de invierno, su madre dejó de darle dinero y John volvió a casa. Lamentablemente, se llevó su nuevo estilo de vida con él. El ambiente del hogar se volvió cada vez más hostil, con discusiones y gritos como comunicación dominante entre John y su madre.

Asumir el asiento del conductor requiere que usted haga dos cosas. La primera es que crea que tiene el *derecho* de conducir. La segunda es que crea que tiene el *poder* de dirigir el volante.

El derecho de conducir

A veces, la forma más poderosa de ayudar a alguien que se ama es haciéndose a un lado y cuidándose usted. Piense al respecto. Si está molesto(a), asustado(a) o deprimido(a), ¿realmente cuán eficaz cree que puede ser su ayuda para otra persona? Se necesita mucha energía para mantener la calma y pensar claramente cuando se siente molesto(a), asustado(a) o deprimido(a), y pensar con calma y claridad es exactamente lo que se necesita cuando el consumo excesivo de alcohol está involucrado. La droga hace que sea imposible que la persona que bebe sea racional. Si usted sacrifica su propio bienestar para cuidar solo a quien bebe, ¿quién queda para ayudar a la relación?

Si el problema de la bebida de una persona ha agotado su autoestima y seguridad, usted no está solo(a). Este es un resultado común de amar a alguien que bebe. La gente que siente su vida fuera de control automáticamente busca algo o a alguien a quien culpar. Su ser querido que bebe no es diferente. Cuanto más pierde el control, más necesita culpar a alguien. Lamentablemente, el blanco más fácil para la culpa es la persona que esté más cerca. En este caso, es usted. Sin duda, usted ha sido el blanco de acusaciones como "Si no reclamaras tanto, no bebería" o "Tú no lo entiendes". Mes a mes y año a año, estas interacciones desgastan su autoestima, hasta que usted casi empieza a creer que *usted* es el problema. Cuando esto ocurre, su propia desdicha se suma a la creada por el problema de la bebida, y su capacidad de ayudar en la situación, básicamente, se va por el desagüe como los cubos de hielo de la noche pasada.

Deje de culparse. Independientemente de lo que le haya dicho la persona que bebe (o cualquier otra), la bebida de alguien más no puede ser su culpa. Sí, sus conductas tienen un efecto en el panorama general del estilo de vida de quien bebe, pero *usted no hizo que esta persona se dedicara a consumir alcohol en exceso.* Todo el mundo tiene motivos de estrés en su vida, algunos más complicados que otros. Pero no todo el mundo los enfrenta emborrachándose. Incluso si usted no es el cónyuge, el padre, el hijo, el tío, el sobrino, el amante o el amigo perfecto, usted no puede ser la causa de que alguien beba. Por las más diversas razones, la persona que bebe responde a la vida bebiendo. Simplemente podría ser alguien que responda durmiendo, comiendo o meditando. Apenas estamos en las etapas iniciales de la comprensión de por qué la gente responde como lo hace. De lo único que podemos estar seguros es de que *usted no causó el problema, y no debe pagar por él.* De hecho, en el momento en que deje de pagar y empiece a cuidarse, tendrá la energía para concentrarse en interactuar con su ser querido que bebe de una forma más positiva. Esto ayudará a que motive a quien bebe a querer alcanzar la sobriedad y lo(a) ayudará a encontrar una forma de vivir más feliz para usted, la persona que bebe y su familia. Si realmente ama a su ser querido, demuéstrelo amándose a sí mismo(a).

Usted no es el problema, pero puede ser parte de la solución. Infórmese bien, asigne la responsabilidad a quien le pertenece y aprenda a aceptar la felicidad.

Prueba positiva: ¡no es su culpa!

¿Alguno de estos pensamientos le resulta familiar? *Simplemente no sé cómo ayudarlo. Si yo fuera un mejor esposo... Si no hubiera vuelto a trabajar cuando estaba tan pequeño... Si yo fuera una hija mejor... Otras personas ayudan a sus seres queridos, ¿por qué yo no puedo?* Es muy probable que este tipo de pensamiento haya cruzado su mente en algún momento. Cuando lleva meses o años en una relación problemática, es natural que empiece a dudar de sí mismo(a). Además, si usted junta esta inclinación natural con las acusaciones de quien bebe y las acusaciones sutiles y no tan sutiles de otra gente, es casi imposible no sentirse culpable. Piense en cómo era su ser querido antes de que empezara todo esto. Recuerde cómo fue empeorando poco a poco su consumo de alcohol. Piense en qué cambió. ¿Puede recordar cómo fue aumentando la bebida de su ser querido? Recuerde cómo los problemas asociados con la bebida también empeoraron: el humor de la persona se volvió errático y difícil de predecir y la diversión compartida desapareció.

¿Cada vez pasan menos tiempo agradable juntos? Si su ser querido también es su amante, ¿han dejado de querer tener sexo? ¿Su ser querido está molesto la mayor parte del tiempo y lo(a) culpa a usted de sus problemas?

Las siguientes preguntas son las más difíciles, entonces piense con detenimiento. ¿Usted quería que todas estas cosas negativas sucedieran? ¿Le pidió a su ser querido que bebiera cada vez más hasta que el alcohol empezara a dominar su vida? ¿Obligó a su ser querido a beber? ¿Todos sus amigos desarrollaron problemas con la bebida? ¿Usted disfruta que el alcohol sea el factor central de su vida? Por supuesto que no. Usted no pidió esto. Usted no trabajó para esto. Usted no causó esto.

Usted solo puede ser culpado(a) por algo que causó. Que usted tenga una relación con esta persona no hizo que ella desarrollara un problema con la bebida. Todo el mundo responde a los factores de estrés de la vida de forma diferente. Algunas personas hacen yoga o trotan, otras patean a su perro, otras le gruñen al mundo... Y otras beben. La respuesta de cada persona es un poco diferente. Su ser querido responde a la vida bebiendo. Si no tuviera la relación que tiene con usted, habría otra persona o situación para culpar por la bebida. El punto es que usted no tiene el crédito ni la culpa de ello. Es hora de que se quite ese peso. Usted vive con el problema, pero usted no es la causa de él.

Usted tiene el poder

Asumir el control, conducir la relación, por así decirlo, está dentro de su poder. Al trabajar en sus mapas conductuales, empezará a ver que usted tiene el poder. A medida que lo vea, empezará a creer en ello.

A menudo es más fácil ver nuestros propios patrones de conducta si primero aprendemos a identificarlos en otros. Analice cuidadosamente el siguiente escenario y las dos reacciones posteriores.

John regresa a casa tarde y borracho después de clases y le dice a su mamá que tuvo problemas con el auto. Ella sabe perfectamente que él estaba bebiendo y que el auto funciona bien. La madre está harta de estas excusas ridículas y...

Reacción N° 1	**Reacción N° 2**
. . . así se lo dice. Le grita y lo acusa de ser un mentiroso. John le dice que ella es una bruja histérica y sale de la casa golpeando la puerta. La madre sabe que va a beber más.	. . . decide que ya no se lo va a aguantar. Le dice: "John, los dos sabemos que no has ido a clases durante todo este tiempo y me duele que me mientas. Vete a dormir y cuando se te baje el alcohol, lo hablamos. Mientras tanto, me voy a acostar. Buenas noches". Cuando su madre sale de la habitación, John se deja caer sobre el sofá y enciende la televisión.

Como puede ver, en la Reacción N° 1 la madre básicamente le echa gasolina al fuego. John llegó borracho y a la defensiva (si no tuviera que defenderse no habría mentido), y la reacción de su madre disparó una reacción muy violenta. Al explotar, le facilitó a él reaccionar como lo hizo. Por eso, aunque tal vez ella se haya sentido mejor por "decir lo que pensaba", no mejoró la relación, no cambió el consumo de alcohol de su hijo y no mejoró su propia vida. De hecho, si gritar y reclamar fueran eficaces para cambiar una conducta, John habría dejado de beber el día que volvió a la casa.

La Reacción N° 2 muestra un efecto igualmente poderoso de la conducta de la madre sobre John. Solo que, en este caso, disparó una reación no combativa. Al mantener la calma y hacer saber a John cómo ella se sentía (en oposición a señalar lo que estaba mal en él), transmitió su mensaje y evitó transformar la interacción en otra pelea y otra excusa para que él siguiera bebiendo. Claro, John podría haber optado por volver al bar de cualquier forma, pero en esa situación habría sido más difícil culpar a su madre.

De la misma forma que la conducta de la madre afecta la conducta de John de forma diferente según cómo reaccione ella a él, su conducta puede tener un efecto positivo, negativo o neutro sobre la conducta de su ser querido. Use la Actividad 13 para explorar las formas en que su conducta puede influir en la conducta de la persona que bebe. Al completar la tercera sección, piense en mantener la calma y la lucidez durante la interacción, evitar la confrontación *(lo que no se debe confundir con evitar los problemas)* y no aceptar la responsabilidad de la conducta de la persona que bebe. Asimismo, busque formas positivas, no negativas, de elaborar su comunicación. Por ejemplo, si desea que su cónyuge se quite las botas llenas de lodo antes de entrar a la casa, un pedido negativo podría sonar así: "Cariño, detesto cuando andas por la casa con tus botas sucias. Por favor, quítatelas antes de entrar". Un pedido positivo le da vuelta a ese mensaje de modo que el oyente escuche una frase cariñosa en el pedido para cambiar: "Cariño, realmente te agradezco cuando te quitas las botas antes de entrar a la casa. Me facilita mucho la limpieza". Aunque a veces sea muy difícil reforzar a alguien que no ha puesto ni la mitad de energía que usted ha invertido en la relación, recuerde que se atrapan más moscas con miel que con vinagre. Si desea que la persona sea receptiva a su empuje para el cambio, mantenga la interacción positiva.

En la Actividad 13, le pedimos que analice cómo podría reducir la probabilidad de que su ser querido se comporte de formas indeseadas. No obstante, antes de hacer el ejercicio, échele un vistazo a la forma en que el esposo de Marge concluyó cómo él podía afectar su comportamiento.

Describa algo que su ser querido hace y realmente a usted le incomoda y le gustaría que dejara de hacer.

Marge se despierta en la mañana con una resaca horrible después de beber toda la noche. Se arrastra por la casa y refunfuña que se siente demasiado mal para ayudar con los niños o la casa.

Describa que podría hacer usted y aumentaría la probabilidad de que la persona que bebe haga lo que usted acaba de describir o qué empeoraría la situación.

Castigo el comportamiento dejando de hablarle. Cuanto más habla o trata de disculparse, más me alejo y no le respondo. Se pone furiosa y, por lo general, sale de casa y se va a beber.

Describa qué podría hacer usted y reduciría la probabilidad de que la persona que bebe haga lo que usted acaba de describir o qué mejoraría la situación.

Podría decirle: "Sabes que no apruebo que bebas y pases la noche fuera, pero quiero escuchar lo que tienes que decir. También quiero que sepas que, cuando te sientas mejor, estoy dispuesto(a) a hablar contigo al respecto pero, en este momento, tú no pareces estar en tus cabales y yo aún estoy muy molesto(a) para hablar de anoche contigo. Hablemos en la cena".

En la segunda respuesta, el esposo de Marge le habla de sus sentimientos y le indica que está dispuesto a comentar la situación, pero en un momento en el que ambos estén en mejores condiciones de hacerlo. Con tranquilidad, le muestra su preocupación pero no le resta seriedad a la situación. Además, al mantener la calma y postergar la conversación hasta que ambos estén mejor, le brinda a su pareja la oportunidad de recuperarse y hacer planes sobre cómo hablar del tema. Esto le permite ser proactivo en vez de reactivo: siempre la mejor posición si desea mantener el control y aumentar la probabilidad de lograr su meta, cualquiera que sea.

El siguiente ejemplo usa una de las opciones de Mark en la Actividad 10 (capítulo 4). Puede usar el plan de Mark como modelo para hacer el suyo si le resulta útil. Lea la actividad y escriba sus respuestas en su cuaderno.

Actividad 13. Conductas con poder

Paso 1: Copie una de sus opciones del Paso B, Actividad 10 (en el capítulo 4), aquí.

Reírse de mí cuando le pido que no beba

Paso 2: Describa qué podría hacer usted y aumentaría la probabilidad de que la persona que bebe haga lo que usted acaba de describir o qué empeoraría la situación. (Probablemente usted tenga ejemplos de su experiencia real).

Ponerme a la defensiva o tratar de discutir con ella. Tratar de explicarle que alguien tiene que estar bien y cuidar la casa. A veces le digo que solo quiero hacer algo para ayudarla, y se enoja muchísimo. Si empiezo a llorar, me atormenta más.

Paso 3: Describa qué podría hacer usted y reduciría la probabilidad de que la persona que bebe haga lo que usted acaba de describir o qué mejoraría la situación.

A veces, cuando me enojo, simplemente me voy. Por lo general no me sigue; solo se calla. Nunca menciono a su mamá pero, tal vez, si mencionara lo que ella diría si la viera atormentándome, se detendría. Vale la pena tratar.

Felicidades, acaba de diseñar su primera "intervención conductual". Esa es una frase pomposa que, en resumen, significa que usted planificó conductas (suyas) que cambiarán intencionalmente la conducta de otra persona (su ser querido que bebe) en la dirección deseada. Usted sabe cómo puede empeorar la situación que describió en la Actividad 13 y cómo puede mejorarla.

A continuación, hay otra Actividad 13 completada. Revise las respuestas de la pareja de Harris, junto con nuestro comentario, para ver qué puede aprender.

Describa algo que su ser querido hace y realmente a usted le incomoda y le gustaría que dejara de hacer.

Siempre que salimos a cenar con mi hermana y su esposo, Harris bebe gin tonics hasta que e mpieza a hablar alto y se pone majadero. Al final, nos avergüenza a todos. Incluso un par de veces nos han pedido que nos vayamos del restaurante.

Describa que podría hacer usted y aumentaría la probabilidad de que la persona que bebe haga lo que usted acaba de describir o qué empeoraría la situación.

Ya hemos pasado por esto tantas veces que realmente me saca de quicio. Termino gritándole, en realidad susurrándole bien alto por el lugar donde estamos, algo como: "No te atrevas a pedir ni un trago más. Me estás avergonzando de nuevo". Esto generalmente lo enoja y pide un trago doble.

Describa que podría hacer usted y reduciría la probabilidad de que la persona que bebe haga lo que usted acaba de describir o qué mejoraría la situación.

Primero, podría recordar que su conducta no se refleja en mí. Luego, podría respirar hondo y decirle: "Sé que disfrutas los tragos, pero para mí es muy importante que ya no pidas más hoy. ¿Podrías hacer eso por mí?". Si insiste en seguir bebiendo, le diré: "Si eliges beber hoy, es cosa tuya. Pero yo no tengo que sentarme aquí a verte. Me voy a casa. Cuando estés sobrio, me gustaría que hablemos al respecto". Y me voy.

En este ejemplo, puede ver algunas diferencias muy importantes entre la primera y la segunda respuesta. En la primera, la pareja deja que Harris controle la situación al enojarse. Su respuesta sugiere que acepta cierta responsabilidad por la conducta de Harris. (¿Por qué otro motivo la conducta de él la avergonzaría?). En comparación, la segunda respuesta ayuda a distanciarla a ella de la conducta de él, lo que, por su parte, la ayuda a mantener la calma y evitar un enfrentamiento. Empieza cuidándose ("Podría recordar que su conducta no se refleja en mí"), de modo que puede evitar estallar y darle a él una excusa para pedir un trago doble. Luego, reconoce los sentimientos de Harris y expresa los suyos, junto con el pedido de que no pida otro trago. Si no tiene éxito, se retira de la situación. Aquí el punto importante es que la conducta de la esposa estaba diseñada para darle a Harris todas las oportunidades de cambiar su patrón (sin quedar mal), mientras protegía su propio bienestar. Esto no siempre podría funcionar exactamente como usted quiere, pero garantiza que no se enganche en el patrón negativo y que empiece a establecer un patrón nuevo.

Al pensar cómo usted puede afectar la conducta de su ser querido, tenga en mente estos puntos:

- Si se enoja, pierde el control de su conducta y de la situación en general. En esencia, usted le da el control al alcohol.
- Cuando sea posible, elabore su mensaje en términos positivos. De esta forma, es más probable que lo escuchen.
- Aunque es importante ver cada situación tal y como es (lo bueno, lo malo y lo feo), es igualmente importante no hacer una tormenta en un vaso de agua. En otras palabras, concéntrese en el aquí y el ahora cuando pueda. No transforme la crisis de la noche en una discusión sobre cómo se arruinó toda su vida. Ver una catástrofe en cada situación tiende a disparar emociones extremas y pérdida del control.
- El progreso ocurre cada vez que intenta cambiar su forma de responder a una situación difícil. Independientemente de que su intento sea completamente, parcialmente o para nada exitoso, haber hecho el esfuerzo debilita el patrón de conducta negativo e improductivo que usted ha practicado antes. El progreso viene de muchos tamaños y muchas formas. Asuma el mérito de cada una de ellas.

A medida que avanza, recuerde todos los días que puede aprender a cambiar su conducta y que ésta puede ayudar a su ser querido a cambiar. Usted sí tiene el poder.

Resumen de la acción

El trabajo que realizó en este capítulo es comparable a meter la llave en su auto para arrancarlo. Si no lo enciende, ni siquiera el motor más afinado puede funcionar. De forma similar, si no cree que tiene el derecho y el poder de asumir el control de su vida, no podrá usar ninguna de las herramientas que le ofrecemos. Así que recuerde que usted no es el motivo por el que su ser querido abusa del alcohol u otras drogas; cada uno de nosotros es responsable solo de nuestra propia conducta. Dicho esto, tenga en mente que puede cambiar cómo responder a su ser querido y, de esta forma, activar cambios positivos en su vida.

Repaso

- Niéguese a asumir la responsabilidad de la conducta de otra persona. Usted no es el problema.
- Configure su radar para detectar los casos en los que podría cambiar su reacción a la conducta de la persona que bebe. Al avanzar por este programa, desarrollará varias herramientas que lo(a) ayudarán a cambiar su forma de responder. El primer paso es reconocer las interacciones en las que puede aplicarlas. ¡Encienda el radar!

Kathy y Jim: un nuevo tipo de amor

Kathy sabía lo que era sentirse responsable. Se sentía responsable de proteger a los niños de la bebida de Jim (tanto de su conducta como de su ejemplo). Se sentía responsable de facilitarle las cosas a Jim en el empleo cuando la resaca era demasiado fuerte para ir a trabajar (después de todo, alguien tenía que garantizar que tuvieran un techo sobre su cabeza). Se sentía responsable de protegerlo de la burla de la familia y de protegerlos a ellos de las explosiones de cólera de Jim. Se sentía responsable de presionarlo a beber con sus reclamos. Incluso se sentía responsable de sentirse tan triste. Y, de repente, algo cambió.

Kathy se preguntó por qué todo era su responsabilidad. Y no había respuesta para esa pregunta. Sí sentía que los niños eran su responsabilidad pero todo lo demás... Simplemente, no se le ocurrió ningún motivo por el que fuera su responsabilidad mejorar la imagen de Jim o resolver sus metidas de pata. En particular, no había razón para que asumiera la culpa de la bebida. Ella nunca le pidió que bebiera. Nunca "hizo" que nadie bebiera y había tenido relaciones cercanas con otros miembros de la familia, amigos y antiguos novios. Otras personas en la vida de Jim habían sido mucho menos cariñosas con él que ella y él nunca las culpó. Simplemente no había evidencia de que la conducta de Jim fuera su culpa.

Kathy decidió que al menos parte del motivo por el que se sentía tan responsable por Jim era porque lo quería mucho. De cierta forma, concluyó que, al asumir la responsabilidad de este cambio asustador en sus vidas, se había estado esforzando por arreglarlo. Cuando por fin aceptó que no era su responsabilidad, ocurrieron dos cosas. Una: dejó de maltratarse. Pudo hacer una pausa. La segunda consecuencia fue que adquirió lucidez y pudo pensar racionalmente en lo que, desde una perspectiva realista, *podía* controlar. Concluyó que su amor por Jim podía ser la motivación para cuidarse, de modo que tuviera la energía para cambiar su forma de lidiar con él. Así,

Kathy se eximió del ciclo interminable de culpa/enojo y empezó un nuevo camino hacia una vida mejor.

capítulo 6

Qué empiece la diversión

Vanessa y Martin

Cuando Vanessa cumplió veintiún años, ya era experta en cuidar a su papá. Su madre había fallecido poco después de que Vanessa cumpliera trece años y Martin, su padre, nunca se había recuperado de la pérdida. Al principio, bebía para "adormecer el dolor" y luego para "olvidar". A medida que fue pasando el tiempo, la gente se acostumbró a verlo borracho y empezó a evitarlo. Finalmente, parecía que bebía apenas para llenar el vacío que había quedado de lo que era su vida. En todo este proceso, Vanessa fue la única persona que se quedó a su lado. De hecho, se había perdido la adolescencia criando a su hermana menor, peleando y poniéndole trampas a su padre para tratar de que dejara el alcohol y dedicándose a sacar adelante su hogar. Vanessa había tenido que madurar antes de tiempo y llegó al tratamiento sintiéndose impotente y resentida, además de culpable por sentirse así.

Si le echó un vistazo al índice de este libro antes de empezarlo, es probable que este capítulo le haya llamado la atención. ¿Qué hace un título como este en medio de un libro serio sobre un problema serio? Bien, es muy fácil. Usted merece divertirse un poco.

Piense en todo el trabajo y la energía que ha invertido lidiando con los problemas causados por el abuso del alcohol. ¿Cuántas veces ha sacado a su familia de una crisis o ha mantenido a su ser querido a salvo escondiéndole las llaves del auto? ¿Alguna vez le ha tocado proteger a sus hijos de la agresión verbal o física? ¿Ha asumido el papel del padre *y* la madre o del único proveedor? ¿Cuánto se ha esforzado para mantener el delicado equilibrio entre una vida cuerda o alucinada con una persona que bebe? Probablemente, la respuesta sea "mucho". De hecho, nos imaginamos que ha trabajado tan duro para mantener su vida de pie que no le ha podido dar la mínima atención ni el tiempo a disfrutar de esa vida. Es hora de cambiar eso.

A partir de ahora, empiece a recompensarse por sus esfuerzos. De hecho, recompénsese solo por ser usted. Como dice el título, es hora de que empiece la diversión.

La autorrecompensa (que es de lo que estamos hablando aquí) no es muy diferente del tipo de recompensas que les da a la familia, los amigos o los compañeros de trabajo. Usted les sonríe, les dice que hicieron un buen trabajo o, a veces, los recompensa con objetos tangibles como dinero, regalos o tiempo especial. Recompensarnos a nosotros solo requiere pequeños ajustes con respecto a la forma en que recompensamos a los demás. En vez de sonreírle al mundo exterior, sonría consigo mismo en su interior. Decirse que ha hecho un buen trabajo requiere menos recursos que decírselo a los demás; no tiene que decirlo en voz alta, basta pensarlo. Puede recompensarse con cosas físicas, tan fácilmente como recompensa a otros. De hecho, es más fácil porque no tiene que adivinar cuál sería una buena recompensa. Usted sabe lo que le gusta.

Debido a que uno de los principales objetivos de este programa es mejorar su calidad de vida, es esencial que introduzca algo bueno en cada día. No, no necesita renunciar a su empleo para tener tiempo para ver partidos y tomar baños de burbujas. Lo único que tiene que hacer es decirse algo bonito todos los días y planear ratitos, la mayor parte de los días, para autorrecompensas un poco más grandes. Y no se preocupe si no ha logrado nada muy relevante. Recompénsese apenas por haber llegado al final del día. De hecho, vamos aún más allá: *¡recompénsese por recompensarse!*

Como ya le sugerimos, la autorrecompensa viene de muchas formas. La más simple y la menos costosa es hablar consigo mismo(a) en un tono positivo, lo que significa apenas decirse cosas agradables como: "Soy una persona dedicada" o "Esta vez manejé la situación mejor". Claro que estas conversaciones consigo mismo(a) varían según la situación. Las llamamos autorrecompensas de Nivel 1. Las recompensas de Nivel 2 son un poco más complicadas en términos de planificación y gastos. Son gratis o cuestan poco pero requieren tiempo. Los ejemplos serían un alto en las tareas domésticas para leer un libro; un baño caliente demorado en la tina; un paseo en bicicleta por el parque; o cualquier actividad que le dé placer. Las autorrecompensas de Nivel 3 son las que, por lo general, guardamos para las "Conquistas" con "C" mayúscula. Por ejemplo, podría recompensarse con un masaje profesional (implica tiempo y dinero) después de haber evitado exitosamente perder el control cuando su pareja llega a casa borracha, mucho tiempo después de que la cena se volvió carbón.

Dentro de poco, le daremos una actividad para que desarrolle sus opciones de autorrecompensa y haga planes para integrarlas a su vida. Pero, primero, necesitamos hablar sobre cuánto incluir o excluir a su ser querido que bebe en su sistema de autorrecompensas.

Divertirse con la persona que bebe, o no

Si la persona que bebe es su cónyuge o su pareja doméstica, es posible que haya fuerzas poderosas motivándolo(a) a usted a incluirla en sus autorrecompensas. Después de todo, la persona a la que usted ama suele ser con la que quiere pasar tiempo. Sin embargo, antes de decidir recompensar su arduo trabajo con una cena con su ser querido, piense con calma en lo que esta persona le agregará a esa actividad. Si hay posibilidades de que no llegue a la cena, que aparezca borracha, o que arruine la velada de otra forma, su autorrecompensa podría transformarse en un castigo. (Si esto describe su situación, ármese de valor. Parte de una buena terapia para el consumo de drogas es trabajar con los seres queridos del consumidor para mejorar la vida juntos. Por eso, si y cuando su ser querido se ponga en tratamiento, ese proceso debería ayudarlo a ser una pareja más agradable y, en ese momento, usted obtendrá placer de incluirlo en sus planes).

Por otro lado, incluir a la persona que bebe en su diversión también puede servir para motivarla a dejar su estilo de bebida pautado por el alcohol. Al incluirla en actividades que no se pueden hacer si se bebe (a estas se les llama "actividades competidoras") y que pueden disfrutar los dos, usted limita el tiempo disponible para la bebida y maximiza el tiempo agradable que pasan juntos. Por eso, puede ser bueno para usted, su ser querido y su relación.

Tras examinar ambos lados de la moneda, usted es quien debe determinar cuánto involucrar a su ser querido en sus autorrecompensas. Sin conocerlo(a) personalmente, nuestra recomendación genérica es que planifique la mayoría de sus autorrecompensas en torno de si mismo(a) y de amigos y familiares confiables e incluya a su ser querido solo de forma limitada. A medida que la conducta de esa persona mejore y se vuelva más confiable, usted podrá aumentar su participación. Mientras tanto, no deje que la persona que bebe arruine su diversión.

Empiece a disfrutar

Tome algunos minutos para empezar a agregar un poco de diversión a su vida. Use la Actividad 14 para empezar a planificar más placer en sus días. La actividad tiene tres columnas, una para cada nivel de autorrecompensa que comentamos. Recuerde que las autorrecompensas de Nivel 1 son objetos o actividades gratuitos e/o instantáneos. Los ejemplos incluyen decirse cosas positivas (la autorrecompensa más barata, más portátil y más poderosa), un momento para sentarse frente a una chimenea encendida, o poner su música favorita mientras realiza las tareas del hogar. Las recompensas de Nivel 2 implican cierto tiempo y/o gastos. Los ejemplos podrían incluir tiempo para leer una novela o una llamada de larga distancia a un amigo. El Nivel 3 incluye todas las otras cosas que requieren más de algunos minutos y más de unos cuantos dólares. Según su gusto (y su presupuesto), podrían ir desde una cena hasta un crucero por el Caribe.

Lea la lista que completó Vanessa a continuación, luego, piense en qué le gustaría hacer y la forma en que le gusta pensar en sí mismo(a) y escriba en su cuaderno todas las cosas que pueda en cada categoría.

Actividad 14. Mi diversión

Autorrecompensas de Nivel 1 (gratis, instantáneas)	**Autorrecompensas de Nivel 2 (tiempo, bajo costo)**	**Autorrecompensas de Nivel 3 (tiempo, dinero)**
Decirme: "Puedo hacerlo"	*Comprar maquillaje*	*Comprarme flores*
Hacer una oración	*Llamar a una amiga*	*Regalarme zapatos nuevos*
Sonreírle a mi reflejo en el espejo	*Ir a una reunión*	*Inscribirme en un gimnasio*
	Leer una novela durante media hora	*Ir al gimnasio*

Salir adelante con un poco de ayuda de sus amigos

Las personas afligidas tienden a alejarse de la gente que es más probable que las ayude y apoye. En vez de dejar que los amigos y familiares les extiendan una mano, se alejan de quienes se preocupan por ellas y tratan de hacerlo todo solas. Aunque no hay investigaciones que apunten exactamente a las causas, la experiencia indica que es en parte por vergüenza y en parte por culpa. Todos estos son sentimientos muy reales y comunes para la gente que vive con alguien que bebe. Sin embargo, aislarse es contraproductivo e innecesario. Decida en este momento hacer a un lado los sentimientos y pensamientos que lo(a) han alejado de la gente que lo(a) apoya e incorpore en su vida el mensaje de la antigua canción de los Beatles: "Puedes salir adelante, con un poco de ayuda de tus amigos". De esta forma.

Primero, piense en las personas que integran su círculo de familiares, amigos y conocidos. De todas esas personas, hay algunas de las que se siente más cercanas, algunas con las que se divierte más y algunas que calificaría como las últimas personas sobre la faz de la tierra con las que quiere pasar tiempo. Empiece tachando al último grupo de la lista de su apoyo potencial. Ahora, le queda una lista de gente con la que puede llenar varias necesidades de su vida.

Probablemente, la mayoría de las personas de su lista son aquellas con las disfrutaría pasar tiempo ocasionalmente, solo para divertirse un poco. No obstante, con algunos cuantos, es posible que usted quiera hablar de su situación. Necesitará dos abordajes diferentes para cada grupo de personas. Primero, hablemos de cómo puede aumentar su contacto con el primer grupo, los amigos casuales.

Crear un círculo social

Si usted se ha mantenido al margen debido a la bebida de su ser querido, puede ser difícil volver a entrar al mundo social. No obstante, recuerde que la dificultad está en su cabeza. Cuando invita a alguien a ir al cine o a almorzar, su incomodidad proviene de su preocupación sobre cómo reaccionará la persona; tal vez piense que usted es atrevido(a) o que está desesperado(a) o que es un tonto(a) o quién sabe qué más. No obstante, si se pone en los zapatos del otro e imagina que alguien lo(a) invita para encontrarse, ¿qué pensaría? Es probable que se sienta halagado(a), que crea que a la persona le agrada usted y, en general, que le guste la idea. ¿Por qué cree que otra gente juzgaría una invitación de una forma más dura que usted? Incluso si la persona no puede ir, no pasa nada y es probable que se vuelvan a comunicar y se pongan de acuerdo para intentarlo en otro momento. Cuanta más gente trate de contactar, mayor probabilidad tendrá de hacer nuevos amigos y aumentar el placer en su vida.

Encuentre a un confidente

Acercarse a las personas con las que quiere compartir sus problemas puede ser un poco más difícil. Sin embargo, es posible. De esta forma.

Primero, identifique su meta. ¿Desea que esta persona solo lo(a) escuche, que lo(a) aconseje, que lo(a) proteja físicamente, que le preste dinero, o se lo(a) lleve a una isla desierta? Tenga muy claro qué está pidiendo. Mantenga su meta simple y concreta. Por ejemplo, algunas metas razonables serían: "Quiero alguien con quien pueda hablar de mis frustraciones por el problema de bebida de mi esposa. No quiero sentirme juzgado o desvalorizado".

Una vez que tenga una meta, piense en quién sería la persona correcta. ¿En quién puede confiar, quién es un amigo lo suficientemente cercano? Decida con quién compartirá sus confidencias.

Luego, decida *cómo* se acercará a esa persona. ¿Qué le dirá? Nuestra sugerencia es el abordaje directo. En vez de darle vueltas al asunto o dar indirectas sobre lo que necesita, simplemente dígalo. Por ejemplo: "Dave, tú y yo hemos sido amigos durante muchos años, y sabes que la bebida de Gina es un problema. Quiero saber si tienes tiempo para conversar porque necesito pensar qué hacer con mi vida. Solo necesito que me escuches y me apoyes. ¿Podrías hacer eso por mí?". Note que esta persona fue muy directa y específica sobre lo que quiere de Dave.

Una vez que elija las palabras, hay dos pasos más. El primero, si está nervioso(a) por pedir ayuda, es practicar la conversación. Puede practicar imaginando que habla con la persona o ensayando la conversación en voz alta. El espejo puede ser una "pareja" útil para practicar pequeñas charlas como esta. Independientemente de cómo lo haga, el punto es superar los nervios lo suficiente para poder *hacerlo*.

Lo que nos lleva al paso final. ¡Hágalo! Es difícil enfrentar los problemas por su cuenta. Todos necesitamos una mano amiga de vez en cuando, y podemos salir adelante con una pequeña ayuda de nuestros amigos.

Si no se siente seguro(a) por su capacidad de hablar de forma eficaz en situaciones delicadas, use la Actividad 15 para identificar a alguien en quien le gustaría confiar y escriba las palabras que usará para perdirle apoyo a esta persona. Tener un plan escrito facilita la tarea. A continuación, vea cómo Vanessa decidió pedirle apoyo a una amiga de toda la vida. Complete su propia actividad en su cuaderno.

Actividad 15. Pedir ayuda

¿A quién le pedirá apoyo?

Erica: hemos sido amigas desde el kinder y vive cerca de mi casa, así que será fácil vernos.

Repita las siguientes afirmaciones:

1. No hay nada malo en pedirle ayuda a la gente. Todos necesitan ayuda de vez en cuando.
2. Los problemas que tenemos no son mi culpa. Aunque puedo mejorar o empeorar las cosas, no soy yo quien tiene el problema de bebida que está destruyendo nuestra vida. Estoy trabajando en la solución para nuestros problemas.
3. Ayudar a los demás hace que la gente se sienta bien consigo misma, así que no hay problema en pedirle ayuda a esta persona.

Escriba su pedido. Dígale a la persona cuál es el problema y sea muy claro en lo que está pidiendo.

Erica, realmente necesito hablar contigo de un problema. Hemos sido amigas toda la vida y sé que puedo confiar en ti. Antes de que me digas nada, solo quiero que me escuches un par de minutos. Necesito que seas mi amiga, en confianza.

Sabes que he pasado mucho tiempo en casa, cuidando a mi papá. Bien, el problema de papá está mucho peor de lo que te puedas imaginar. Y cada vez se sale más de control, y simplemente no sé qué hacer. Necesito hablar con alguien que no me juzgue ni me regañe. Te quiero y necesito que me apoyes. ¿Puedo contar con tu ayuda en todo esto?

Cuando les hablamos a los clientes sobre las autorrecompensas y el pedido de ayuda a los amigos y familiares, siempre están plenamente convencidos de que son ideas sensacionales y que tienen que ponerlas en práctica. Al final de la sesión, se van con la intención de seguir nuestro consejo... y luego algo sucede y no siguen adelante. La semana siguiente, cuando les preguntamos cómo les fue, nos dicen que la "vida" se les complicó y no tuvieron tiempo para autorrecompensarse ni comunicarse con los amigos. Les decimos que es una excusa muy pobre. No fue la vida lo que se complicó. Fue la falta de planificación. La vida siempre está allí, independientemente de que trate de encontrar tiempo para hacer ejercicio o llamar a un amigo o hacer una siesta. Usted *planea* el tiempo y *saca* el tiempo para las cosas que le importan. No deje la diversión perdida al fondo de su programación, llenándose de polvo. Si realmente quiere devolverle a la vida el placer y el apoyo, saque el calendario en este momento y separe tiempo para completar las actividades de este capítulo. Programe también sus recompensas de Nivel 1, 2 y 3, así como el momento en que llamará a la gente para que lo(a) ayude a salir adelante y divertirse.

Resumen de la acción

Cuidar a los demás empieza por cuidarse usted. Empiece a trabajar en la recuperación de su vida social. Pida compañía. Pida ayuda. Sea agradable consigo mismo(a).

Repaso

- Planifique sus recompensas de Nivel 1, 2 y 3 y póngalas en práctica.

- Implemente un plan de acción para incluir a otra gente en su vida.

Kathy y Jim: el Palacio del Placer

Cuando Kathy y Jim empezaron a salir, uno de sus lugares favoritos para salir los viernes era una combinación de restaurante y salón de baile llamado el Palacio del Placer. Por un poco menos de diez dólares, podían comerse una hamburguesa y unas papas fritas y bailar hasta que les dolieran los pies. Cuando Kathy empezó a pensar en agregarle diversión a su vida, empezó a pensar cada vez más en el Palacio del Placer y a llamarle a esta parte del programa su proyecto de reconstrucción... porque estaba reconstruyendo el Palacio del Placer.

El primer paso en el proyecto de reconstrucción de Kathy fue hacer una lista de elogios que ella sentía que se merecía y prometerse que se iba a detener frente al espejo cada vez que usara el baño y elogiarse. Se decía: "Soy una buena madre... una esposa leal... atenta... organizada... atractiva... Tengo un futuro".

Kathy también se programó una manicura y pedicura todos los meses (Nivel 2) y se inscribió en un curso universitario nocturno sobre literatura romántica (Nivel 3). Además, Kathy decidió que era hora de confiarle a su hermana todo lo que estaba pasando y de admitir que le caería muy bien contar con ayuda. Así que pensó detenidamente cómo le pediría a su hermana que la escuchara y la ayudara sin criticar a Jim. (Kathy sabía que los viejos hábitos son difíciles de arrancar y que, si su hermana le decía algo malo de Jim, ella lo defendería y terminaría discutiendo con su hermana).

Kathy hizo planes muy específicos, fue al punto de lo que iba a decir y se apegó a ellos. El efecto de los elogios en el espejo del baño sorprendió a Kathy. Kathy se dio cuenta de que cada ciertas horas salía del baño sintiéndose un poco mejor consigo misma y un poco más segura de su capacidad de lograr sus metas. No se imaginaba que algo tan fácil pudiera tener un efecto tan grande.

Cuando Kathy llamó a su hermana para pedirle que se encontrarán para hablar de algo importante, la hermana de Kathy se asustó un poco. No sabía si eso significaba que Jim le había pegado a Kathy de nuevo (su hermana sabía sobre la primera vez, aunque Kathy pensaba que se lo había podido ocultar) o si (eso esperaba) Kathy lo iba a dejar. Kathy fue muy clara con su hermana con respecto al tipo de ayuda que necesitaba y su hermana le prometió apoyarla de la forma en que ella se lo pedía. Al final del encuentro, Kathy sintió que se había quitado un peso de los hombros. Saldría adelante con un poco de ayuda y la reconstrucción del Palacio del Placer.

capítulo 7:
No propicie el propiciamiento

Vanya y Juan

Vanya y Juan llevaban juntos poco tiempo cuando Vanya empezó a pensar que había cometido un terrible error. Se conocieron en la iglesia. A él le atrajeron la vivacidad y el ingenio de ella. A ella él le parecía muy guapo y le encantaba su estilo rudo. Juan nunca se graduó de la secundaria y trabajaba en una empresa de construcción. Trabaja duro y se divertía con la misma intensidad, a diferencia de los hombres con los que Vanya había salido antes. Lo que le faltaba en delicadeza, decía ella, le sobraba en masculinidad. Había algo bruto y vital en él que atrapaba su imaginación y, luego, su corazón. Al principio, su vida juntos era emocionante... Y luego las emociones se transformaron en algo mucho menos interesante. La bebida de Juan aumentó, junto con sus consecuencias negativas.

No asuma las soluciones

Al ser la pareja saludable de la relación, usted ha asumido la tarea de hacer que las cosas funcionen y de recoger los pedazos cuando se caen. Es común que las personas en su posición ignoren sus necesidades con el fin de "cuidar" a la persona que bebe y a la familia. Lamentablemente, al ser tan útil, usted también ha logrado dos cosas muy poco útiles. La primera es que usted les salva la vida a los demás a costas de agotar la suya. Cada vez que ignora sus necesidades para cuidar a los otros, gasta un poco más de sus reservas de energía. Eventualmente, estará tan exhausto(a) que corre el riesgo de colapsar (física, mental o motivacionalmente), o seguirá tratando de ayudar pero sus esfuerzos se volverán cada vez menos eficaces. Va a quedar vacío(a).

La otra consecuencia de ser quien soluciona todo es que le facilita a la persona que bebe mantener su patrón de conducta actual. Mientras usted esté allí para limpiar el desorden, esconderle las cosas al jefe y, generalmente, arreglar lo que se rompa, la persona que bebe no necesita cambiar. El término popular para describir este patrón en el que la persona bebe y usted organiza todo es "propiciamiento". Como usted siempre está disponible para solucionar los problemas, muestra que acepta la bebida. Sus palabras podrían ser lo contrario cuando regaña, reclama y alecciona, pero su conducta grita: "¡Aquí estoy para facilitarte todo!".

Cuanto más usted da, más la persona que bebe toma, hasta que su vida deja de pertenecerle. Todo lo que usted hace se centra en evitar las consecuencias negativas de la conducta de su ser querido que bebe, en limpiar el desorden o en sentirse lastimado(a) y molesto(a) por caer en esta trampa. Lo que empezó como una buena intención de ayudarle a su ser querido se transforma en un veneno para la relación porque le facilita al otro la bebida y lo(a) deja a usted sintiéndose usado(a) y molesto(a).

Para ilustrarlo, consideremos a Juan y a Vanya. Juan bebe mucho y ha perdido varios empleos por ello. Su patrón típico es controlar su consumo lo suficiente durante la semana para no causar problemas pero embriagarse el fin de semana y no poder trabajar el lunes por la mañana. Después de varias "ausencias" y reportarse enfermo, lo despiden. Así ha sido por años y a Vanya le preocupa que Juan pierda el empleo que acaba de encontrar. Juan funciona muy bien las dos primeras semanas y, luego, fiel a su estilo, se encuentra a sus amigos para ver fútbol el domingo y beber. El lunes por la mañana, Vanya no logra sacarlo de la cama y él le pide que llame a su jefe y diga que está enfermo. Pensando solo en salvar el empleo, que la familia necesita desesperadamente, Vanya llama. Aparentemente, es lo que haría cualquier pareja amorosa, ¿cierto? Por supuesto. Pero si nos fijamos con detenimiento, verá que Vanya le está enviando un mensaje silencioso a Juan. Le está diciendo que puede beber todo lo que quiera y ella, a través de sus acciones, acepta ser la responsable de esa conducta. Juan puede beber sin costo.

Cualquiera puede ser un propiciador. Vea si identifica las conductas propiciadoras en los siguientes ejemplos. Estas conductas surgen mucho en nuestras consultas.

> Alan tiene veintipocos años. Sus amigos lo describen como el "alma de la fiesta original" y a él le enorgullece hacerle honor al título. La mayoría de las noches se las pasa bebiendo y luego duerme hasta después del medio día. Sobra decir que no logra conservar ningún empleo y, como resultado, aún vive con sus padres. A los padres de Alan les preocupa mucho su conducta pero lo aman y hacen lo que pueden para ayudarlo. No le reclaman por sus hábitos ni le piden que les pague renta ni contribuya de ninguna forma en el hogar. Creen que si le brindan un entorno seguro y de aceptación, Alan eventualmente va a crecer y sentar cabeza.

> George está tan preocupado por la posibilidad de que su esposa tenga un accidente con el auto al volver a casa del bar que hace cuestión de tener siempre su bebida favorita en casa para que ella no se detenga a tomarse un trago en el camino después del trabajo. "Después de todo", dice, "ella va a beber de cualquier modo, así que es mejor que lo haga en casa donde no puede matarse en un accidente".

Alicia tenía dieciséis años cuando le hicieron la primera multa por conducir ebria. Un viernes por la noche, al volver de un partido de fútbol en la secundaria, la detuvo un oficial de tránsito por conducir muy despacio, y no pasó la prueba del alcoholímetro. Cuando la policía les avisó a sus padres, corrieron a la estación, pagaron la fianza, se llevaron su auto y la llevaron a casa donde la metieron a la cama y la arroparon. Luego, contrataron a un abogado costoso para que eliminara la acusación en su contra. Sintiendo que habían salvado a su hija de un trauma significativo, los padres de Alicia la hicieron prometer que no iba a volver a beber pero no le quitaron el auto porque lo "necesitaba" para ir a la escuela.

Los padres de Alan, los padres de Alicia, George y Vanya tenían buenas intenciones, pero todos son culpables de solucionar o propiciar. Mediante el amor y la ignorancia, están facilitándoles la vida a sus seres queridos para que beban con impunidad. Juan nunca tiene que arrastrar su cuerpo dolido fuera de la cama ni enfrentar a su jefe con sus excusas. Alicia aprendió que puede burlarse incluso de la ley y Mami y Papi lo van a resolver; no tiene por qué cambiar. Alan no tiene que hacer nada. Se divierte y sus padres se encargan de todo lo demás. Mientras ellos no requieran ningún cambio de su parte para seguir manteniéndolo, garantizan que él no cambie. George también propicia la bebida de su esposa al facilitarle las cosas en casa. No tiene que pensar en cuándo o dónde beber, cuáles son las posibles consecuencias ni enfrentar el hecho de que la bebida le rompe el corazón a su esposo. Para ninguna de estas personas la bebida tiene costos. Tienen lo que se podría decir un pase libre.

Lo más difícil es dejar que alguien a quien se ama experimente las consecuencias naturales de su conducta. Pero, si realmente ama a la persona, debe hacerlo. Piense en las conductas solucionadoras que usted podría tener para propiciarle la bebida a su ser querido y piense en las consecuencias que es hora de que esta persona experimente.

La Actividad 16 lo(a) ayudará a anotar sus pensamientos. Como puede ver en el ejemplo, Mark (del capítulo 4) se dio cuenta de que una buena parte de lo que hacía para motivar a María a cambiar, en realidad tenía el efecto contrario y le facilitaba seguir bebiendo. Complete la actividad en su cuaderno.

Actividad 16. Conductas solucionadoras

¿Cómo le facilita a su ser querido la bebida y cómo sería si no lo(a) tuviera a usted o a alguien como usted?

Compro alcohol, limpio, invento excusas cuando ella no puede ir a sus compromisos, le digo que no es su culpa, la llevo cuando pierde las llaves o la licencia, finjo que me creo sus mentiras porque estoy demasiado triste para cuestionarlas, la llevo a la cama cuando está demasiado borracha para caminar

Los viejos hábitos son difíciles de perder

Al avanzar a sus metas y alejarse de su patrón solucionador/propiciador, experimentará intensamente la verdad de esta frase: Los viejos hábitos son difíciles de perder... *muy difíciles*. Usted y su ser querido han interactuado de la misma forma durante tanto tiempo que ya perfeccionaron el baile. Pueden disparar los puntos álgidos del otro casi como si levantaran un dedo mentalmente. Además, lo conocido siempre es más cómodo que lo nuevo (al menos en el campo emocional), de modo que incluso el cambio para mejorar inicialmente es incómodo. Su ser querido que bebe reaccionará al cambio y usted verá su *propia* resistencia, aunque usted sea quien lo está generando.

Lo hemos visto repetidas veces. Alguien llega al tratamiento porque su vida con la persona que bebe se ha vuelto insoportable y cualquier tipo de cambio parece una bendición. Luego, la relación empieza a cambiar y la misma persona que llegó a la clínica desesperada por salir de su situación se echa para atrás.

"Lo amo. Es un buen hombre. El licor es lo que es malo".

"Es mi hija, no puedo abandonarla".

"Llevamos juntos diecisiete años, no puedo cambiarle las reglas ahora".

"¿Qué pasa si trato de cambiar y me abandona?".

"Es mi papá. Estoy en deuda con él".

"Si no tapo las cosas, ¿qué pensará la gente de nosotros?".

Hemos oído miles de razones para dejar que las cosas sigan iguales cuando la gente enfrenta la incomodidad natural de lo desconocido. No obstante, la verdad es que los sentimientos que la gente tiene cuando decide hacer un cambio (por ejemplo, cuando usted empezó este libro) son los sentimientos reales. Su frustración, enojo, depresión y deseo de un cambio siguen siendo reales. Cuando usted se descubre pensando "Las cosas no están tan mal", es probable que apenas esté reaccionando al estrés del cambio. Es difícil pero, si usted reconoce lo que está haciendo y no pierde de vista su meta, puede avanzar. Nada cambia por arte de magia. Su ser querido que bebe no se despertará mañana siendo una nueva persona y usted no podrá ayudarlo haciendo lo que viene haciendo por años. No ha funcionado.

Hábitos que no funcionan

Usted y su ser querido que bebe son únicos, pero ciertos hábitos son tan comunes que podríamos apostar que se reconoce en al menos algunos de los siguientes.

Arreglar

Usted "arregla" lo que su ser querido que bebe rompe. Cada día, usted recoge los pedazos. La resaca de la persona que bebe es muy fuerte para ir a trabajar, y usted es quien llama al jefe para "explicarle". O llega a casa demasiado ebria, vomita todo el baño y usted limpia. El teléfono suena a las 2:00 a. m. Es su ser querido que

(¡por suerte!) olvidó dónde dejo el auto y necesita que usted vaya a recogerlo... y usted va.

Desde su punto de vista, podría parecer que arreglar las cosas es simplemente lo más humano o sensible. Después de todo, nadie deja a una persona que ama durmiendo en su vómito o en una esquina de la calle. Estamos de acuerdo. Si considera las consecuencias de corto plazo, sería inhumano hacerlo. No obstante, piense en las consecuencias de largo plazo. Cada vez que usted arregla la situación, su ser querido que bebe tiene otra poderosa experiencia de aprendizaje. ¿Qué aprende? La persona que bebe aprende que, independientemente de cuán irresponsable sea su conducta, ¡no hay consecuencias! Usted se encargará de todo. Claro que tal vez tenga que escuchar sus reclamos al día siguiente ... Pero ¿qué importan un par de quejas si uno obtiene lo que quiere sin tener que pagar por ello?

En vez de arreglar

Si quiere que su ser querido que bebe cambie su estilo de vida, usted tiene que dejarlo responsabilizarse de él. Si llega a casa ebrio y deposita la cena y los cócteles sobre su ropa, déjelo que duerma sobre ella. En la mañana, cuando se despierte con el hedor de la noche anterior, habrá aprendido una lección más constructiva que si usted lo limpia todo y lo arropa en su cama deseándole dulces sueños. De forma similar, cualquiera con edad suficiente para tener resaca durante la semana tiene edad suficiente para llamar a su jefe a la mañana siguiente. Si su ser querido se pone agresivo cuando bebe y les hace una grosería a sus padres, deje que sea quien se disculpe y vuelva a arreglar la relación. Deje de dar pases libres. No es fácil (usted también tendrá que aguantar el hedor de la noche anterior) pero, a largo plazo, valdrá la pena.

Reclamar

Pensamos en llamar a este hábito "instruir" o "enseñar" porque "reclamar" tiene una connotación desagradable, y su intención no es desagradable. Pero, seamos honestos. Desde el punto de vista de quien bebe, sus comentarios bienintencionados son pura y simplemente reclamos.

Por ejemplo, su ser querido llega a casa borracho y usted le recuerda el terrible impacto que la bebida tiene en su vida juntos. Usted está molesto(a), preocupado(a) y tiene el derecho de expresar esos sentimientos. Sin embargo, la persona se encoge de hombros y se va a dormir. Este patrón lleva años. La persona llega tarde. Usted reclama.

Lo que podría estar pasando, en realidad, es que usted está reforzando (recompensándola) por llegar tarde a casa y ebria. Un hecho de la naturaleza humana es que no desperdiciamos mucha energía en conductas que no compensan. Si alguien hace lo mismo repetidamente, puede apostar que hay algo satisfactorio en la situación.

Un ojo entrenado puede ver lo obvio: sus sermones no deben molestar mucho a la persona puesto que mantiene la misma conducta mes tras mes. Incluso, podría disfrutar la atención o el hecho de tenerlo(a) a usted a su entera disposición. Aun si usted siente que está eligiendo esperar y sermonearla, es por la conducta de la persona que usted lo hace. Podría haber una lucha de poder aquí.

La persona que bebe también podría sentir cierto tipo de respaldo de su parte porque la está esperando. Piense al respecto. Tal vez haya cierto confort en saber que, independientemente de cuánto beba o qué tan tarde llegue, usted estará allí con su cancioncita de siempre al llegar a casa. Esto quiere decir que la lección para quien bebe es que el alcohol no le quita ninguna de las comodidades del hogar. Es un pase libre.

En vez de reclamar

Pruebe usar frases que empiecen con “Me siento”, de modo que su ser querido sepa que lo(a) ha lastimado a usted, pero sin ataques. No obstante, primero piense en lo que quiere lograr con sus palabras.

¿Solo quiere asegurarse de que su ser querido sepa que lo(a) ha lastimado? Si es así, dígaselo y disfrute de la pelea resultante. Por otra parte, si está tratando de hacer que su ser querido que bebe se comporte diferente, tenga esa meta en mente y use sus palabras para indicarle que su conducta lo(a) está lastimando ahora.

Por ejemplo, ¿recuerda en el capítulo 5 cuando la madre estaba reclamándole a John por volver tarde a casa después de la universidad porque se había quedado bebiendo con sus amigos? Nos imaginamos que su meta era que John llegara a casa sano y salvo y a tiempo para comer con la familia, pero cada vez que le reclamaba a John, él se iba a seguir bebiendo o se enojaba y se portaba grosero. Sin duda es hora de probar algo diferente. En vez de discutir con John, la madre podía haber usado una frase que empezara con "Me siento". Podría decir: "Me siento mal cuando sé que estás bebiendo por ahí" o "Te extraño cuando no estás en casa para cenar con la familia". Y nada más. Luego, cuando John esté sobrio y ella sienta que está de buen humor, la madre puede acercarse y decirle, de la forma más positiva posible, lo que le gustaría ver en el futuro y lo que hará si eso no sucede. Por ejemplo, podría decirle: "Me preocupo por ti cuando llegas tarde a casa pero, a partir de ahora, no voy a esperarte sentada. Voy a hacer algo por mi cuenta. Así que, si llegas tarde y no estoy en casa, no te preocupes. Quiere decir que me fui a visitar a mi madre o a una reunión de Al-Anon".

Proteger

Aunque proteger a quien se ama parece una buena idea, podría no serlo. Tal y como sucede con arreglar y reclamar, proteger puede tener un efecto positivo y uno negativo. A veces, al proteger a la gente, usted le impide que aprenda a protegerse por su cuenta.

Considere a la esposa que siempre llama al trabajo de su marido para avisar que está enfermo. Cada vez que inventa excusas para cubrirlo, apoya la bebida. Él bebe sin enfrentar ninguna consecuencia. No tiene que arrastrarse al trabajo sintiéndose terrible. No tiene que lidiar con la incomodidad de mentirle a su supervisor. Ni siquiera tiene que levantarse temprano para hacer la llamada. No tiene que sufrir las repercusiones de no ir a trabajar sin haberse reportado enfermo. Lo único que tiene que hacer es seguir bebiendo todo lo que quiera, con la comodidad de que su esposa pagará los platos rotos. Para él, es un negocio redondo.

La ciencia y la experiencia nos dicen que si no se le exige a la persona que bebe que asuma la responsabilidad de las consecuencias negativas de la bebida, hay pocas posibilidades de que su conducta indeseada vaya a cambiar. De hecho, lo más probable es que las cosas poco a poco empeoren. Si usted quiere que mejoren, si realmente quiere ayudar a su ser querido que bebe, debe dejar de protegerlo.

Con frecuencia, la gente nos cuenta que le compra licor a la persona que bebe, con el fin de tenerlo en casa, sano y salvo. La justificación es algo como: "Si le compro su licor favorito, se vendrá a beber a casa y no correrá el riesgo de tener un accidente en el auto o de que le hagan una multa". Una variación es: "Si llamo y digo que está enfermo cuando está de resaca, no correrá el riesgo de que lo despidan, y nuestra vida no se va a descalabrar". Suena terriblemente razonable pero, ¿lo es?

Para empezar, comprarle alcohol a alguien que bebe es darle permiso para beber. Si le da permiso para beber en casa, hay un paso muy corto para ver esto como un permiso para beber en cualquier lugar. Además, ¿qué pasa si la persona llega a casa y bebe durante una hora o dos y *luego* decide irse a un bar? Sus esfuerzos habrán sido totalmente contraproducentes. Aunque sienta que está protegiendo a su ser querido, esta conducta en realidad alimenta el problema.

En vez de proteger

Una forma más constructiva de "ayudar" sería hacer una lista de actividades sin bebida que la persona disfruta, en especial las que son difíciles de hacer si bebe, e involucrar a su ser querido en una de ellas en el tiempo en que normalmente bebería. También podría considerar tener sus bebidas sin alcohol favoritas y las comidas que prefiere para brindarle como alternativa al licor.

Responda las siguientes preguntas para ver si usted es "protector(a)". Lea cada afirmación y, en el espacio que se brinda, anote cuántas veces ha hecho eso en los últimos seis meses. Por ejemplo, si ha llevado licor a su hogar tres veces durante los últimos seis meses, coloque un 3 al lado de esa acción.

Cantidad de veces	**Acción protectora**
________	Recogió a su ser querido en un bar en mitad de la noche
________	Llamó al jefe de la persona que bebe para "explicarle" una ausencia
________	Pagó una deuda en un bar para evitar que el dueño hiciera algo contra su ser querido
________	Le inventó excusas a la familia porque la persona que bebe no fue a las reuniones familiares
________	Les inventó excusas a los amigos porque la persona que bebe no fue a los encuentros planeados
________	Les inventó excusas a los miembros de la familia por la conducta de su ser querido cuando se ha emborrachado y se ha puesto desagradable
________	Les inventó excusas a los amigos por la conducta de su ser querido cuando se ha emborrachado y se ha puesto desagradable
________	Llevó licor a la casa para que la persona no saliera a beber
________	Se rehusó a hacer planes con los miembros de la familia porque no quiso correr el riesgo de exponer a su ser querido que bebe ante ellos durante un periodo particularmente malo
________	Se rehusó a hacer planes con sus amigos porque no quería correr el riesgo de exponer a su ser querido ante ellos
________	Contó historias sobre otras personas que beben más que su ser querido
________	Pagó la fianza de su ser querido que bebe para sacarlo de la cárcel

________ Ayudó a su ser querido a buscar artículos que perdió mientras bebía
________ Le lavó la ropa vomitada
________ Actuó como enfermero(a) cuando la persona estaba borracha
________ Curó las lesiones relacionadas con el alcohol de su ser querido
________ Les ocultó los problemas a la familia y los hijos
________ Persuadió a los miembros de la familia a que no hablaran de los problemas de la bebida
________ Ha sido el reloj despertador de su ser querido y se ha asegurado de que llegue al trabajo a tiempo
________ Ha preparado alimentos específicos para ayudar a curar la resaca
________ Le ha dicho a su ser querido que su conducta inapropiada no era tan mala
________ Ha consolado a su ser querido que bebe cuando siente culpa o remordimiento
________ Ha minimizado la gravedad de la conducta de su ser querido
________ Ha reducido sus propios gastos porque su ser querido gasta demasiado en bebida

Descubra su puntuación sumando todas sus respuestas. Si su puntuación es mayor que cero, es hora de que empiece a dejar que su ser querido asuma la responsabilidad de su bebida. Cualquier puntuación superior a cero indica que usted se está castigando por la conducta de su ser querido... una estrategia perdedora. Usted es quien paga, y la persona que bebe aprende que está bien. ¡***No*** está bien!

Desechar lo viejo

Ahora que vio cómo sus antiguas conductas podrían realmente apoyar la bebida, veamos por qué los esfuerzos pasados por hacer que su ser querido dejara de beber fallaron. No se trata de lamentarse por los intentos fallidos, pero necesita desechar lo viejo para abrirle espacio a lo nuevo. Para ello, piense en las estrategias que ha usado a lo largo de los años para hacer que su ser querido dejara el alcohol. Estimule su memoria con los siguientes ejemplos. Marque cada estrategia que haya probado y agregue cualquiera que no hayamos incluido.

¿Alguna vez...

____ le pidió que dejara de beber o que bebiera menos?
____ ocultó el licor o lo lanzó a la basura?
____ le dio a su ser querido información impresa sobre AA u otras formas de dejar la bebida?
____ lo motivó a consultar a un consejero espiritual?
____ se separó por un tiempo de su ser querido?
____ ocultó su billetera, chequera o dinero?
____ les pidió a amigos o empleadores que intervinieran?
____ se emborrachó para mostrarle a su ser querido qué se siente?
____ amenazó divorciarse?
____ amenazó llevarse a los niños?
____ tapó los errores de su ser querido causados por la bebida e hizo que esa persona se sintiera culpable por ello?
____ evitó a amigos y familiares debido a los problemas con la bebida e hizo que su ser querido se sintiera culpable por ello?
____ han discutido por el tema de la bebida?
____ le dijo a su ser querido que había perdido su confianza y respeto?
____ acusó a su ser querido de avergonzarlo(a) en público?
____ llamó a la policía o al 911 para que detuvieran la bebida de su ser querido?
____ asumió la tarea de buscar alcohol escondido en el auto y en la casa?
____ razonó con la persona sobre las ventajas y las desventajas de la bebida?
____ le suplicó a su ser querido que dejara de beber?
____ (Complete con otras tácticas que haya probado y no incluimos aquí).

Si ha hecho cualquiera de estas cosas repetidamente y su ser querido sigue bebiendo, es un hecho que estas estrategias no funcionan. Así que revíselas, estúdielas y hágalas a un lado. Olvídese de esas estrategias improductivas y sustitúyalas por algo más eficiente. ¿Qué tiene que perder? Si esto no funciona, no estará peor que cuando empezó y nuestra experiencia nos dice que más del 75 por ciento de la gente que usa esta estrategia tiene resultados satisfactorios. No hay motivo para pensar que no sea su caso.

Recibir lo nuevo

Todas esas tácticas insatisfactorias que ha usado antes están a punto de ser sustituidas por nuevas técnicas poderosas. Las actividades agradables que enumeró en el capítulo 6 poco a poco sustituirán las negativas, como evitar a los amigos por la vergüenza y quedarse en casa para vigilar a su ser querido que bebe. Los siguientes tres capítulos (8, 9, y 10) le brindan los aspectos prácticos para sustituir las conductas propiciadoras por otras constructivas.

Resumen de la acción

Revise sus interacciones con su ser querido y trate de detectar qué podría estar haciendo que propicia que esa persona siga bebiendo. Póngales atención a los arreglos, los reclamos y la protección.

Repaso

- Arreglar los problemas causados por su ser querido debido al alcohol solo le facilita seguir cometiendo los mismos errores una y otra vez. Permitir que la persona experimente las consecuencias de la vida real de su conducta tiene más probabilidades de producir un cambio positivo.

- En vez de desperdiciar su energía reclamando y recordándole a su ser querido las consecuencias negativas de la bebida y las drogas, dígale con calma cómo se siente con lo que está ocurriendo y, luego, ponga su atención en otra cosa.
- A veces, al tratar de proteger a alguien, en realidad dañamos a esta persona. Asegúrese de que sus esfuerzos por mantener a su ser querido sano y salvo sean constructivos, como involucrarlo en actividades agradables sin bebida, y no destructivos, como mantener licor en casa para evitar que conduzca ebrio.

Kathy y Jim: pagar los platos rotos

El concepto de propiciar abrumó a Kathy la primera vez que lo oyó. "¿Quiere decir que todos estos años he estado empeorando todo?", comentó desolada. "¡Estaba tratando de ayudar, no de facilitarle la bebida!".

Kathy pronto se tranquilizó y entendió que no estaba haciendo nada "malo". Apenas hacía lo que le parecía correcto, aunque los resultados no fueran los pretendidos. Pero, ahora, tenía el compromiso de hacer cambios efectivos y productivos, así que revisó sus respuestas típicas a la bebida de Jim e identificó varias conductas propiciadoras que se dispuso a cambiar.

Aunque había muchas cosas que Kathy decidió cambiar, para ella, la más importante era su hábito de proteger a Jim de decepcionar a los niños. Antes, cuando él llegaba a casa en uno de "aquellos" días, Kathy buscaba rápidamente algo para que los niños hicieran fuera o en su habitación para que no vieran a Papá tropezándose o arrastrando las palabras. Ella sabía que para Jim era muy importante que los niños lo respetaran y se esforzaba mucho para que él no les diera una mala impresión. Pero ya no más.

La siguiente vez que Jim llegó a casa tambaléandose, Kathy no se los ocultó a los niños. Vieron a Papá tropezarse en la puerta y no lograr colgar su abrigo en el armario. Jim trató de hablar con ellos pero sus palabras no se entendían y vio a los niños retroceder. Estaban asustados y fue evidente. Jim trató de nuevo de preguntarles cómo había sido su día, pero la más pequeña empezó a llorar y corrió a esconder su carita en la falda de Kathy. Jim se quedó inmóvil por un momento. Luego dijo "Mierda" y se fue a la habitación. Kathy lo oyó ducharse y meterse a la cama.

Algo cambió esa noche.

capítulo 8

Solución de problemas

Richard y Louise

Richard y Louise llevaban siete años de casados cuando ella empezó a hacerse un trago todas las noches, al volver del trabajo. "Necesito relajarme", decía. Al principio, Richard no le dio mucha importancia, pero conforme fue pasando el tiempo, Louise aumentó de un trago a dos o tres todas las noches y eventualmente adoptó el hábito de saltarse la cena, beber toda la noche y caer dormida en el sillón reclinable.

Richard probó todo lo que sabía para hacer que Louise dejara la bebida. La regañó, haciendo que se sintiera culpable y mal. Le suplicó, apelando a su sentido del deber familiar. Se enfureció con ella, y la amenazó varias veces con dejarla o echarla a la calle. Nada funcionó.

Finalmente, Richard decidió ver el problema desde una óptica diferente . . .

Los problemas de siempre bajo una óptica diferente

Al recorrer el camino del cambio, usted enfrenta el desafío de pensar en nuevas formas de lidiar con las situaciones con las que ha lidiado miles de veces antes... pero de formas que no funcionaron muy bien. La estrategia para solucionar los problemas que enseñamos está diseñada para ayudarlo(a) a diseñar soluciones que funcionen. Al seguir estos pasos, usted podrá generar varias soluciones posibles y tomar la mejor decisión sobre cuál usar.

Paso 1: Definir el problema

La clave para la solución del problema es producir una descripción realmente específica del mismo. Cuanto más específica y completa sea su descripción de lo que debe cambiar, más fácil será cambiar. Por ejemplo, cuando Richard describía vagamente el problema que tenía con Louise como "ella bebe demasiado y arruina nuestro tiempo juntos", le costaba mucho pensar en estrategias para cambiar su situación. Trató de hablar con ella, le gritó, lloró, ignoró el problema... Pero, de alguna forma, siempre sentía que estaba usando las herramientas equivocadas para el terreno en que se encontraba. Cuando por fin se sentó y se preguntó exactamente cuáles situaciones y conductas la hacían "beber demasiado", pudo dividir el caos absoluto en que sentía que se había transformado su vida en problemas menores y más manejables. En este caso, pudo definir el problema como el patrón de respuesta de Louise a un día estresante en el trabajo con exceso de bebida. Cuando Richard vio las cosas de esta forma, se dio cuenta de que su respuesta al estrés le daba un buen punto de partida. Así, definió el problema como proponer una nueva forma de reducir los efectos del estrés laboral y ayudarla a relajarse sin beber.

Paso 2: Lluvia de ideas

La mejor forma de pensar en nuevas ideas es desactivar su editor interno. En otras palabras, hacer una lista de todas las soluciones posibles en las que pueda pensar... *independientemente de que tengan sentido, sean realistas o ridículas*. La lista de Richard de todas las formas posibles (realistas y ridículas) en que podía ayudar a Louise a relajarse sin beber en exceso se incluye a continuación. Como puede ver, fue capaz de apagar esa voz interna que llamamos nuestro editor; es decir, la voz que nos dice: "Esa es una idea tonta" o "No va a funcionar". Una vez que Richard completó la lista con todas las ideas que se le ocurrieron, pasó al Paso 3.

La lista de Richard con las posibles formas de ayudar a Louise a relajarse

• Decirle que se calme	• Limitarla a un solo trago	• Decirle egoísta	• Hacer que se sienta culpable.
• Ofrecerle té	• Ofrecerle preparar la cena	• Recordarle que todos tenemos días malos	• Poner una grabación de relajamiento
• Deshacerme de los niños	• Prepararle un baño	• Planear unas vacaciones	• Tener sexo salvaje
• Frotarle el cuello	• Hacerle un masaje	• Hacerle un lavado de cabello	• Poner música tranquilizadora
• Alquilar su pelicula favorita	• Cantarle	• Hacerle un berrinche	• Caminar en el parque
	• Bailar con ella		• Darle helado

Paso 3: Evaluar y seleccionar una solución

Cuando su lista esté tan larga como es posible y haya logrado mantener a su editor interno en silencio, es hora de que organice y seleccione sus ideas. Algunas de ellas obviamente serán poco realistas y puede descartarlas de una vez. Ahora, revise el resto de la lista y evalúe cada idea según la probabilidad de que funcione y la facilidad de ponerla en práctica. Sobre todo, si se supone que la actividad va a competir con la bebida, recuerde que debe ser satisfactoria para la persona que bebe. Además, no elija su idea favorita e ignore el resto. Podría descubrir que la favorita no funciona y necesitar un plan B. Califíquelas todas y luego haga un círculo alrededor de la que consideró que tiene más probabilidades de funcionar y es más fácil de realizar. Esta es su primera opción para solucionar su problema. Este es su plan.

Puede ver lo que hizo Richard con su lista de la lluvia de ideas en el Paso 3. ¡Por suerte, decidió que deshacerse de los niños no era opción! También eliminó algunas otras ideas que no le parecieron realistas. Como puede ver, concluyó que frotarle el cuello y ofrecerle preparar la cena mientras tomaba un baño eran sus dos principales opciones.

La evaluación y la selección de Richard

Opciones rechazadas	*Posibilidades*	*¿Qué tan probable?*	*¿Qué tan fácil es?*
Decirle que se relaje	*Ofrecerle preparar la cena*	*Mucho*	*Mucho*
Deshacerse de los niños	Prepararle un baño	Mucho	Tal vez
Hacer un berrinche	Hacerle un masaje	Mucho	Tal vez
Hacer que se sienta culpable	Cantarle	¡No!	Mucho
Recordarle que todos tenemos días malos	Ofrecerle un té	Tal vez	Mucho
Decirle egoísta	Alquilar su película favorita	Tal vez	No es práctico
Tener sexo salvaje	*Frotarle el cuello*	*Mucho*	*Mucho*
Caminar en el parque	Planear unas vacaciones	Tal vez	Tal vez
Limitarla a un solo trago	Hacerle un lavado de cabello	¡Ni idea!	No es práctico
Poner una grabación de relajamiento	Poner música tranquilizadora	Tal vez	Mucho
Bailar con ella	Darle helado	Tal ve	Mucho

Paso 4: Inténtelo y haga el seguimiento

Una vez que tenga un plan de acción, inténtelo. Pero no haga lo que ha hecho todos estos años: intentarlo una y otra vez. Esta vez, inténtelo como un científico. Esto significa implementar su plan y darle seguimiento. Es mejor escribir cómo manejará el problema la próxima vez que ocurra y tomar notas lo antes posible después de intentarlo. De esta forma, podrá decir exactamente qué tan bien funcionó o, si no fue así, cuáles partes deben ajustarse. Algunas veces, podrá ajustar un poquito su plan para que funcione. En otras, tendrá que volver al Paso 3 y seleccionar una nueva solución.

Al final del Paso 3, Richard escribió su plan para la próxima vez que Louise volviera a casa después del trabajo de mala cara. A continuación, puede ver sus notas sobre cómo funcionó su plan las primeras veces que lo puso en práctica.

Plan: Cuando Louise llegue a casa reclamando de su jefe, le frotaré el cuello y le diré cuánto los niños y yo la queremos. Luego, le sugeriré que tome un baño caliente mientras preparo la cena.

5 de oct.: llegó a casa de mal humor y le froté el cuello y le dije cosas bonitas. Pero realmente quería que estuviéramos juntos, así que le sugerí que preparáramos la cena juntos. Todo empezó bien, hasta que los niños empezaron una competencia de gritos y el humor de Louise se fue al suelo. Cuando terminé de poner los niños a dormir, ella estaba ebria y se había quedado dormida en el sofá.

Revisión del plan: cumplirlo hasta el último detalle la próxima vez y ¡volver a intentarlo!

11 de oct.: otro día malo en el trabajo para ella. Esta vez, después del masaje en el cuello y las palabras bonitas, le ofrecí preparar la cena mientras ella tomaba un baño. A Louise le encantó la idea y subió muy contenta. Cuando estaba en medio de la preparación de la cena, oí que los niños golpeaban la puerta del baño preguntando cuándo Mamá empezaría a trabajar en los disfraces de Halloween. Louise terminó de bañarse de una vez y bajó las gradas, claramente molesta. Insistió en que un trago con la cena la ayudaría a tranquilizarse pero... Pasó lo de siempre.

Revisión del plan: mantener a los niños alejados de ella y tranquilos.

15 de oct.: aquí vamos de nuevo. Esta vez, hice todo como lo había planeado y mantuve a los niños conmigo en la cocina.

Louise pudo sumergirse a gusto en la tina y bajó a cenar con una sonrisa en el rostro. En un momento, durante la cena, sugirió que nos tomáramos un trago juntos, pero le dije cuánto estaba disfrutando el simple hecho de que estuviéramos juntos y ella no insistió. ¡Éxito!

Paso 5: Evaluar, refinar o probar otra idea
Este paso realmente ocurre con el Paso 4. Al implementar sus planes y darles seguimiento, tendrá ideas sobre cómo mejorarlos. Tal y como vio en las notas de Richard, cada vez que describió cómo habían salido las cosas, también ajustó su plan para volverlo más eficaz.

Recuerde siempre que los cambios en los que está trabajando se refieren a la forma en que viven usted y su ser *querido*. Por definición, son dinámicos o constantes. Nunca ocurrirá que usted decida responder a una persona o situación de cierta forma y no tenga que modificarla. De un día a otro, de un mes a otro, cambiamos. Nuestros planes y enfoques de la interacción también tienen que cambiar. No se desanime si sus planes no funcionan a la perfección la primera vez o la quincuagésima. Simplemente, siga dándoles seguimiento y refinándolos. Se volverá un proceso natural.

Resumen de la acción

Si no funcionó antes, es poco probable que funcione ahora. Si el problema sigue allí, examínelo bajo otra óptica.

Repaso

- Definir el problema.
- Hacer una lluvia de ideas con soluciones (saque a su editor interno de ahí).
- Evaluar sus soluciones y seleccionar una para probar.
- Intentarlo y hacer seguimiento.
- Evaluar, refinar o probar otra idea.

Kathy y Jim: encontrar nuevas rutas

A medida que Kathy poco a poco fue haciendo cambios en sus formas de responder a la conducta de Jim con la bebida, empezó a sentirse muy bien con respecto a su futuro. Él aún bebía más de lo que debía para la relación, pero la violencia física llevaba meses sin ocurrir y el humor general de Jim en la casa había mejorado mucho. Faltaba un poco más de esfuerzo antes de que Kathy estuviera dispuesta a aceptar la situación como algo permanente. En particular, Kathy realmente quería que Jim pasara más tiempo con los niños pero, cuando se lo sugería y él aceptaba llevarlos al boliche el viernes siguiente, saboteaba los planes y se tomaba un par de cervezas cuando llegaba a casa después del trabajo. Entonces Kathy desistía de la idea porque no quería que bebiera y subiera a los niños al auto en ese estado.

Kathy decidió que sus sugerencias, regaños molestos y trucos tácticos no iban a lograr el objetivo. Entonces decidió ver el problema bajo otra óptica. Primero, puso el dedo en la llaga (es decir, lo definió claramente). Ella sabía que Jim amaba a sus hijos y quería tener una relación con ellos. Al mirar el patrón de las salidas frustradas del padre y los niños, identificó lo que pensaba que era el problema real. Ella siempre comentaba el tema durante la semana y Jim, que quería estar con los niños, aceptaba la idea y hacía planes para el fin de semana (viernes). El problema era que entonces él volvía a casa del trabajo al final del día, cansado y un poco irritado. Por otra parte, los chicos estaban entusiasmados y listos para irse al boliche con su papá. La combinación resultante era un padre cansado e irritado y una sala llena de niños ruidosos... No era exactamente una receta de éxito. Kathy hizo una lista de posibles soluciones, incluso ensayar con los niños la conducta apropiada para cuando el papá llegara a la casa y tenerlos listos para salir en el momento en que Jim llegara, de modo que no hubiera tiempo para tomarse ninguna cerveza. Sintió que la mejor solución era lo que ella llamó en tono jocoso el "uno-dos y gancho al hígado". Volvió a sugerirle a Jim que llevara a los niños al boliche pero, cuando él aceptó llevarlos el viernes siguiente, ella le respondió que al final de una semana de trabajo pesada, le parecía que sería mejor dejar a los niños donde sus padres y salir solos ellos dos a cenar (el primer golpe). Luego (el segundo golpe), el sábado por la tarde, después de haber dormido lo suficiente y haber descansado en la casa, el boliche sería una salida agradable, no solo para los niños sino también para Jim. Jim pensó que esta era una excelente idea y estuvo de acuerdo con el plan.

Cuando llegó el fin de semana, Jim y Kathy disfrutaron su cena en un restaurante; él iba a pedir una cerveza pero vio la mirada de decepción de Kathy y se detuvo. El sábado por la tarde, todos disfrutaron el boliche, incluso Kathy que pudo tener una tarde tranquila en casa como resultado.

capítulo 9
Comunicación

Harold y DeeAnne

"Cada vez que tratamos de hablar de algo más personal que los resultados del fútbol, es una pelea garantizada", nos dijo DeeAnne cuando llamó a la clínica. "Parece que se esfuerza por hacer las cosas que me enojan. Incluso cuando le pido con toda la gentileza del mundo que deje de hacer algo o que haga algo por mí, empieza a gritar y lo usa como excusa para tomarse un trago más. ¡Sabe cuánto detesto que beba tanto!"

En el centro de cualquier relación está la comunicación. Si las personas que forman parte de la relación no pueden encontrar una forma de decirse lo que necesitan, lo que quieren y lo que valoran del otro, la relación está en terreno frágil.

Comunicarse

En el capítulo 5, hablamos un poco sobre el estilo de comunicación y dimos ejemplos de cómo traducir sus afirmaciones de negativas a positivas. Por ejemplo, en vez de decir "Detesto que bebas", podría volver la frase más positiva diciendo "Me encanta estar contigo cuando estás sobrio(a)".

Ambas afirmaciones buscan el mismo resultado (la sobriedad) pero una usa palabras combativas y la otra palabras amorosas.

Cuando las relaciones pasan por momentos difíciles, ya sea que tengan que ver con la bebida o no, hay cuatro cambios predecibles en la forma en que la pareja se comunica: dejan de usar afirmaciones que (1) son *positivas (**P**ositive),* (2) empiezan en *primera persona **(I)**,* (3) muestran *comprensión (**U**nderstanding)* y (4) demuestran la disposición de *compartir (**S**hare)* la responsabilidad de la situación. En otras palabras, sus patrones de comunicación dejan de ser PIUS (por sus siglas en inglés). A medida que la relación se vuelve cada vez más conflictiva, las conversaciones pierden sus componentes positivos y se concentran casi exclusivamente en lo negativo. Los participantes tienden a hacer afirmaciones con "tú" en lugar de frases con "yo" y dejan de hacerle saber a la otra persona que entienden cómo se siente ella. Finalmente, dejan de compartir la responsabilidad de su vida juntos y se concentran en tratar de culpar al otro.

Las afirmaciones PIUS transmiten el mensaje de una forma más suave. El oyente no se siente atacado y, por lo tanto, es menos probable que contraataque. No es difícil aprender un estilo de comunicación más gentil, pero requiere práctica. Cuando la pareja ha estado atacándose durante cierto tiempo y tiene un historial de sentimientos heridos, cambiar la forma de comunicarse al principio es como nadar contracorriente; es posible pero hay que concentrarse. Sin embargo, lo que encontrará es que, si usted hace el esfuerzo de mejorar su forma de comunicarse, la persona que bebe tendrá menos excusas para responderle negativamente.

Afirmaciones positivas

Como ya hablamos de usar afirmaciones positivas, no nos repetiremos aquí. Aun así, es útil revisar ejemplos de cómo las afirmaciones negativas se pueden transformar en frases positivas. Tome el tiempo para leer la siguiente lista y piense en algunas de las frases que le ha dicho a su ser querido recientemente.

Negativo(a)	Positivas
1. Tú siempre arruinas la velada.	1. Disfruto tanto estar contigo cuando no bebes.
2. Tú haces que sea imposible controlar nuestra cuenta bancaria.	2. Por favor, ayúdame a llevar el control de la cuenta bancaria anotando los gastos.
3. Tus amigos y tú hacen un desorden completo.	3. Me alegra que a tus amigos les guste venir. ¿Podrías ayudarme a mantener la casa limpia para que sea un lugar agradable de visitar?
4. Tú siempre me avergüenzas.	4. Me haría tan feliz si esta noche tomaras algo sin alcohol.
5. No voy a tener sexo contigo cuando estés ebrio(a).	5. Me encantaría hacer el amor contigo cuando estés sobrio(a).
6. No soporto que me mientas.	6. Quiero creerte pero en esa historia hay algo que no calza.
7. Tú nunca me escuchas cuando te estoy hablando.	7 Entiendo que algunas de nuestras conversaciones son incómodas, pero me encantaría si pudieras ayudarme a resolver las cosas.
8. Eres un(a) HdP. Tomaste dinero de mi billetera sin pedirlo. ¡Te voy a matar!	8. Es muy triste que tengas que tomar mi dinero. Asumo que tendré que guardarlo en un lugar más seguro.
9. Qué no te vuelva a ver gritarles a los niños de esa forma, grandísimo(a) agresor(a).	9. Yo sé que lidiar con los niños puede ser frustrante, pero ayúdame a darles un buen ejemplo hablándoles con calma.
10. No te soporto, imbécil egoísta. Faltaste al aniversario de mis padres a propósito.	10. Tal vez no te quedó claro que hoy era la celebración del trigésimo aniversario de mis padres. Me habría gustado que fueras.
11. ¿Por qué no levantas el trasero del sofá y buscas trabajo? Ya llevas seis meses desempleado(a). ¿No tienes un mínimo de autoestima?	11. Sé que estar sin trabajo debe ser difícil para ti. ¿Hay algo que pueda hacer para ayudarte?

Afirmaciones en primera persona ("yo")

La forma más rápida de generar una pelea es hacer que alguien se sienta atacado. Y la forma más sencilla de hacerlo es empezar sus frases con la palabra "tú". En el momento en que la mayoría de las personas escuchan esta palabra, se preparan para el ataque... Y por un buen motivo. Empezar una frase con "tú" alerta al oyente de que está a punto de convertirse en el centro de atención. Debido a la naturaleza habitualmente conflictiva de su relación, su ser querido que bebe espera que este enfoque sea un ataque. Por eso, se prepara para pelear o correr. De ahí a una pelea, es cuestión de segundos. Cuando le hable a su ser querido acerca de los problemas o de asuntos emocionales, concéntrese en decirle cómo se siente o qué quiere, no lo que él está haciendo mal. Los siguientes ejemplos lo van a aclarar.

Ejemplo de afirmaciones en primera persona ("yo")

Venenosas	**Sin el veneno**
1. Tú eres tan desconsiderado(a): ¿por qué no avisas que no vienes a cenar?	1. Me entristece mucho cuando no llegas a cenar y no me avisas.
2. Tú estás a punto de tener un accidente por conducir cuando bebes.	2. Me asusta mucho que bebas tanto.
3. Tú no deberías beber esta noche.	3. Me alegraría tanto si no bebieras esta noche.
4. Tú eres un asco.	4. Para mí es importante tener la casa ordenada. ¿Podrías recoger tus cosas?

Afirmaciones comprensivas

Hay otra pieza del rompecabezas de la comunicación que los ayudará a entenderse mejor, independientemente de los problemas que comenten. Trate de incluir "frases comprensivas" en sus conversaciones. Es decir, deje que su ser querido sepa que usted lo entiende y que le importan sus sentimientos. Por ejemplo, digamos que usted está tratando de convencer a su ser querido de salir a buscar empleo. Puede usar todas las técnicas que ya comentamos y decirle: "Amor, me preocupa mucho nuestra situación financiera actual. Realmente ayudaría mucho que envíes algunas solicitudes de empleo hoy". Ese sería un excelente punto de partida. No obstante, sería aún mejor si le agrega una frase comprensiva para que su ser querido sepa que usted toma en cuenta lo difícil que le resulta. En ese caso, podría decir: "Amor, sé lo frustrante que te resulta buscar empleo con el mercado tan duro, pero estoy muy preocupado(a)...".

Mostrarle a la otra persona que usted entiende cómo se siente, hace que sea más fácil que lo(a) escuche sin que ella sienta que tiene que defenderse.

Compartir la responsabilidad

Hemos explorado ampliamente cómo su conducta está entrelazada con la de su ser querido que bebe. Aunque usted no sea la causa del problema, está íntimamente involucrado(a) y tiene un efecto en él. Por eso, tiene lógica compartir un poco de la responsabilidad de las cosas que no andan bien. (No en todos los casos, sino en los que sea apropiado).

Cuando usted le pide a su ser querido que cambie, junto con el reconocimiento de lo difícil que resulta, hágale saber que usted se ve como parte del panorama general. No obstante, tome en cuenta que no necesita asumir la responsabilidad de todo lo que anda mal ni de la conducta de la persona que bebe. Apenas necesita reconocer que usted es parte de la situación. Aquí hay algunos ejemplos de cómo podría hacerlo.

- "Entiendo que te molesta que los niños hagan tanto ruido. Tal vez puedo ponerlos a jugar en su habitación para que puedas concentrarte en los requisitos del anuncio de empleo".
- "Yo sé que también tengo la culpa de que discutamos tanto. Voy a tratar de ser más comprensivo(a) y espero que también trates de ponerte en mi lugar con respecto a los problemas".

- "Sé que a veces reacciono de forma pesada cuando bebes, incluso si no es para tanto. Trabajemos juntos para resolver nuestras diferencias".

Una de las formas más fáciles de mostrar que usted se ve como parte de la situación y de bajarle el tono a una situación emocional es decir algo como: "¿Puedo ayudarte? Pareces molesto(a)".

Comunicación PIUS en acción

Este es el momento de ver cómo DeeAnne suavizó su enfoque de comunicación con Harold. Las Actividades 17 y 18 muestran los cambios que hizo. A revisar los ejemplos, piense en cómo aplicaría el estilo PIUS a su vida. Luego, trabaje con ambas actividades en su cuaderno.

Actividad 17. Discusiones anteriores

Piense en las tres últimas discusiones que haya tenido con su ser querido y empezaron con intentos suyos de decirle algo. Describa cada una con la mayor cantidad de detalles que pueda.

Discusión N° 1

Harold y yo íbamos a encontrar a unos amigos para cenar y, en el camino le pedí: "Por favor, hoy no bebas porque siempre te emborrachas y me avergüenzas". Él respondió que no siempre se emborrachaba y que si me avergonzaba tanto, por qué salía con él. Yo le grité algo... ni siquiera recuerdo qué fue... y terminamos devolviéndonos para la casa.

Discusión N° 2

Era viernes por la noche y llegué tarde a casa después del trabajo... una reunión había durado más de la cuenta. Cuando entré, alrededor de las 7:00, Harold estaba estirado en el sofá con una docena de cervezas en el suelo y cinco de las botellas ya vacías. Como sabía que solo había llegado una hora antes que yo, era obvio que se había tomado esas cinco rápidamente y no estaba en condiciones de ayudarme a preparar la cena o hacer la lista de compras del supermercado. "Otra vez estás borracho", le dije. "Vete a la mierda" me contestó. No nos hablamos el resto de la noche.

Discusión N° 3

Después de una velada muy agradable, viendo una película juntos, pensé que era un buen momento para reforzarle a Harold la sobriedad. Le dije: "Eres mucho más agradable cuando no estás borracho", pensando que lo estaba elogiando. Pues él no lo tomó bien y me gritó: "Ya vas de nuevo, molestándome con tus reclamos de lo que bebo". Reaccioné diciéndole que si él no fuera un borracho, yo no tendría motivos para reclamar y, a partir de ahí, la velada estaba arruinada.

La siguiente actividad requiere que elija una de las tres discusiones que describió en la Actividad 17 y cree una comunicación PIUS.

Actividad 18. Planificación de PIUS

Seleccione una discusión de la Actividad 17 y vuelva a escribir su parte, de forma que sea positiva (P), empiece con afirmaciones en primera persona-"yo" (I), muestre comprensión (U) de las luchas o el punto de vista de su ser querido y comparta (S) la responsabilidad con él.

La próxima vez que Harold y yo tengamos una velada agradable en la que él no beba, no voy a mencionar la bebida. Una forma más positiva de hablar de la velada es concentrarme solo en el hecho de que esté sobrio, en vez de compararlo con las veces en que no lo está. Además, creo que tengo que hacerle saber lo contenta que me pone estar con él cuando está sobrio y que sé que no siempre es fácil para él. Finalmente, debería decirle que me considero parte de la situación y comparto la carga con él. En resumen, le diré algo como: "Amor, gracias por esta velada maravillosa. Me encanta estar contigo así (él sabe que me refiero a que está sobrio, no necesito decírselo), y sé que no siempre es fácil para ti, y eso lo vuelve aún más especial. ¿Qué puedo hacer para mejorar las cosas para ti?"

Tras planear su comunicación PIUS, DeeAnne la ensayó mentalmente para garantizar que, cuando se presentara la oportunidad, estaría lista. Haga lo mismo.

Resumen de la acción

La forma en que le habla a su ser querido no solo refleja cómo se siente con respecto a él, sino también establece el tono de sus reacciones hacia usted. Practique el uso del estilo de comunicación PIUS que comentamos en este capítulo. Si es necesario, hágalo como tarea. Anote frases negativas que haya usado con su ser querido antes y practique volver a escribirlas en formato PIUS. Luego, asegúrese de usar este estilo para decirle a su ser querido lo que le gustaría que hiciera y cómo responderá a esa conducta. Cuanto más claridad y "PIUS" le inyecte a la comunicación de sus solicitudes y planes, más fácil será que su ser querido coopere.

Repaso

- Elabore sus comunicaciones en términos positivos.
- Hable en primera persona ("yo").
- Deje claro que entiende la posición de su ser querido.
- Afirme su intención de compartir la responsabilidad de la situación a la que se refiere.

Kathy y Jim: desarrollar un nuevo estilo

Kathy sabía que tenía que encontrar una forma de decirle a Jim que ya no aceptaría que les dijera groserías, ni a ella ni a los niños. El problema era que, cada vez que ella había tratado de decírselo, él le respondía exactamente de la forma que ella intentaba detener. Esta vez lo planeó diferente. En vez de esperar que pasara para llamarle la atención, esperó a tener una discusión en la que él no uso groserías. Luego, le dijo: "Jim, sé que estás molesto conmigo y que tenemos que hablar al respecto. Pero primero quiero decirte que me siento muy bien de que podamos tener estas discusiones sin decirnos groserías. Muchas gracias". Esto sorprendió a Jim. Casi olvidó qué era lo que le había molestado y el resto de la discusión perdió buena parte del veneno y él y Kathy hablaron con calma del tema.

capítulo 10

Elementos básicos de la conducta

Ladonna y Keith

> Ladonna sabía que la bebida de Keith había empeorado mucho durante el año anterior, a pesar de que siempre lo defendía ante sus padres e insistía en que ellos exageraban. En privado, le suplicaba que bebiera menos, le rogaba que dejara de beber y, últimamente, todos los días terminaban a gritos. Aunque sabía que tenía razón y él no, también sabía que insistir en ese punto no era útil. Ambos necesitaban cambiar y decidió que, como ella era la persona sobria, lo haría primero.

Este capítulo es su "caja de herramientas". Hasta ahora, le hemos mostrado cómo dirigirse a las conductas que necesitan cambiar y cómo abordar ese cambio. Ahora, uniremos todas las piezas para lograrlo. Usted reconocerá algunas de estas estrategias a partir de ejemplos de los capítulos iniciales. Otras serán cosas que ya sabe y hace. Si una buena parte de este material le resulta familiar, excelente. Será más fácil de usar. Si las ideas son nuevas para usted, no se preocupe; las aprenderá.

Recompensas, castigos e indiferencia

Los psicólogos y muchas sabias abuelas saben que la clave para el cambio en la conducta está en las recompensas, los castigos y la indiferencia. Los psicólogos llaman las recompensas "refuerzos", todos llaman los "castigos" tal cual y "la indiferencia" simplemente significa ignorar la conducta no deseada (los psicólogos la llaman "extinción").

Recompensas

El viejo dicho "Atrapas más moscas con miel que con vinagre" resume a la perfección la función de las recompensas. Si quiere que alguien haga algo, recompénselo por ello. Haga que la persona se sienta bien. Cuanto más frecuentes y poderosas sean las recompensas por una buena conducta, mayor es la probabilidad de que la persona la repita.

Por ejemplo, considere a Sammy, cuya madre está agotada de tratar de que arregle su habitación. Tras meses de reclamar y de ver cómo cada vez crece más la pila de cosas en el suelo, la mamá decide que es hora de un soborno. Le dice a Sammy que, por cada día que ponga la ropa sucia en el cesto, arregle su cama y guarde sus juguetes en la caja correspondiente, recibirá una moneda. Al final de la semana, la mamá lleva a Sammy a la tienda de juguetes para que gaste el dinero que se ganó. A Sammy le encantan los juguetes, así que piensa que esta es una excelente idea y se transforma en un fan de la limpieza.

La madre usó una recompensa para lograr que Sammy hiciera lo que ella pedía. Lo llamó soborno, pero en realidad fue una recompensa. Los niños tienen la necesidad natural de jugar y los juguetes son una forma excelente de satisfacerla. Por eso, la satisfacción de su deseo de juguetes recompensó la conducta de Sammy. Las ventajas de usar recompensas en una situación como esta son claras. La madre dejó de reclamarle a Sammy, así que su relación mejoró, Sammy cambió su conducta intencionalmente, por lo que la mamá lo dejó tranquilo y le dio un juguete, y la mamá tuvo la satisfacción de poder ver de nuevo el piso de la habitación de su hijo.

Hay otro detalle a considerar en la recompensa que la madre eligió para Sammy. Ella seleccionó algo que *Sammy* valoraba, no algo que ella valoraba. *Una recompensa solo funciona como tal si la persona a la que se destina la desea.* Si la madre hubiera elegido su vegetal favorito, a menos que a Sammy también le encantara, no habría funcionado como recompensa.

Usted puede aplicar el principio de la recompensa a su ser querido que bebe y volverle placentero hacer lo que usted quiere. Incluso si lograra que la persona cambiara a punta de gritos, ¿qué sería más agradable, gritarle o hacer que cambiara por las buenas? Después de todo, su meta final es que la persona que bebe cambie para que ambos disfruten de una relación más feliz.

Cuanto más refuerzo logre la recompensa, mayor la probabilidad de que su ser querido repita la conducta recompensada. Incluso así es cómo funciona el alcohol. La gente sabe que, cuando bebe, olvida sus problemas, se vuelve más romántico, se siente menos ansioso, se siente menos deprimido; en efecto, el alcohol hace que se sienta bien. Lamentablemente, eso solo oculta los problemas en el momento y crea más problemas después. Pero la expectativa inicial de la gratificación inmediata evita pensar en las consecuencias de largo plazo, y los platos rotos se pagan más tarde. Ese es el poder que pueden tener las recompensas positivas.

Un buen ejemplo del uso de una recompensa fue la forma en que Kathy logró que Jim se fuera directamente a casa después del trabajo, al final del capítulo 2. En vez de sermonearlo sobre lo desagradable que era que pasara a tomarse un trago con Charles, le preparó una recompensa si se iba directo a la casa: su comida favorita, una esposa sonriente y la compañía de su amigo.

No hay límite a la variedad de palabras, objetos y situaciones que pueden ser recompensas. Cualquier cosa que haga que alguien se sienta bien/feliz es una recompensa. Eso incluye desde una sonrisa hasta una comida, sexo, regalos y actividades. Si a su ser querido que bebe le gusta, es una recompensa. Y recuerde que beber también es una recompensa. La suma de *sus* recompensas debe ser mayor que la del alcohol.

Recompensar a las personas que se aman es fácil. Lo difícil es asegurarse de saber lo que su ser querido considera una recompensa. Esto puede ser particularmente complicado si el alcohol cambió a la persona y los antiguos placeres perdieron su encanto. Haga una lista de las recompensas que cree que le gustarán a su ser querido. Si se le ocurren cosas que su ser querido pueda disfrutar más que beber, mucho mejor. Como mínimo, asegúrese de que sean lo suficientemente satisfactorias para llamarle la atención. En el siguiente ejemplo, puede ver que Ladonna incluyó sabiamente sus sonrisas, abrazos, besos y palabras agradables en su lista. Después de todas las peleas entre ella y Keith, pensó que el simple hecho de mostrarle la parte de ella de la que él se había enamorado en primer lugar le resultaría muy grato a Keith. ¡Tenía razón! Después de leer la lista de Ladonna, escriba su propia lista en su cuaderno.

Actividad 19. Cambio en la conducta que se va a recompensar

Enumere las conductas que quiere que su ser querido tenga con más frecuencia y las recompensas que serían apropiadas para cada una de ellas. Una buena idea es pensar en más de una recompensa para cada conducta, en caso de que la situación complique poner en práctica su idea original. También puede reutilizar ideas.

Conductas	***Recompensas***
Mantenerse sobrio. No beber.	• Decirle a Keith cuánto disfruto su compañía cuando está así. Acurrucarme con él en el sofá. • Decirle que lo amo y ofrecerme a hacerle su comida favorita. • Ponerme la ropa íntima que a él más le gusta e invitarlo a un viaje inesperado a la habitación.

Quedarse en casa después de la cena, en vez de irse al bar.	• Poner la música favorita de Keith y decirle cuánto me gusta pasar la noche con él. Tal vez invitarlo a bailar en la sala como hacíamos cuando éramos novios. • Ofrecerle un masaje en la espalda. • Sorprenderlo con una película de acción y un bol gigante de palomitas de maíz: su "cita" favorita cuando éramos más jóvenes.

Castigos

Todos saben castigar. Alguien dice o hace algo que no le gusta y usted dice o hace algo que a esa persona no le gusta para que se sienta mal. Cuando su ser querido llega a casa ebrio, usted grita o llora o le lanza algo. Eso es un castigo. ¿O no?

Si su relación se ha deteriorado hasta el punto de que casi todas sus interacciones son negativas, podría ser que su ser querido experimente sus gritos o las cosas que lanza como recompensas. Claro que no es exactamente lo mismo que si hace algo amoroso y lo disfruta activamente. No obstante, la atención por una molestia suele ser mejor que la falta completa de atención. Así que cuando usted hace un escándalo, su ser querido se siente conectado con usted. Aunque la conexión sea desagradable, hay una conexión. Además, si sus interacciones se transforman en escenas muy emocionales, su ser querido (y usted también) podría experimentar una cierta adrenalina que podría ser satisfactoria. Asimismo, después de una pelea, por lo general, hay una reconciliación y un periodo similar a una luna de miel, en el que ambos tratan de ser más agradables de la cuenta y esto, de cierta forma, vuelve a reforzar la pelea. Así que el mensaje en este punto es ser muy cuidadoso si planea usar los castigos para ayudarle a su ser querido a cambiar. Con frecuencia, pueden ser contraproducentes y, además, no son tan poderosos para activar cambios duraderos como las recompensas.

En la mayoría de las situaciones, puede defender su punto de vista de la misma forma o incluso con más eficiencia usando recompensas o la indiferencia (consulte la siguiente sección). Los castigos siempre deben ser su última opción. Si gritar y pelear no ha funcionado antes, es muy probable que tampoco lo haga ahora. Sería más eficaz algo que llamamos "replanteamiento positivo". Por ejemplo, su ser querido llega a casa ebrio a las dos de la mañana y quiere tener sexo con usted. En vez de ceder con tal de que se calle o de gritarle que es un(a) ebrio(a) asqueroso(a), pruebe esto. Dígale a la persona que disfruta hacer el amor pero solo cuando está sobria y atenta a sus necesidades, y estará feliz de tener sexo con ella cuando cumpla con estas condiciones. De esta forma, transforma un castigo potencial (rechazo) en una promesa de recompensa cuando su ser querido se comporte de forma apropiada.

El tipo de castigo que le recomendamos que considere al rediseñar los mapas de su ser querido es quitarle la recompensa. Eso significa quitar algo positivo, en vez de introducir algo nuevo y desagradable en la situación. Kathy lo hizo al prometerle a Jim una cena amorosa y una noche agradable si llegaba a casa a las 5:30. Cuando no lo cumplió, le dejó una cena fría y le quitó su compañía. Fue castigado sin la teatralidad y el peligro potencial de una pelea.

Tenemos una advertencia acerca del uso de castigos. Ponga atención a las señales de peligro físico de parte de su ser querido. Usted sabe qué tan lejos puede llegar su castigo, así que esté atento(a) a sus instintos. No hay ninguna ventaja en castigar a su ser querido que bebe, hasta el punto de que se genere una pelea violenta o que se vaya de la casa dando un portazo. Sabemos qué tan tentador puede ser castigar a alguien que lo(a) haya lastimado, pero tenga cuidado de que ese castigo no sea contraproducente. Tenga en cuenta siempre cuál es su meta final y pregúntese si esta estrategia lo(a) acercará a esa meta o solo le dará la satisfacción momentánea de la venganza. Si se trata de la segunda opción, no lo haga.

La indiferencia

En vez de usar castigos cuando su ser querido haga algo inapropiado, es más seguro y más poderoso actuar con indiferencia. Es muy similar a retirar una recompensa prometida, como lo describimos en la sección anterior.

Cuando su ser querido presente una conducta inadecuada, hágale saber que no quiere estar cerca de esta conducta y luego váyase. Si hay otras personas en la misma situación, sugiera que se vayan a otro lugar o simplemente ignore a la persona que bebe. A todo costo, no le permita que lo(a) arrastre a una pelea, lo que podría ser satisfactorio en última instancia y alejarlo(a) en vez de acercarlo(a) a su meta.

Por ejemplo, ustedes dos están acurrucados en el sofá para una sesión de videos, con el acuerdo de que la bebida de la noche será el chocolate caliente. A media película, su ser querido saca una cerveza de la refrigeradora. "Amor, recuerda que acordamos que hoy no habría alcohol para poder disfrutar nuestra compañía" le dice usted. "Ya sé", responde la persona, "pero es que una cerveza caería perfecta ahora". "Por favor, no lo hagas", dice usted. "No seas tan fastidioso(a)", insiste. En este punto, podría ponerse a pelear con la probabilidad de resultados desagradables, sin mencionar que aún va a pasar la noche con usted. O, usted podría decir: "Lamento que elijas beberte esa cerveza en vez de ver el resto de la película conmigo. Yo prefiero estar contigo cuando no bebes, así que me voy". Luego, toma su abrigo, y se va a casa de un amigo o familiar o simplemente sale de la habitación. Sin escándalo, pero también sin recompensa por beber. Usted usó la indiferencia y dejó a la persona lidiando con eso sola. Este es un mensaje importante.

Un pensamiento adicional

Antes de que cerremos el tema de las recompensas, los castigos y la indiferencia, debemos agregar unas palabras sobre el mundo real. Aunque nuestros ejemplos son un reflejo de la vida real, los hemos simplificado para transformarlos en anécdotas educativas claras. Sus experiencias con estas estrategias a veces serán tan tranquilas (o incluso más) que las que describimos, pero a veces no será así. Descubrir nuevas formas de vivir juntos es complicado y, una vez que las aplica, podrían tardar un poco en funcionar. A veces, los planes son contraproducentes y usted termina preguntándose si estos métodos valen la pena el esfuerzo. Solo podemos decirle lo que la experiencia nos ha enseñado.

Si lleva años tratando de vivir con su ser querido, es evidente que usted valora la relación. Eso significa que el esfuerzo vale la pena. Muy pocos de nuestros clientes han llegado al programa y han experimentado cambios positivos sin esfuerzo. No obstante, la mayoría ha logrado esos cambios. A veces, requiere meses de trabajo pero, eventualmente, la mayoría de quienes usan este enfoque son capaces de mejorar su calidad de vida y muchos de ellos logran que su ser querido busque tratamiento. Solo se requiere que usted persista lo suficiente para que el proceso funcione y siga trabajando en el proceso. Defina sus estrategias, deles seguimiento, reevalúelas y revíselas. Luego, inténtelo de nuevo. Usted puede lograrlo.

Ahora, todo junto

Ya aprendió sobre las recompensas, los castigos, la indiferencia, la solución de problemas, la elaboración de mapas, la definición de metas y la comunicación PIUS. Ahora, ¿cómo juntarlo todo? De hecho, es más fácil de lo que podría pensar. Para empezar, vuelva a los mapas de bebida que elaboró (en el capítulo 2) de la conducta actual de su ser querido y a las revisiones que hizo. Luego, examine sus respuestas para responder lo siguiente:

1. ¿Usted hace algo que pensaba que desmotivaría la bebida pero en realidad la recompensa?

2. ¿Hay una respuesta típica suya que recompensa una conducta que no quiere recompensar? Si es así, ¿cómo puede alterar su conducta para usar la indiferencia o, si es adecuado y seguro, el castigo?
3. ¿Está usando castigos cuando podría estar usando la indiferencia o la recompensa? Trabaje para cambiar la situación, de modo que pueda concentrarse en lo positivo y ofrecer una recompensa, en vez de concentrarse en lo negativo.
4. ¿Las formas revisadas de empezar las conversaciones o responder a su ser querido usan frases positivas, en primera persona ("yo"), muestran que entiende lo difícil que le resulta a esa persona cambiar e indican que usted comparte la responsabilidad de la situación?

Al responder cada pregunta, busque formas de mejorar sus planes usando las técnicas que ha aprendido. Una vez que tenga planes con los que se sienta a gusto, practíquelos. Lo ideal es que encuentre a alguien que lo ayude a ensayar las situaciones descritas en los mapas de bebida. Si no tiene a nadie para hacer el juego de roles, ensaye los planes en su imaginación. Usted se sorprenderá al ver cuán eficaz pueden ser los ensayos mentales para mejorar su desempeño en la vida real.

Ahora que está listo(a) para empezar a hacer algunos cambios poderosos en su forma de interactuar con su ser querido que bebe, es importante informarle qué está pasando. No, no necesita decirle que empezó un programa para hacerlo(a) dejar la bebida. Lo que tiene que decirle es que lo(a) ama y quiere mejorar su vida juntos. Asegúrese de usar la comunicación positiva para transmitir el mensaje de forma cariñosa, concentrado en cómo se siente usted y mostrando claramente que entiende las dificultades involucradas y que comparte la responsabilidad. Aquí hay algunos ejemplos.

- "Yo te amo *(oración en primera persona, "yo", con su sentimiento)* tanto que me asusta cuando veo que bebes. Sé que para ti es difícil dejar la bebida *(comprensión),* así que dejaré de reclamarte, pero tampoco puedo soportar seguir siendo testigo de ello. Quiero que las cosas mejoren, así que ya no seré parte de tu vida con el alcohol *(compartir la responsabilidad).* A partir de ahora, cuando bebas, saldré de la casa hasta que vuelvas a estar sobrio(a)".
- "Me importas y sé que estás bajo mucho estrés *(comprensión/frase positiva),* pero no puedo lidiar con lo que está pasando *(afirmación en primera persona).* Necesito hacer algunos cambios en mi vida *(afirmación en primera persona).* No puedo seguir como estamos *(compartir la responsabilidad).* ¿Estás dispuesto(a) a ayudarme *(compartir responsabilidad)*?"
- "Nuestras peleas por la bebida ya han desgastado mucho a esta familia *(compartir la responsabilidad).* Sé que te molesta tanto como a mí *(comprensión)* y haré lo que sea necesario para ayudarnos *(afirmación en primera persona/ compartir la responsabilidad).* Te amo y quiero que hagamos un plan juntos para que nuestra vida sea más feliz *(positiva/compartir la responsabilidad)*".
- "Las cuentas se están acumulando y estoy preocupado(a) *(afirmación en primera persona).* ¿Qué podemos hacer *(compartir la responsabilidad)*? Te amo muchísimo y me preocupa nuestro futuro *(positiva/ afirmación en primera persona)*".

¡IMPORTANTE! Si su ser querido responde a una de estas nuevas comunicaciones de forma positiva y reconoce el problema y la necesidad de cambiar, podría ser un buen momento para sugerir que vean a un terapeuta juntos. En el próximo capítulo, hablaremos más sobre cómo abordar la idea del tratamiento pero, por ahora, tenga en cuenta que cualquier remordimiento de parte de esa persona es una excelente oportunidad para tocar el tema. Si lo hace y ella reacciona negativamente, no diga nada más por ahora. Habrá otras oportunidades... E intentos más exitosos.

Prueba, te va a gustar

Al fin y al cabo, usted está pidiendo que usted y su ser querido cambien la forma en que viven al cambiar la conducta cotidiana. Puede ser asustador, en especial para la persona dependiente del alcohol que debe enfrentar el futuro sin su muleta emocional. En vez de tratar de convencer a alguien a que cambie algo "para siempre", pida cambios pequeños y cómodos. Pídale a su ser querido que considere no beber apenas durante esta visita de sus padres o comprometerse a llegar a casa a tiempo para la cena el lunes de esta semana. Pida algo pequeño para que sea fácil de lograr. Será más fácil obtener un compromiso de esa forma, y la probabilidad de que se cumpla el compromiso será mayor. Su tarea será garantizar que cumplir la promesa sea igual de satisfactorio o aún más que beber.

Hay mil y una áreas en las que puede adoptar el enfoque "prueba, te va a gustar". Siempre que le pida un cambio a su ser querido que bebe, piense en cómo puede hacer que ese cambio sea un pasito que la persona pueda dar fácilmente y usted pueda recompensar. A continuación, incluimos algunos ejemplos de cómo nuestros clientes han usado este enfoque con éxito a lo largo de los años.

- En vez de tratar que alguien se comprometa a ayudar a mantener organizada toda la casa para siempre, concéntrese en una conducta a la vez: "Amor, yo sé que te molesta que deje mi maquillaje en el lavatorio del baño, así que lo recogí. Si recoges las toallas mojadas del suelo y las cuelgas, prometo que no vuelvo a dejar mi maquillaje en el lavatorio". Cuando logre el cambio con las toallas, puede pasar a los platos de la cena y así sucesivamente.

- Cambiar la forma en que uno de los padres se relaciona con un niño pequeño no es más fácil que cambiar la forma en que usted y su ser querido que bebe se relacionan. Si quiere mejorar la conducta de su ser querido con sus hijos, evite pedirle que "sea más agradable" o "más comprensivo". Esos son dos grandes cambios globales y es difícil definirlos. Es mejor pedir un pequeño cambio en la conducta. Por ejemplo, podría decir: "Me incomoda mucho cuando le gritas a Billy por su habitación. Si tratas de hablarle con calma del desorden, yo lo ayudo a recogerlo".
- Muchas parejas discuten por dinero más que por cualquier otra cosa. Esto puede ser un problema particularmente grave si uno de los miembros bebe en exceso y está desempleado o gasta el dinero de forma inapropiada. De nuevo: es más fácil pedir una pequeña modificación en la conducta que cambiar todo el estilo de vida de quien bebe. Un primer paso podría ser: "Entiendo que estás bajo mucha presión y no quiero aumentarla. Pero me preocupa que no podamos pagar las cuentas. ¿Crees que podríamos planear un presupuesto doméstico, de modo que tengamos suficiente para cubrir los gastos de la casa?"
- "Tú ya no hablas conmigo" es una frase que, hasta donde sabemos, nunca ha producido un aumento en la comunicación. Si quiere abrir las líneas de comunicación, pida un cambio pequeño como: "Últimamente no hemos estado en la misma frecuencia. Me gustaría sacar un rato contigo para hablar de la relación. ¿Podemos sacar solo treinta minutos mañana por la mañana para hablar?". No necesita pedir un compromiso de un mes para esta actividad. De hecho, no necesita insistir en los treinta minutos. Diez también sirven. Pida la cantidad de tiempo y de días que cree que serán fáciles para su

ser querido. Luego, independientemente del resultado de las conversaciones, recompense el hecho de que su ser querido sacó el tiempo para hacer esto por usted. Un beso, un abrazo o apenas un agradecimiento sincero puede abrir a la persona para otras comunicaciones.

- El sexo y las muestras de cariño suelen ser lo primero que se hace a un lado por el problema de la bebida. Si su ser querido ha reclamado de su falta de deseo y usted no quiere besar a una botella, trabaje en un beso sobrio a la vez. Haga que llegar a la cama sobrio sea tan interesante como pueda. Por ejemplo: "Si llegas a casa directo después del trabajo, le pediré a mi mamá que cuide a los chicos y me podré aquel nuevo negligé que te gusta tanto. Una cosa podría llevar a la otra. ... ¿Qué te parece?"

Note, cómo en todos los ejemplos, el hablante usa el patrón PIUS. Las comunicaciones son positivas y clara mente comparten la responsabilidad de la situación. Cuando corresponde, demuestran comprensión y emplean afirmaciones en primera persona. También es importante ser consciente de que cada una de estas personas primero se aseguró de que las recompensas que ofrecieron fueran atractivas para sus seres queridos. Recuerde que Sammy no habría limpiado su habitación por la promesa de comer berenjena, aunque esta sea la comida favorita de su madre.

Haga su propio seguimiento

Cuando los clientes trabajan con nosotros en la clínica, pueden darse el lujo de venir al consultorio con regularidad y revisar su progreso: lo que intentaron, lo que salió bien, lo que no funcionó y cómo pueden mejorarlo. Lamentablemente, no tenemos el lujo de reunirnos con usted en privado y orientarlo(a) durante este proceso. Sin embargo, podemos contarle que es lo más cercano a ello. Mantenga un registro escrito de sus planes, cómo/cuándo los usa, qué sucede y cómo los revisa. En otras palabras, haga su propio seguimiento como si se estuviera reuniendo con nosotros regularmente para revisar sus resultados.

Debido a que usted está tan íntimamente involucrado en todo lo que pasa, será muy difícil que analice de manera objetiva lo que ocurre con solo revisarlo mentalmente. Ponerlo en el papel es la mejor forma de ayudarse a dar un paso atrás y ver el panorama completo de cómo su conducta afecta a su ser querido que bebe. Lleve un registro de todo lo que ocurra. Verá que, con el tiempo, se volverá más fácil recordar anotar las cosas y disfrutará revisar sus notas. Después de todo, son los mapas que está siguiendo en dirección a un futuro más feliz.

También es buena idea repetir periódicamente las actividades de referencia del capítulo 2. De esta forma, tendrá una forma de medir los cambios en su ser querido y en su vida. Es muy probable que los resultados sean satisfactorios. Si no es así, en el capítulo 12 hablamos de las opciones que tiene para mejorar su vida, incluso si su ser querido que bebe no cambia.

Resumen de la acción

Ahora usted cuenta con herramientas adicionales que lo(a) ayudarán a hacer cambios poderosos y satisfactorios en su vida. Para cada secuencia de bebida que trace, planifique sus estrategias para cambiar el curso de los eventos. Haga que las recompensas sean su herramienta más usada y busque oportunidades para recompensar a su ser querido por sus conductas positivas. También recuerde que conductas positivas pueden ser simplemente la ausencia de conductas negativas. *Cada caso en el que su ser querido esté sobrio es un motivo para recompensarlo.* Use sus sonrisas, sus palabras y sus acciones para que la sobriedad resulte más atractiva que la bebida.

Repaso

- Las recompensas deben ser atractivas para su destinatario.
- Los castigos no son tan eficaces para lograr cambios de conducta duraderos como las recompensas.
- La indiferencia (extinción) es un complemento útil de las recompensas.
- Use todas las herramientas que haya aprendido para hacer que *no* beber sea igual o más interesante que la bebida para su ser querido.

Kathy y Jim: hacer cambios

Kathy por fin empezó a sentir que estaba a cargo de su vida, después de trazar el mapa de las tres secuencias de bebida más comunes de Jim, desde los disparadores hasta las consecuencias, y de planear cómo lidiaría con cada una de ellas. Aunque se veía tentada a seguir haciéndole ver a Jim que era un cretino, Kathy se obligó a concentrarse en las cosas que quería que él hiciera, en vez de las que no quería que hiciera, y encontró formas positivas de explicárselas a él.

Una pelea frecuente que Jim y Kathy tenían era sobre cómo estaban criando a su hijo, Ted. Jim sentía que Kathy era demasiado blanda con él y constantemente les gritaba a a ambos por el comportamiento de Ted. Kathy sentía que, por todo el estrés con el que tenían que vivir sus hijos por la bebida de Jim, ellos no debían ser tan duros con respecto a cosas como mantener la habitación arreglada y el uso del teléfono.

Ted era el mayor, tenía once años y parecía que se portaba mal para llamar la atención de Jim. Kathy sabía que si Jim fuera un poco más cariñoso con Ted, su conducta mejoraría. No obstante, a pesar de todos los sermones y peleas, Jim seguía explotando cada vez que Ted se pasaba de la raya aunque fuera mínimamente. De hecho,

Kathy había trazado el mapa de una secuencia típica: Jim llegaba del trabajo y Ted corría a contarle a su papá algún evento del día. Jim le pedía a Ted que esperara que se quitara el abrigo y se sirviera un trago y a Ted se le bajaba el ánimo. En cuestión de momentos, Ted botaba algo (a veces a su hermanita) o dispersaba sus tareas o juguetes en la mesa de la cocina. La reacción de Jim prácticamente inevitable era gritarle preguntándole: "¿Qué demonios te pasa?". Ted lloraba y se iba a su habitación dando un portazo. Jim tocaba la puerta y le decía a Ted que no podía salir hasta que él se lo permitiera. Y así se iba cualquier esperanza de pasar una velada agradable juntos.

Cuando Kathy vio claramente la relación entre la conducta de Jim y de Ted, planeó mejores formas de organizar su rutina al final del día. Para empezar, habló con Ted para que esperara hasta que su papá estuviera sentado en el sofá, sin zapatos, para acercarse a contarle las cosas de la escuela. Luego, se concentró en inyectar una pequeña interacción positiva en la relación de Jim y Ted. En vez de tratar de convencer a Jim de que necesitaba ser más positivo con su hijo si quería que mejorara su conducta, lo abordó a través de su sentido de la paternidad (y su ego) y le puso un enfoque positivo a la situación. Le dijo: "Jim, sé cuánto significa Ted para ti, y a él también le encanta pasar tiempo contigo. Realmente quiere ser como tú. ¿Por qué no te vienes a casa directo del trabajo hoy y lo llevas a comer a Pizza Factory? Pueden divertirse con algún videojuego lejos del caos de la casa. Yo me quedo en casa con los más chicos y Ted y tú diviértanse solos".

La respuesta de Jim a la invitación de Kathy para que saliera con su hijo la sorprendió. Ella imaginaba que él no aceptaría la idea porque estaba cansado del trabajo y necesitaba pasar al bar para hablar de algo con sus amigos, sabía que se Ted se iba a portar mal en el restaurante o cualquier otra excusa de las que había usado antes para no pasar tiempo con los niños. Sin embargo, esta vez *aceptó*. Kathy casi había empezado a discutir con él al respecto por la pura costumbre. Pero no lo hizo, sino que lo abrazó y le dijo que Ted estaría encantado. También lo llamó al trabajo unos veinte minutos antes de la hora de salir para recordarle sus planes para esa noche y decirle que Ted estaba tan animado que ya había hecho toda su tarea y había ordenado su habitación. Jim se rió y le dijo que se iría a casa después del trabajo y así lo hizo.

capítulo 11
Tratamiento

Linda y Ron

A Linda le preocupaba Ron, su hermano gemelo, desde que estaban en la secundaria. Ahora que compartían un apartamento en la universidad, vivía en estado de pánico al ver que se iba de fiesta toda la noche, dormitaba entre las clases de la mañana y, en términos generales, estaba perdiendo el control de su vida. Cuando trataba de hablarle al respecto, él le recordaba que ella era su hermana y no su madre. Inevitablemente, si le sugería que hablara con alguno de los orientadores de salud mental del campus, él explotaba y salía del apartamento dando un portazo. Al cambiar su forma de hablarle y aprender a dejar de facilitarle la bebida, pudo reducir las peleas y restaurar cierta armonía en su relación. No obstante, seguía convencida que el consumo de alcohol de Ron no era apenas "diversión universitaria", como él decía, y que necesitaba ayuda profesional.

En muchos aspectos, lograr que su ser querido que bebe se ponga en tratamiento es, al mismo tiempo, el punto alto y el punto bajo de este proceso. Representa el punto alto porque, para muchas personas que beben, el tratamiento es la única forma en que logran aprender a vivir sin licor. También puede ser el punto bajo porque, como sabe, es difícil cambiar y el tratamiento será una lucha para su ser querido. Por supuesto que las luchas de su ser querido también se vuelven sus luchas y, como siempre, sus esfuerzos siguen siendo críticos en todo esto.

Lograr que su ser querido que bebe se ponga en tratamiento requiere la misma atención a los detalles y planificación que todo lo que ha hecho hasta ahora. En el mejor de los casos, la mayoría de la gente que consume alcohol en exceso es ambivalente con respecto al tratamiento. Incluso cuando se concientiza de cuánto dolor y sufrimiento causa su bebida, la idea de dejarla es asustadora. Usted tendrá que ser sensible a estos miedos a la hora de abordar el tema.

Motivos para beber

Seguir bebiendo tiene costos y beneficios para su ser querido. Los costos son claros y puede enumerarlos mejor que nosotros. Sin embargo, aunque los beneficios sean menos obvios, son igualmente importantes. Cada persona tiene una experiencia única con el alcohol, pero es útil revisar algunos de los motivos más comunes que tienen las personas para no dejar de beber. Algunas de ellas, todas o ninguna podrían aplicarse a su ser querido. Una tarea importante para usted es pensar en los beneficios de la bebida que disfruta la otra persona. Si es posible, hable con él o ella al respecto. Si no, use el conocimiento íntimo que tiene, sus poderes de observación y su capacidad de pensamiento crítico. La Actividad 20 lo(a) ayudará en esto. Lea cómo Linda completó la actividad con respecto a la bebida de Ron y use su cuaderno para completar la suya.

Actividad 20. ¿Por qué beber?

La siguiente lista ayudará a que fluya su inspiración creativa. Marque las razones para beber que usted cree que podrían aplicarse a su ser querido. Complete la lista con su propia reflexión sobre la conducta de la persona que bebe o hable con ella al respecto. Después de revisar su lista, escriba un resumen.

__*X*__El alcohol sabe bien.
__*X*__El alcohol se siente bien.
_____Emborracharse lo(a) hace evitar sentimientos desagradables.
_____Emborracharse le permite evitar situaciones desagradables.
_____Beber le da seguridad en situaciones sociales.
__*X*__Beber le da seguridad en situaciones románticas.
__*X*__Beber alivia el estrés.
_____Beber es una forma de pasar tiempo con amigos y/o familiares.
_____Beber es el único pasatiempo que tiene.
_____Beber es una buena excusa para no poder trabajar.
_____Beber es la forma más fácil de escapar del dolor o el aburrimiento.
_____Beber adormece los malos sentimientos.
_____¿Otros?

Cuando no bebe, Ron es un chico tímido. Así que, además de que le gusta el sabor del alcohol, disfruta el "valor en una botella" que le brinda socialmente. Todo esto le ha facilitado realmente acostumbrarse a beber. Ahora, me imagino que también tiene una adicción física al alcohol, así que hay tanto atractivos físicos como emocionales para seguir bebiendo.

Recuerde que, si le pide a su ser querido que renuncie a la bebida, debe estar listo(a) para ayudarlo a encontrar algo igualmente satisfactorio para sustituirla.

En el capítulo 2, usted calculó cuánto tiempo su ser querido gasta en actividades con y sin bebida. Si renuncia a esas actividades, tendrá que llenar su tiempo con algunas actividades más saludables. Esté preparado(a) para ofrecerle a su ser querido otras actividades igualmente satisfactorias a elegir. Por ejemplo, si gasta una hora o dos todos los días después del trabajo socializando con amigos en el bar, su ser querido necesitará otra actividad social sin bebida para ocupar ese tiempo. Lo mismo aplica para los fines de semana y las noches. Dejar un vacío creará un agujero pidiendo a gritos que lo llenen... Y si lo deja por su cuenta, su ser querido lo llenará con la vieja y conocida bebida. Su trabajo en esta etapa es darle a su ser querido tantos motivos interesantes para no beber como los que él podría encontrar para beber.

Prepárese para la sobriedad de su ser querido y ayúdela preparando una lista de actividades satisfactorias y sin alcohol que se puedan disfrutar en lugar de beber. Asegúrese de que las actividades que seleccione sean interesantes para su ser querido y no solo para usted. Incluso si a usted no le interesa el licor, recuerde que satisface muchas necesidades de su ser querido. Planifique en función de ello. De hecho, consulte al experto. Hable con su ser querido sobre el tema. Use su estilo de comunicación PIUS para preguntarle qué pueden hacer juntos y sea lo suficientemente placentero para renunciar al licor en ese periodo. La Actividad 21 lo(a) ayudará a hacer esta lista. Revise la lista de Linda en el ejemplo que se incluye a continuación y haga su propia lista en su cuaderno.

Actividad 21. Actividades por las que vale la pena mantener la sobriedad

- *Correr temprano por las mañanas (a Ron le encantaba el atletismo en la secundaria)*
- *Conversaciones personales conmigo toda la noche (solíamos hacer esto regularmente antes de que me enojara tanto por su consumo de alcohol)*
- *Andar en patineta por el campus después de que la multitud se va, por las noches*
- *Comer montones de palomitas viendo películas extranjeras en el cine local*

Las actividades sin bebida que prepare para la sobriedad de su ser querido también son poderosos incentivos en dirección a esa sobriedad. Al trabajar en los mapas de bebida y hacer planes para motivar la sobriedad, use estas actividades como incentivos y recompensas. No necesita esperar a que su ser querido se ponga en tratamiento para empezar a disfrutar estos momentos juntos sin bebida. Ofrézcale el placer de su compañía, a cambio de la sobriedad durante el tiempo y con la frecuencia que su ser querido logre mantenerse sobrio. Con suficientes interacciones positivas de este tipo, la sobriedad extendida y, en última instancia, el tratamiento serán el próximo paso.

Seleccionar el tratamiento

Si no hace nada más, al menos haga esto: *tenga un tratamiento listo para acudir en el momento en que su ser querido diga que le interesa*. Ese interés aumentará y luego se evaporará si no aprovecha el momento. Por cada motivo que a usted se le ocurra para buscar la sobriedad, su ser querido tiene dos para evitarla. Cuando la balanza al fin se incline a favor de que la persona considere el tratamiento, usted no puede darse el lujo de dejar que la balanza cambie de lado mientras busca un programa adecuado.

Hay disponibles varias opciones de tratamiento. Aunque todas tienen defensores, no todas han demostrado producir resultados constantes. Describiremos las opciones de tratamiento más populares y le contaremos lo que se sabe de su eficacia. No obstante, tome en cuenta que, una vez que su ser querido tenga la intención de ponerse en tratamiento, usted podría tener que alterar su elección para adecuarse a las preferencias de la otra persona. Piense en lo que conoce de los gustos y el estilo de su ser querido al hacer su selección.

El primer paso al explorar las opciones de tratamiento es entender la diferencia entre tratamiento y apoyo. Cuando hablamos de "tratamiento", nos referimos a un programa de intervención activa que toma a su ser querido de la mano y le *enseña* a vencer al licor. Esto es diferente de los grupos de apoyo que brindan motivación e intervención en casos de crisis pero no le enseñan ni ayudan a la persona a practicar nuevas conductas lejos de la bebida. Hablamos de destrezas específicas. Un programa de tratamiento debe enseñarle a la persona habilidades para resistirse a la bebida y reconstruir su vida. De preferencia, el programa también involucrará activamente a los seres queridos de quien bebe, así como nos hemos aproximado a su ser querido al ayudarlo(a) a usted en este libro. Por eso, al evaluar los programas de tratamiento, pregunte específicamente cómo pretenden enseñarle a su ser querido a vivir sin o manejar el alcohol. Si no escucha estrategias específicas dirigidas claramente a las conductas problemáticas, siga buscando.

Logre que su ser querido alcance la sobriedad: alternativas a los reclamos, las súplicas y las amenazas se basa en un modelo que la investigación ha comprobado que es eficaz. La descripción genérica del programa con el que usted ha venido trabajando es terapia cognitiva-conductual o terapia de entrenamiento de habilidades. En nuestra clínica, el programa se llama Community Reinforcement and Family Training (CRAFT/Refuerzo comunitario y capacitación familiar) y se deriva de un programa anterior llamado Community Reinforcement Approach (CRA/Enfoque de refuerzo comunitario), que trata directamente a la persona que bebe. El CRA sigue siendo el tratamiento que usamos en nuestra clínica y ha ayudado a muchas personas con problemas de bebida a reemplazar el alcohol por un estilo de vida positivo.*

Puede encontrar programas similares al CRA y complementarios a lo que ha hecho aquí buscando tratamientos que incluyan frases en sus descripciones como "capacitación en destrezas sociales", "terapia conductual marital", "tratamiento cognitivo-conductual", "terapia racional-emotiva", "tratamiento motivacional" o "terapia concentrada en las soluciones". Es importante tener en cuenta que los diferentes profesionales y centros de tratamiento tendrán su propio "sesgo", por así decirlo, con respecto a los modelos de tratamiento. Esto significa que ofrecen programas de diferente duración, diferente formato de aplicación (individual, familiar, grupal) y, probablemente, usan un lenguaje ligeramente diferente para describir los mismos tratamientos. Al investigar las diversas opciones en su comunidad, recuerde que usted busca un tratamiento que ayude a su ser querido a descubrir los disparadores y refuerzos de sus conductas nocivas, que le enseñe a cambiar los disparadores y refuerzos que se pueden cambiar y a cambiar sus respuestas a los que no pueda cambiar.

Hay cientos de programas de tratamiento a elegir y está fuera del alcance de este libro siquiera empezar a describirlos. No obstante,

*Para obtener una descripción detallada del CRA, consulte: Meyers, R. J. y J. E. Smith. 1995. *Clinical guide to alcohol treatment: The community reinforcement approach*. Nueva York: Guilford Press.

basta decir que el programa que seleccione debería atender al menos a las tres destrezas que mencionamos y ser un lugar cómodo para usted y su ser querido. No tenga reparos en hacer llamadas, preguntar, entrevistar a los profesionales e informarse sobre los servicios complementarios que el programa ofrezca. Usted es el "cliente" y tiene el derecho de asegurarse de seleccionar el mejor "producto" para usted y su ser querido. Use el directorio telefónico y busque centros de salud mental y rehabilitación para casos de alcohol y drogas. También consulte a la agencia estatal local que atiende casos de consumo de alcohol y drogas.

A lo largo de los años, ha habido un amplio debate sobre si funciona mejor el tratamiento con internación o ambulatorio. No obstante, desde la perspectiva del costo-beneficio, no parece que la terapia con internación (que es mucho más cara que la ambulatoria) aumente mucho los índices de éxito (Miller y Hester 1986). De todos modos, usted debería explorar todas las opciones, puesto que no hay una forma única, y lo que funciona o no para su vecino, podría funcionar o no para usted. Antes de que se enamore de cualquier lugar, consulte a su seguro de salud si lo cubre.

Hay una amplia diversidad en los programas ambulatorios. Además de los diferentes enfoques que puedan tener, también varía la estructura. Podrían ofrecer sesiones semanales individuales, terapia de grupo o incluso sesiones nocturnas para ajustarse a los horarios laborales. Muchos programas también brindan programas de tratamiento diarios que requieren asistencia de la mañana a la tarde, todos los días. Muchos programas ambulatorios requieren que los pacientes asistan a grupos de autoayuda, como Alcohólicos Anónimos (AA), además de la terapia, y otros grupos usan el formato de los Doce Pasos como tratamiento. A fin de cuentas, ningún tratamiento puede funcionar si la persona que bebe no *asiste y participa* durante el tiempo suficiente para que les permita funcionar.

Junto con un programa de tratamiento activo, a mucha gente le resulta útil usar a un buen grupo de apoyo, como Alcohólicos Anónimos (AA) y Narcóticos Anónimos (NA) para su ser querido y Al-Anon y Nar-Anon para usted. De hecho, el apoyo social y la ayuda para estructurar el tiempo que antes se gastaba consumiendo alcohol o drogas es extremadamente útil para mucha gente.

Entreviste a los profesionales de tratamiento

Cuando decida cuál es el mejor enfoque para usted y su ser querido que bebe, tome el tiempo para entrevistar a diferentes profesionales que responden a su modelo ideal. Diferentes terapeutas que usan el mismo enfoque, trabajan diferente con clientes diferentes. Infórmeles a los terapeutas que quiera entrevistar lo que está haciendo. La mayoría de ellos estarán dispuestos a reunirse con usted (con frecuencia sin cobrarle) para comentar el enfoque que usan. Como mínimo, el profesional debería estar dispuesto a dedicarle algunos minutos al teléfono para responder sus dudas sobre su abordaje.

Cuando entreviste a los profesionales, hágales todas las preguntas que se le ocurran y comente todo lo que le preocupe. (De hecho, prepare una lista de preguntas con anterioridad, de modo que no pase nada por alto). Un buen centro (o terapeuta) no solo será receptivo a sus dudas sino también lo(a) ayudará a pensar en preguntas específicas si no está seguro(a) sobre qué preguntar. Es de interés del lugar que todos los clientes entiendan qué les ofrecen y cómo funciona el programa.

Algunas de las preguntas más obvias incluyen las siguientes:

- ¿Cuánto cuesta el programa?
- ¿Mi seguro lo cubre?
- ¿Cuánto dura cada sesión?
- ¿Con qué frecuencia mi ser querido deberá asistir a las sesiones?

También querrá saber si ell tratamiento solo se brinda en grupos o hay opciones de terapia individual, de parejas y familiar.

Si su ser querido tiene mucho tiempo de beber en grandes cantidades y muestra señales de dependencia física, podría necesitar internarse en un hospital o unidad de desintoxicación antes de empezar el tratamiento. Usted debería descubrir si el centro de tratamiento tiene acceso a este tipo de ayuda médica. Si no es así, pregunte cómo podría conseguirla, además de la psicoterapia.

La bebida suele ocultar otros problemas, como la depresión o los trastornos de ansiedad, y cuando una persona deja de beber, estos problemas se vuelven evidentes. Por eso, es importante garantizar que el programa tenga al personal apropiado para lidiar con problemas de salud mental. En ciertos casos, la persona requiere medicamentos para ayudarla en el periodo difícil de reajuste y abstinencia.

Pídale al(a la) terapeuta que describa su filosofía y le brinde una descripción detallada del propio tratamiento. Nuestra recomendación, a partir de la investigación científica, es que busque tratamientos que correspondan a las categorías de la terapia conductual o la terapia cognitiva-conductual, ya sea para la persona o para la pareja o la familia. Si está considerando otro abordaje o alguien trata de convencerlo de alguno en particular, pida una lista de investigaciones con resultados publicados que respalden el tratamiento. Investigue todo lo que pueda antes de decidir.

También es importante que sepa cuáles son las calificaciones del(de la) terapeuta. ¿Tiene alguna certificación como orientador(a) para casos de consumo de alcohol o licencia como psicoterapeuta? Si no es así, le recomendamos que busque otra opción. También debería saber hace cuánto tiempo la persona trabaja con consumidores de alcohol. No existe una cantidad de experiencia perfecta para usar como referencia, pero si no le quieren brindar esta información es señal de que debería buscar otra alternativa. Hay puntos positivos y negativos con respecto a la cantidad de experiencia de los terapeutas. Más experiencia puede ser sinónimo de mayor eficacia, pero los terapeutas recién graduados tienden a estar más actualizados en el campo. Al final, lo que cuenta es encontrar a alguien con quien usted se sienta a gusto y en quien pueda confiar.

Finalmente, pregunte cómo planea el(la) terapeuta involucrarlo(a) a usted en el programa. Si a la persona le sorprende su pregunta, quiere decir que no es el(la) terapeuta correcta para usted. Usted necesita a alguien que trabaje con los dos (y con otros miembros de la familia, si es necesario) para cambiar no solo a la persona que bebe sino también su entorno. No hay mucha probabilidad de éxito si no cambian ambos.

La oportunidad

Con el tratamiento listo para el momento en que su ser querido dé señales de que está preparado, usted puede empezar a buscar la oportunidad. Así es. No se trata simplemente de llegar corriendo a casa a informarle a su ser querido que encontró un plan de tratamiento espectacular. Si alguna vez ha hecho esto, ya sabe cuál es la respuesta más probable.

La mejor forma de evitar el rechazo y de aumentar la probabilidad de que su ser querido esté abierto a la idea de tratamiento es buscar los momentos en que su motivación se dispara. Podría ser cuando su ser querido está particularmente insatisfecho consigo mismo o cuando ustedes dos se estén llevando mejor que nunca y la otra persona quiere complacerlo(a). Usted conoce a su ser querido mejor que nadie, así que esté alerta a los momentos de receptividad.

Así como ha planeado y practicado cuidadosamente los cambios que ha hecho para mejorar su forma de relacionarse con su ser querido, encontrar la oportunidad de sugerir el tratamiento también requiere una reflexión cuidadosa. Como dijimos: usted conoce mejor que nadie a su ser querido, así que no podemos decirle qué debe buscar. Sin embargo, podemos guiar su reflexión con las preguntas de la Actividad 22. Para Linda fue una grata sorpresa darse cuenta que había diversas condiciones en las que Ron estaría anuente a la idea de la terapia. Lea las respuestas de Linda en el ejemplo y anote las suyas en su cuaderno.

Actividad 22. Abrir la oportunidad

1. ¿Cuándo sería más probable que su ser querido estuviera dispuesto a probar algo nuevo como forma de tratamiento? *Posiblemente al final de una de nuestras conversaciones relajadas por la noche.*
2. ¿Hay alguna hora particular en el día en que esa persona se sienta más relajada? *Tarde por la noche.*
3. ¿Hay más probabilidades de que su ser querido esté más abierto a anaizar la opción del tratamiento cuando están ustedes dos solos o con otra gente? Si es con otras personas, ¿quiénes? *Solos.*
4. ¿Hay más probabilidades de que su ser querido esté abierto a la idea de tratamiento tras varios días de sobriedad o mientras sufre las consecuencias de una borrachera? *Creo que sería cuando esté de resaca.*
5. ¿Su ser querido estaría más abierto a sus sugerencias cuando llevan varios días sin pelearse o al reconciliarse después de una pelea? *Cuando no peleamos por varios días.*
6. ¿Su ser querido estaría dispuesto a ponerse en tratamiento si fuera por su relación? (Esto es lo que llamamos el enfoque de la "puerta trasera": hacerlo para mejorar la relación y, coincidentemente, también mejora la salud y la conducta de la persona que bebe). *No creo que esto sea relevante.*
7. Revise sus intentos pasados de hacer que su ser querido se pusiera en tratamiento. ¿Qué funcionó? ¿Qué no funcionó? *He tratado montones de veces de convencerlo, he discutido, le he gritado, lo he minimizado. Nada funcionó.*

Una vez que identifique algunas situaciones (o estados de ánimo) que cree que serían favorables para sugerir el tratamiento, piense en varios escenarios. Trate de prever con la mayor cantidad de detalles posibles cuál sería el lugar, qué diría usted y cómo podría responder su ser querido. Asegúrese de pensarlo a fondo. ¿Qué diría usted si la persona responde positivamente y qué diría si no es así? En otras palabras: ¡planifique, planifique, planifique!

Por ejemplo, tal vez haya notado que su ser querido se siente realmente culpable después de haber sido agresivo con usted y le parece que este sería un buen momento de sugerirle el tratamiento. La conversación podría ser algo así.

La persona que bebe:	No sabía lo que hacía. Lo siento mucho. ¿Cómo puedo compensarte?
Usted:	De hecho, hay algo que puedes hacer. Sé que no querías lastimarme, pero lo hiciste. Tengo a un(una) terapeuta que puede ayudarnos a dejar de hacer esto. Realmente quiero que vayamos juntos. ¿Estarías dispuesto(a) a intentarlo?
La persona que bebe:	Creo que sí.
Usted:	Muchas gracias. Voy a llamar ahora mismo para programar una cita.

Si la persona que bebe lo duda, una buena respuesta sería la siguiente:

Usted:	Vayamos solo una vez o dos a ver si nos ayuda. Si no te gusta, podemos suspenderlo.
La persona que bebe:	Está bien, pero no prometo nada.
Usted:	No hay problema. Yo igual te agradezco que estés dispuesto(a) a considerarlo. Eso me hace sentirme bien.

El hecho es que la persona que bebe suspenderá el tratamiento de cualquier forma si no le gusta, así que de nada sirve insistir. Su ser querido tiene el control de dónde y cuándo hace lo que hace, así que reconozca ese control. Exigirle a alguien que haga algo, por lo general, hace que quiera hacer lo contrario. En nuestra experiencia, hemos encontrado que, una vez que la persona que bebe inicia el tratamiento y el terapeuta calma sus miedos, la persona acepta la ayuda. Lo difícil es convencerla a empezar.

Es mejor no *preguntar* si su ser querido quiere buscar ayuda. Afírmelo como un hecho, pero de una forma alentadora, compartiendo la responsabilidad, y no en un estilo dictatorial. Ofrezca el tratamiento como algo que mejorará su vida juntos, en vez de algo para corregir el "defecto" de su ser querido. Este es otro ejemplo.

Es sábado por la mañana y usted está en casa con su ser querido. Aunque la persona bebió la noche anterior, no está de resaca y está de buen humor. Usted se ofrece a prepararle el desayuno favorito y mantiene el buen ambiente mientras hablan de sus intereses comunes. Si el buen humor de su ser querido continúa y usted siente que es un buen momento, podría tener esta conversación:

Usted:	¡Qué mañana tan tranquila! Me gusta esta paz.
La persona que bebe:	Sí, realmente es una mañana agradable.
Usted:	Últimamente he estado pensando... Siento que las cosas han mejorado entre nosotros, pero quiero que estemos aún mejor. De verdad te amo.
La persona que bebe:	Y yo a ti.
Usted:	He estado viendo a un terapeuta para que me ayude a resolver las cosas. Creo que está funcionando.
La persona que bebe:	No sabía que estabas haciendo terapia. ¿Qué pasa?
Usted:	Mira, yo te quiero tanto que quiero hacer todo lo posible para que nuestra vida sea más feliz. ¿A ti no te gustaría eso?
La persona que bebe:	Espero que esto no sea lo que creo que es. Todo estaba tan bien esta mañana. ¿No puedes parar con ese temita?

Usted:	Solo quiero que las cosas estén tan bien como sea posible. ¿No estarías dispuesto(a) a ir conmigo solo una vez a reunirnos con mi terapeuta? Hazlo por nosotros.
La persona que bebe:	¿Esto es algún tipo de terapia matrimonial? No necesitamos esa tontería; estamos bien.
Usted:	Estamos bien, pero podríamos estar mejor. No te va a pasar nada si me acompañas una vez.
La persona que bebe:	Lo voy a pensar. ¿Ahora podemos cambiar de tema?
Usted:	Claro. Podemos volver a hablar de ello después.

En este ejemplo, presentamos un modelo de cómo mantener la interacción positiva y evitar el enfrentamiento. Recuerde: no fuerce nada. No presione si su ser querido se resiste. Una vez que haya roto el hielo, será más fácil mencionar el tema la próxima vez que aparezca la oportunidad. Podrían ser necesarios varios intentos hasta que su ser querido acepte la ayuda, pero si evita pelear por el tema, puede seguir mencionándolo hasta que la otra persona ceda.

Incluso puede seguir aumentando la presión de acuerdo con la situación. Puede ser más incisivo(a) (sin enfrentamientos) si siente que la resistencia de la persona se va debilitando o puede aumentar las recompensas prometidas. También puede reducir lo que le pide a su ser querido y pasar de "ven a la terapia conmigo" a "ven a una sesión" o apenas "habla con mi terapeuta por teléfono y descubre qué tiene que decir". Algunas personas se ven tentadas a conocer al(a la) terapeuta porque les dicen que el(la) terapeuta ha oído hablar tanto de ellas que solo quiere conocerlas. No hay límites con respecto a la creatividad que pueda aplicar para mantener la oportunidad abierta y motivar a su ser querido a dar un paso al frente.

A lo largo de los años, en nuestro trabajo con los clientes, hemos descubierto algunas estrategias que funcionan bien con la mayoría de la gente. Sin embargo, como siempre, evalúe cada una para ver si es apropiada a su situación. Solo las primeras dos sugerencias se aplican a cualquier persona.

1. La seguridad está primero. Independientemente de todo el cuidado que le haya puesto a sus planes para sugerir el tratamiento, abandónelos de inmediato si su ser querido muestra señales de violencia. Olvide el tema, tranquilícelo y espere otra oportunidad. Ella *llegará* y la meta es que usted pueda aprovecharla.
2. Asegúrese de que el(la) terapeuta y el programa que haya elegido le resulten cómodos a su ser querido. Esto significa que no debe conseguirle un(a) terapeuta evangélico(a) a una persona atea o sesiones grupales a alguien que sufre de ansiedad social. Trate de buscar compatibilidades entre la terapia/el(la) terapeuta y su ser querido. Por otro lado, prepárese y prepare a su ser querido para un proceso difícil. Como sabe, los cambios no son fáciles. No obstante, tenga en cuenta que el objetivo es la felicidad y la mayoría de las cosas que valen la pena cuestan.
3. Si usted está en terapia, a veces es útil contárselo a su ser querido e invitarlo a que lo(a) acompañe. Pero recuerde usar la comunicación PIUS y hacer que la invitación sea positiva. Podría decir algo como: "He estado en terapia porque estoy pasando por momentos difíciles y sería maravilloso si también pudieras venir para ayudarme... A mi terapeuta le encantaría conocerte".
4. Otra opción, si usted está en terapia, es pedirle a su terapeuta que llame a su ser querido y lo invite a asistir a una sesión. De nuevo: la invitación debería ser positiva y transmitir la idea de que el objetivo del(de la) terapeuta es conocer a una persona importante en su vida para entender mejor *su*

relación. Además, pídale a su terapeuta que simplemente invite a su ser querido a *una* sesión. Si la sesión sale bien y la persona se siente cómoda, la pueden invitar a volver a una segunda sesión.

5. Si usted no está en terapia, puede introducir el tema preguntándole a su ser querido si estaría dispuesto a acompañarlo(a) a usted a ver a un terapeuta. En vez de poner todo el peso sobre su ser querido ("Tú necesitas tratamiento porque eres un/a borracho/a"), enfatice su compromiso con la relación y con el hacer lo necesario para tener una vida feliz juntos ("Realmente quiero ser una mejor pareja en este matrimonio y me ayudaría que me acompañaras a ver a un terapeuta"). Una vez que su ser querido haya aceptado trabajar para mejorar su vida juntos, abordar el tema del alcohol será una parte natural de ese proceso.
6. Si la persona que bebe se rehusó a ponerse en tratamiento pero sabe que usted está involucrado(a) en un programa, usted podría darle una tarjeta con una cita programada para ella. Esto a veces tiene más peso que una invitación verbal. Si su ser querido falta a la cita, siempre puede comentar después al respecto y, posiblemente, programar otra.
7. Usted puede mencionar que escuchó hablar de un programa nuevo/eficaz/interesante e invitar a su ser querido a probarlo con usted, sin compromiso.
8. Si su ser querido ha estado enfermo, usted puede decir que está preocupado por su salud y que al menos debería buscar ayuda para sus problemas físicos.
9. Apelar a los amores de su ser querido. Pídale que busque ayuda por la seguridad de su trabajo, los niños, su matrimonio, su vida sexual, su salud, etc. A menudo, el incentivo más poderoso es el miedo de perder uno de los grandes amores.

10. Si la persona que bebe está constantemente renuente a la idea del tratamiento, usted podría tratar solo de analizar el tratamiento con ella. Esto significa que, en vez de recomendárselo, pregúntele a su ser querido bajo qué condiciones consideraría que el tratamiento es adecuado. Esta podría no llevar a nada, pero también podría darles la oportunidad de comentar con calma su situación actual y comparar qué tan parecida o diferente la perciben. Lo que es más importante: usted aprende por dónde debe presionar para motivar a su ser querido que bebe. Por ejemplo, la persona podría decir que, siempre y cuando su matrimonio aguante tal y como está, no se necesitan cambios. O su ser querido podría pensar que su consumo de alcohol en realidad no le está causando a nadie ningún problema serio. En ambas situaciones, usted tiene la oportunidad de decirle a su ser querido, al estilo PIUS, la más pura verdad.

A menudo, a los clientes les preocupa que, si preparan todo según nuestras indicaciones, y su ser querido descubre que el tratamiento estaba arreglado de antemano, podría sentirse manipulado. Esto es posible. No obstante, recuerde que lo(a) instamos a que sea honesto con la persona que bebe desde el principio. Usted dejó de fingir que la vida era aceptable para usted. Usted le dijo a su ser querido que no está dispuesto(a) a resolver los problemas de él/ella y en cuáles circunstancias disfruta estar con él/ella. En cierto punto del proceso, también es posible que le haya contado a su ser querido que usted está en terapia y espera que el crecimiento personal que experimenta también ayude a que relación crezca. Dígale que usted está en tratamiento y tiene a un(a) terapeuta que lo(a) está ayudando a trabajar en ciertos problemas. Entonces, puede pedirle que vaya con usted a la terapia, y en ese punto, puede haber arreglado que usted salga de la sesión y se transforme en el tratamiento de la persona; o durante la terapia, podría sugerirse que consiga su "propio" terapeuta. Hay muchas alternativas en este escenario. Si usted ofrece ayuda en el contexto de los pasos amorosos que haya dado para asegurarse de que su ser querido tenga opciones, en caso de que quiera tomarlas, es probable que no se sienta manipulado. Si reacciona con enojo, retroceda y dígale que no quiere presionarlo, que apenas intenta tener opciones disponibles en caso de que las quiera.

Cuando desaparece la oportunidad

A pesar de toda su planificación cuidadosa y la espera paciente de que surja la oportunidad, existe la posibilidad de que su ser querido no la acepte. Todo es perfecto, ustedes dos están casi en luna de miel, usted menciona el tema de forma amorosa y clara, y su ser querido explota. O usted logra que la persona llegue a la sala de espera del terapeuta, y se arrepiente y se marcha. ¿Qué hacer? Muy fácil. Lo mismo que hizo para llegar hasta aquí en primer lugar. Usted le agradece por considerarlo, le recuerda cuánto la ama y disfruta estar con ella cuando está sobria, y planifica y espera otra oportunidad. A veces pasa.

Lo hermoso de las oportunidades es que pueden aparecer, desaparecer, aparecer, desaparecer y volver a aparecer. Si necesita retroceder, no hay problema. El hecho de que haya aparecido una oportunidad, aunque fuera por poco tiempo, significa que puede aparecer. Basta revisar su estrategia para ver si puede mejorarla y esperar el momento. La mayoría de la gente que usa este programa, logra que su ser querido al menos pruebe el tratamiento. Recuerde que este proceso es como un viaje. Los cambios exigen tiempo y el camino tiene sus curvas. Lograr que su ser querido se ponga en tratamiento a menudo requiere varios intentos, pero es posible.

Respaldar el tratamiento

Cuando su ser querido se pone en tratamiento, es importante que usted siga practicando el nuevo estilo de interacción en el que ha venido trabajando. De hecho, su ayuda será más necesaria que nunca. Usted sabe, por experiencia, la dificultad que implica cambiar hábitos antiguos y con qué facilidad una persona se puede desmotivar y volver a los antiguos patrones. Ahora, imagine la dificultad de cambiar si se le suma el desafío de tratar de renunciar a una droga (o drogas) que afectan no solo la mente sino también el cuerpo. En una palabra: infernal.

Muchas personas que beben han abandonado el tratamiento porque fue demasiado difícil cambiarse a sí mismas mientras su entorno seguía igual. En este punto, usted ha hecho cambios excelentes en el entorno de su ser querido. Es fundamental que siga usando recompensas, comunicándose con el estilo PIUS y poniendo atención a los disparadores y patrones que conducen a la bebida, las peleas y otras situaciones difíciles. Su trabajo, a partir de ahora, será seguir esforzándose por mejorar la forma en que ustedes dos interactúan y apoyar el tratamiento. No puede simplemente enviar a su ser querido que bebe para que "lo arreglen". Debe ser un apoyo activo y, si es necesario, un(a) participante involucrado(a) en el tratamiento.

Según el tipo de programa que inicie su ser querido, su papel varía. Nuestra esperanza es que se involucre en un programa de tratamiento activo que se concentre no solo en eliminar el problema de la bebida, sino también en sustituirla por otros patrones de conducta más saludables y productivos. Si ustedes no están en terapia de pareja, obtenga la aprobación de su ser querido para hablar con su terapeuta. Pregunte cómo puede ayudar. O mejor aún: pregúntele a su ser querido cómo puede ayudar. Lo(a) sorprenderán los tipos de ayuda que puede pedir una persona y que a usted nunca se le hubieran ocurrido.

Dos de las formas universalmente apropiadas de apoyar el tratamiento son: eliminar los obstáculos al tratamiento y recompensar a su ser querido por asistir. Facilítele la asistencia al garantizar que sus tareas de cuidado de los niños estén cubiertas, que el transporte esté disponible y que no haya otros eventos programados en ese horario. Y todo lo demás que se le ocurra para eliminar los obstáculos. Recompense a su ser querido diciéndole cuán orgulloso(a), feliz, encantado(a) o emocionado(a) usted está con él por el esfuerzo que está haciendo. No se obsesione con lo mal que estaban las cosas. Más bien concéntrese en el cambio positivo y en su futuro brillante. Facilite todo lo que pueda la asistencia de la persona al tratamiento.

Cuando se debe involucrar a un profesional médico

En la mayoría de los casos, su mejor opción de tratamiento es un profesional licenciado de salud mental (psicólogo clínico, trabajador social clínico, orientador certificado en consumo de alcohol). Estas personas están capacitadas para ayudar a la persona con un problema de bebida a encontrar formas más saludables de lidiar con la vida. No obstante, hay casos en los que se recomienda la asistencia de un profesional médico, como un doctor o un psiquiatra.

Si su ser querido bebe grandes cantidades de licor (más de cinco o seis tragos por día durante muchas semanas), podría necesitar una desintoxicación médica para ayudarlo con los síntomas de la abstinencia. La experiencia anterior es su mejor guía: si su ser querido ha tenido síntomas de abstinencia antes, cuando intentó dejar el alcohol o las drogas, es probable que necesite una desintoxicación médica esta vez. Por lo general, este tipo de desintoxicación tarda de tres a cinco días y se puede hacer ambulatoria o con internación, según la gravedad y los recursos disponibles en su comunidad. Durante la desintoxicación, el personal médico monitorea a su ser querido y le brinda medicamentos que lo ayudan a superar los delirios, los temblores, las convulsiones y otros síntomas de abstinencia que podrían empezar algunas horas después del último trago. Tome en cuenta que la abstinencia psicológica tardará considerablemente más que la física. La psicoterapia es esencial para lidiar con el estrés emocional de renunciar al licor y ajustarse a un nuevo estilo de vida. Superar la abstinencia física es apenas el primer paso.

Otros casos en los que se debería involucrar a un profesional médico incluyen la presencia de problemas en el hígado (algunas señales de esto serían un estómago distendido, ojos y piel amarillentos y heridas que no sanan), consumo de varias drogas o un historial de problemas emocionales o psiquiátricos que requieren medicamentos. Esta lista no es definitiva. Si tiene alguna duda sobre el estado de salud de su ser querido o su capacidad de lidiar con el estrés de renunciar al alcohol, consulte a un médico.

Ayuda para el reso de la familia

Es muy probable que otros miembros de la familia también se hayan visto afectados por el alcohol y es importante buscar terapia familiar o ayuda individual para ellos. Al-Anon es un buen recurso para los miembros de la familia que necesitan el apoyo y la empatía de otras personas que han vivido o aún viven en situaciones similares. La mayoría de las comunidades tienen varias divisiones de Al-Anon en la guía telefónica.

Al mal tiempo, buena cara

Más allá de la emoción de que su ser querido se ponga en tratamiento, tome en cuenta que el proceso podría ser muy difícil para él. Una vez que pase la satisfacción personal inicial de haber dado este paso al frente (posiblemente en cuestión de horas o días), a su ser querido le caerá el peso de la realidad de estar renunciando a un viejo y querido amigo. Va a ser duro y, sin duda, habrá ocasiones en que su ser querido se desquitará con usted. Después de todo, fue su *insatisfacción* con la vida de su ser querido lo que empezó todo el proceso de cambio.

Acepte esa responsabilidad (felicítese en secreto) y tenga su meta en mente. Usted puede tolerar este resentimiento temporal para, eventualmente, vivir la vida que se merece. Siempre y cuando se mantenga a salvo (aún es muy pronto para desechar su plan de seguridad) y siga usando todas las estrategias que ha estado practicando, usted puede superar esto. Y su ser querido también.

Otra advertencia que debemos hacerle es que son más las personas que abandonan el tratamiento que las que se mantienen en él... Al menos al principio. Es muy común que las personas inicien y desistan del tratamiento varias veces antes de empezar a hacer cambios duraderos. No se desanime si su ser querido se pone en tratamiento y lo abandona al poco tiempo. Todos los cambios que usted ha hecho cuentan en la ecuación del éxito y ni siquiera el abandono del tratamiento puede negarlos. Siga esforzándose por hacer su vida más agradable y recompensando a su ser querido por las conductas que evitan la bebida. Continúe cuidándose y evitando facilitarle a su ser querido la bebida sin consecuencias. Podrían ser necesarios varios intentos pero, eventualmente, hay grandes probabilidades de que su ser querido lo logre. Mientras tanto, no pierda de vista los cambios positivos que ha logrado y disfrútelos.

En cierto momento, podría decidir que ha hecho todo lo que ha podido y que lo ha intentado todas las veces posibles. Tendrá que decidir si desiste de la relación en caso de que su ser querido no cambie. En ese punto, tal vez quiera usar esta decisión como el último intento de motivar a la persona que bebe a ponerse en tratamiento al decirle que usted la abandonará a menos que cambie. No obstante, si lo hace, debe estar seguro(a) de estar listo(a) para cumplir su amenaza. De lo contrario, perderá su credibilidad futura. Las amenazas vanas simplemente le dan más poder a quien bebe.

Resumen de la acción

Como ya dijimos, la parte crítica de lo que logre en este paso es tener el tratamiento listo para actuar en el momento en que su ser querido indique que está abierto a la idea. Usted debe ser capaz de dirigir a la persona que bebe a un terapeuta dentro de las veinticuatro a cuarenta y ocho horas posteriores a que haya aceptado la idea. Según nuestra experiencia, este es el periodo máximo de la oportunidad. De hecho, unos minutos después de que su ser querido diga "Necesito tratamiento", la motivación podría empezar a desvanecerse. Si lo compara con una ola que viene y va, corresponde a la brevedad con la que alcanza el punto más alto. No desperdicie un instante de ese tiempo: tenga a mano el tratamiento. Cuanto más rápido agarre la ola, mayor la probabilidad de que su ser querido la surfee en dirección al éxito.

Use los mapas de la bebida que realizó para descubrir cuándo su ser querido estaría más anuente a aceptar el tratamiento y esté alerta a esas oportunidades. Luego, cuando la oportunidad se presente, use sus habilidades de comunicación PIUS para presentar, de forma amorosa pero firme, la opción del tratamiento. Hágalo con la expectativa de que su ser querido aceptará, pero esté preparado(a) para retroceder si ve resistencia o enojo. Tenga en mente la imagen de la ola y sepa que, aunque se haya devuelto al mar, eventualmente regresará adonde usted está sentado(a) esperándola. De la misma forma que cada vez que se cae de la tabla de surf le enseña un poco más sobre cómo mantenerse sobre ella, cada vez que menciona el tema del tratamiento sin una pelea de por medio, se acerca un poco más al momento en que su ser querido lo acepte.

Repaso

- Busque programas de tratamiento que tengan respaldo empírico sólido sobre su eficacia. Recomendamos los que usan métodos descritos con términos como "conductual", "cognitivo-conductual" o "entrenamiento de habilidades" y que involucren a los seres queridos de la persona en bebe en el esfuerzo de cambio.

- Tenga a mano el tratamiento para su ser querido y esté listo(a) para acudir a él en el momento en que la persona acepte intentarlo.
- Use sus mapas de carretera para identificar las oportunidades en las que puede sugerir el tratamiento con probabilidades de que su ser querido esté receptivo a la idea.

Kathy y Jim: generar oportunidades

Las cosas iban bien gracias a que Kathy había incorporado el hábito de trazar el mapa de la bebida de Jim y *planificar de antemano* cómo lidiaría con las diferentes situaciones. Auque él aún bebía bastante, y esto aún era causa de problemas, también aumentaba la cantidad de veces que Jim se iba a casa directo del trabajo y pasaba la noche sobrio con Kathy. También había empezado a llevarse a Ted a comer pizza y a los videojuegos los sábados por la tarde, así como a pasar un poco más de tiempo de calidad con los dos niños menores. Además, Kathy había programado un encuentro regular con su hermana todas las noches de los jueves y Jim sabía que debía estar en casa para cuidar a los niños. No siempre llegaba a tiempo (y Kathy dejaba a los niños donde su madre o en casa de un vecino), pero él aceptaba la responsabilidad de la noche.

La vida realmente había mejorado desde la época en que Kathy sentía que nada valía la pena. Sin embargo, Jim aún bebía y, aunque disfrutaba las tardes con Ted y aceptaba la responsabilidad de las noches de los jueves con los niños, a menudo llegaba a casa borracho o se abría una cerveza antes de salir con Ted. Cuando eso ocurría, Kathy no lo dejaba conducir con el chico y Jim se molestaba y salía de la casa dando un portazo para irse a beber. A pesar de ello, Kathy sentía que finalmente tenía cierto control de su vida y Jim había redescubierto cierto placer en su vida familiar, lo que facilitaba que ella lo tentara a mantenerse sobrio.

Kathy hizo una lista de las veces en que creía que Jim estaría más receptivo a ponerse en tratamiento. Cuando se emborrachaba en vez de salir con Ted los sábados, Jim se levantaba el domingo por la mañana corroído por la culpa. Se disculpaba varias veces y por lo general trataba de abstenerse todo el día para compensarlo. Kathy decidió que ese sería un buen momento para mencionar el tratamiento, así como los viernes por la mañana después de las veces en que había llegado a casa tarde y borracho y encontraba una nota de Kathy donde le decía lo decepcionados que estaban los niños por tener que quedarse con la abuela y no con su papá.

Tras identificar esas oportunidades, Kathy las esperó y se preparó. Encontró a una buena terapeuta cerca de su casa, dispuesta a organizar su agenda y ajustarla a Jim en el momento en que él estuviera anuente. Esta mujer era psicóloga clínica cognitiva-conductual y se concentraba en ayudar a alcohólicos a desarrollar las habilidades necesarias para alejarse del licor y reconstruir su vida. También insistía en que Kathy estuviera preparada para ser miembro activo del equipo de terapia con Jim. Kathy estaba entusiasmada y, mientras tanto, había programado un par de citas para ella, en parte para conocer a la terapeuta y en parte para mantener su propia motivación.

Cuando llegó el momento y Jim empezó a disculparse por otro sábado arruinado, Kathy le dijo: "Jim, sé que quieres que nosotros y los chicos estemos bien. Yo también quiero eso. De hecho, he estado yendo donde una terapeuta maravillosa que me ha ayudado mucho a manejar mis sentimientos. A ella le encantaría conocerte y a lo mejor te ayude. Mañana tengo cita con ella. Realmente puedes hacer la diferencia para nuestra familia si vienes conmigo y hablas con ella". Preparada para retroceder ante la mínima señal de enojo, Kathy quedó encantada cuando Jim le preguntó si esa mujer era una "loquera" y si iba a tratar de enredarle las ideas. Feliz de satisfacer la curiosidad de Jim sobre la psicóloga, Kathy le explicó que simplemente hablaban de varias cosas. “La terapeuta”, le dijo, “me ayuda a pensar en cómo llevarme mejor contigo, así como a controlar mis propios sentimientos para no perder los estribos y empeorar las cosas”. Kathy sabía que era exactamente por eso que Jim había pasado disculpándose toda la mañana. Jim aceptó conocer a la terapeuta y Kathy de inmediato llamó al servicio de mensajería confirmando que acudirían a la cita preprogramada para el lunes en la mañana.

Kathy estaba tan entusiasmada y Jim tan determinado a no actuar como un “loco” que el resto del día fue estupendo. Él no bebió y Kathy se esforzó por hacerle saber a Jim cuánto ella lo amaba y disfrutaba su compañía cuando estaba sobrio.

capítulo 12

Prevención de recaídas

Carlene y Peter

Peter había reducido bastante la bebida en los últimos meses en que Carlene había estado aplicando sus recién aprendidas destrezas de cambio de conducta y comunicación PIUS. Él había estado asistiendo a las reuniones de AA con regularidad y parecía sincero sobre querer abandonar la bebida. Sin embargo, cada tres o cuatro semanas en que tenía un día particularmente difícil en el el trabajo, o en que él y Carlene discutían por dinero, volvía a emborracharse. Carlene se debatía entre querer recompensar su conducta cuando se alejaba de la bebida y el sentimiento de traición por las veces en que él bebía. A pesar de que las cosas habían mejorado, ella aún estaba bastante preocupada.

Llegamos al paso final. Esta debe ser la parte de "y vivieron felices para siempre", ¿cierto? En realidad no. Blanca Nieves y el Príncipe Encantado vivieron felices para siempre. El resto de nosotros vive en el mundo real. Eso significa que disfrutamos los buenos momentos, nos esforzamos por superar los malos ratos y, por lo general, seguimos adelante, un paso a la vez.

La videa real está llena de altibajos, como usted bien sabe, y la diferencia entre la gente atrapada en los malos momentos y quienes salen adelante está en su forma de *interpretarlos*. Por ejemplo, considere a alguien cuya pareja consume alcohol en exceso y cuya vida se consume en la sobrevivencia en esta relación difícil. Esta persona puede mirar la situación y verla horrible y sin salida y renunciar a la esperanza de tener una vida mejor. O la persona puede mirar la situación y ver problemas que se deben solucionar y poner su energía en descubrir cómo hacerlo. (En este momento, la segunda persona debe sonarle muy familiar). De hecho, los verdaderos ganadores en la vida llegan al punto de ver los problemas como *oportunidades*. Cuando algo sale mal o alguien complica las cosas, usted tiene la oportunidad de aprender un poco más sobre lo que activa las cosas o motiva a la gente al aislarlas (las conductas, no a las personas) y descubrir lo que causó el problema.

Lapsus

Todos cometemos errores. Independientemente de que esté aprendiendo a caminar, tratando de perder peso, cambiando su forma de comunicarse, o intentando dejar de consumir alcohol en exceso, se va a equivocar. Es una parte completamente natural de estar vivos.

Cuando alguien trata de cambiar su conducta y comete un error, hablamos de un "lapsus". *Los lapsus son una parte esperada del proceso de cambio.* Los lapsus pueden ser desagradables, por ejemplo, al encontrar a su ser querido ebrio después de tres semanas de abstinencia o verse reproduciendo de nuevo el viejo estilo beligerante de hablar. Sin embargo, que el lapsus sea una oportunidad o una catástrofe depende por completo de cómo lo vea.

Cada vez que usted y su ser querido hacen planes y las cosas no salen según lo esperado, usted tiene la oportunidad de aprender un poco más sobre sí mismo(a). La conducta no ocurre en un vacío, así que si no siguió sus conductas planificadas, ya sabe con seguridad que algo lo disparó a salirse de la ruta. Tome el tiempo para revisar la situación en la que ocurrió el lapsus y descubrir sus disparadores. Por ejemplo, usted había planificado una cena familiar en su restaurante chino favorito y su hijo aparece ebrio tras cinco semanas de abstinencia. Aunque esto parece una recaída con *R* mayúscula, ustedes dos pueden analizar qué antecedió el lapsus de hoy e identificar, por ejemplo, problemas con la novia en los últimos días y la depresión derivada que lo hace pensar que su vida es injusta y que realmente "necesita" sentirse mejor. Tal vez su mejor amigo había salido de la ciudad y no tenía con quién hablar. Ustedes dos podrían decidir que en situaciones similares en el futuro, puede llamarlo(a) a usted, a su padrino de AA o a su tío favorito. Independientemente de la estrategia que preparen, lo importante es que el episodio de bebida no se vea como una falla, sino como una parte natural del proceso de aprender a administrarse mejor. Mantenga su enfoque en las cinco semanas de sobriedad alcanzadas y los cambios positivos que han resultado. No permita que un día de bebida opaque este cambio maravilloso que ya iniciaron.

Usted ya sabe todo lo que necesita para transformar los lapsus en oportunidades de aprendizaje. Usted sabe cómo darle seguimiento a su conducta, cómo trazar el mapa de las interacciones y cuál es la importancia de planificar y ensayar. Lo que falta de aprender, si es que aún no lo ha hecho, es a controlar su reacción emocional a un lapsus durante el tiempo suficiente para aplicar sus destrezas analíticas.

Situaciones de alto riesgo

Puede hacer que sea más fácil evitar una reacción emocional exagerada a un lapsus al preverla y prepararse para ella. Obviamente, no puede saber de antemano cada situación que puede ser un disparador para que usted o su ser querido vuelvan a los viejos hábitos, pero probablemente puede predecir bastantes situaciones de ese tipo. Piense en los cambios que ha hecho en su forma de responder a la ebriedad de su ser querido y reflexione en las situaciones en las que ha sido particularmente difícil mantener su nuevo patrón. Estas son sus situaciones de *alto riesgo* para mantener esta nueva conducta. La Actividad 23 lo(a) ayudará a prever sus situaciones de alto riesgo. Carlene descubrió que era bastante fácil predecir las situaciones que la pondrían más nerviosa. Échele un vistazo a las respuestas de ella y luego anote las suyas en su cuaderno.

Actividad 23. Identificar situaciones de alto riesgo

1. ¿Qué estados de ánimo serían más propensos a producirle un lapsus? *Cuando me deprimo y me conmisero. Realmente en cualquier estado emocional negativo.*
2. ¿En qué momento del día se siente menos seguro(a) de mantener su nuevo patrón de conducta? *Al final del día, después del trabajo.*
3. ¿Qué lugares le resultan particularmente difíciles? *No se me ocurre ninguno.*
4. ¿Hay personas cuya presencia le dificulta conservar su nuevo patrón? *Los chicos que corretean por todo lado mientras trato de hablar con Peter.*
5. ¿Hay algún día que sea especialmente difícil? *No se me ocurre ninguno.*
6. ¿En qué situaciones es más probable que pierda el control? *Definitivamente, cuando llega a casa borracho y es obvio que venía conduciendo en ese estado.*
7. ¿Qué estado de ánimo de su ser querido le dificulta en especial mantener el control? *Cuando está borracho.*
8. ¿Cuáles frases o tono de voz de su ser querido lo(a) sacan de quicio? *Cuando masculla, con esa voz de borracho.*
9. ¿Cuáles conductas de su ser querido lo(a) vuelven loco(a)? *Que beba y conduzca.*
10. ¿Hay ocasiones en las que no se siente físicamente bien y le resulta más difícil mantener su nueva conducta (por ejemplo, cuando le duele la cabeza, está enfermo/a o, si usted es mujer, antes de su menstruación)? *Nada constante.*

Hay tantas situaciones de alto riesgo potenciales como personas. Además, identificar las situaciones que actualmente le resultan de alto riesgo no significa que no surgirán otras nuevas la próxima semana. (Por suerte, las antiguas eventualmente también perderán su poder). Para estar realmente preparado(a), debe preguntarse continuamente: "¿*Qué* facilita que pase por un lapsus?", "¿*Quién* es más probable que dispare un lapsus?", "¿*Dónde* tengo más posibilidades de estar vulnerable a perder el control?" y "¿*Cuáles* pensamientos y sentimientos disparan los problemas?". Tome en cuenta que su ser querido que bebe podría no ser la persona que le genere un lapsus. Si está exhausto(a) por el trabajo o los niños o familiares, podría estar demasiado cansado(a) o estresado(a) para lidiar de forma eficaz con su ser querido. Prevea también este tipo de situaciones de alto riesgo. Forman parte de su vida, así que asegúrese de no pasarlas por alto.

Puede ver que al pensar con calma en todos los estados de ánimo, los momentos, las conductas, etc. que podrían disparar un lapsus, usted puede identificar varias situaciones de alto riesgo. Ahora puede prepararse para ellas. Hágalo usando la misma estrategia de mapeo que usó para analizar la conducta de su ser querido (en el capítulo 2).

Carlene decidió que el disparador más poderoso de lapsus para ella era que Peter condujera a casa ebrio, así que trazó el mapa de esa situación de alto riesgo primero y con bastantes detalles. Era algo más o menos así.

> Peter llega a casa tarde, así que ya sé que viene borracho. ➔ Mentalmente reviso mis planes nuevos y mejorados para lidiar con esta situación. ➔ Por fin aparece y yo empiezo a usar el discurso PIUS que había planificado, pero él masculla algo, tira las llaves del coche en la mesa y se va a la habitación. ➔ Siento un enojo incontrolable e incluso un odio que me sube de abajo arriba. ➔ Pienso en lo ingrato que es y lo poco

que le importamos los niños y yo, no solo para aparecer borracho, sino también para conducir nuestro auto en ese estado. Podría haber destruido el auto (¡¿qué haríamos con eso?!) y matarse o terminar preso. ➔ Exploto y le digo que es un imbécil.

Aunque sé que tengo razón y él no, y que merece sentirse tan mal como, o incluso peor que yo, también sé que insistir en eso nunca ha mejorado las cosas antes y probablemente no lo hará ahora. Así que necesito un plan de acción para manejar esta situación. Voy a examinar cada paso de este mapa de lapsus y a planear una nueva ruta para todos los pasos que pueda. Cuantos más desvíos pueda incluir en él, más fácilmente puedo salir de este camino pedregoso, incluso si pierdo el primer o el segundo desvío. **(Los desvíos de Carlene están impresos en negrita).**

Peter aún no ha llegado a casa, así que ya sé que vendrá borracho. ➔ Reviso mentalmente mis planes nuevos y mejorados para lidiar con esta situación **y hago una lista de los cambios positivos por los que estoy trabajando y comparo la satisfacción que me daría regañarlo con la que tendré al verlo cambiar.** ➔ Por fin llega y empiezo a decirle el mensaje PIUS que había planeado, pero él gruñe, tira las llaves de su auto en la mesa y se mete a la habitación dando un portazo. ➔ Siento una rabia incontrolable que es casi odio y me corroe por dentro, **así que respiro profundamente y me encierro en el baño, paro algunos minutos para recordar lo que estoy tratando de lograr y que si exploto, lo único seguro es que esta escena se seguirá repitiendo.**

➔ Pienso en lo malagradecido que es y lo poco que le importamos los niños y yo, no solo por llegar ebrio, sino también por conducir en ese estado. Podría destrozar el auto (¡¿y quué hacemos nosotros?!) y matarse o terminar en prisión. **Recuerdo que el alcohol cambia el cerebro de la persona y aunque él es responsable de su bebida,**

la conducta que se deriva es resultado del alcohol. Él no trata deliberadamente de hacer que nuestra vida sea un infierno. También recuerdo que mi meta final es que él esté sobrio, no probar que yo tengo razón esta noche. → En vez de "explotar y decirle que es un completo imbécil", **salgo del baño y le digo: "Sé lo que te cuesta controlar la bebida y sabes cuánto me asusta que bebas y conduzcas. Pero en este momento, probablemente lo mejor en que tengamos una buena noche de sueño. Eso sí, por la mañana, quiero que hablemos al respecto. Te quiero. Buenas noches".**

Cuando Carlene completó su nuevo mapa, se detenía un par de minutos, dos o tres veces al día, para imaginarse viviendo la situación que había descrito. No solo repasaba mentalmente cada paso, sino también trataba de experimentar las sensaciones que había descrito. Se imaginaba a Peter gruñendo de la forma más grosera posible y haciéndola a un lado. Experimentaba la rabia y el odio ardiendo en su interior y luego se visualizaba activamente respirando profundamente en vez de explotar, entrando al baño para calmarse y pensar, y así sucesivamente. Esto podría parecer un esfuerzo muy desagradable para el beneficio de un idiota borracho, pero recuerde que se trata del hombre que ella ama y que Carlene cree que aún pueden tener una vida feliz juntos si resuelven el problema de la bebida. Así que el trabajo vale la pena. Podría suceder que justo la reacción tranquila y amorosa de Carlene a la grosería de Peter cuando está borracho sea lo que termine de inclinar la balanza y lo haga sentirse culpable y con ganas de hablar del tratamiento a la mañana siguiente. A veces, de las peores situaciones surgen las mejores oportunidades.

Ataques sorpresa

Por muy preparado(a) que usted esté para las situaciones de alto riesgo que prevé, algunos eventos podrían tomarlo(a) por sorpresa. No hay problema. Usted no puede predecir todos los disparadores, pero puede usar lo inesperado para reforzar su arsenal. En el momento en que las cosas se calmen, tome su cuaderno y describa toda la situación de principio a fin, como si fuera un detective que busca hasta la última pista para resolver un misterio importante. Anote todo lo que haya ocurrido, incluidos los participantes, el lugar, lo que dijeron e hicieron todos, cómo se sintió usted, qué se dijo a sí mismo(a), el estado de ánimo de su ser querido. Todo. Luego, ordénelo en la secuencia en la que ocurrió y busque puntos en los que podría haber actuado diferente. Describa de qué forma. Este ahora es su nuevo plan para esa situación. De esta manera, incluso las situaciones más desagradables pueden ser sorpresa solo una vez. La próxima vez que ocurran, usted estará preparado(a).

Lapsus de la persona que bebe

El mismo enfoque que aplica a sus lapsus es apropiado para su ser querido cuando se aleje de los planes de tratamiento y experimente un lapsus. Nuestra esperanza es que, independientemente del tratamiento que elijan, incluya un enfoque racional para solucionar los lapsus. A menos que su ser querido sea un superhumano, no tenga duda de que habrá lapsus. Podría mantener la abstinencia durante un tiempo y luego emborracharse, o tomar Antabuse (un medicamento que provoca que la persona se enferme si lo consume con alcohol) religiosamente durante un tiempo y luego suspenderlo. Los lapsus podrían manifestarse como ausencias a las sesiones de terapia o como explosiones de mal humor. Usted puede predecir los escenarios más probables mejor que nadie.

Usted puede ayudar a su ser querido que bebe a evitar que los lapsus se transformen en episodios de borrachera (recaídas):

mantenga la misma perspectiva oportunista sobre los lapsus de esa persona tal y como lo hace con los suyos. Por muy difícil que sea, puede ayudar a su ser querido a examinar racionalmente cada lapsus y descubrir los disparadores que requieren un manejo más cuidadoso. Por su cuenta, también puede analizar los lapsus de la otra persona y tratar de ver qué podría haber hecho usted para evitarlos o minimizarlos. Aunque usted no es la causa del problema, recuerde siempre que tiene el poder de ser parte de la solución.

Si están trabajando con un(una) buen(a) terapeuta cognitivo-conductual, usted y su ser querido tendrán mucho respaldo para ayudarlos a lidiar de forma productiva con los lapsus. Todos sabemos que el camino hacia la sobriedad no es plano y aprender a maniobrar alrededor de los baches es una parte crítica de la terapia. Si su ser querido optó por no ponerse en tratamiento sino tratar de combatir el problema solo con su ayuda, usted tendrá que ser especialmente fuerte para mantener una visión positiva de las cosas. Y será particularmente importante que tenga un buen sistema de soporte. Así que, si aún no tiene uno, es hora de trabajar en ello.

Manejar las desistencias

La gente desiste del tratamiento. Las personas que beben, en particular, abandonan el tratamiento. Ayude a su ser querido a ponerse en tratamiento con la expectativa de que se quedará lo suficiente para "graduarse", pero que no lo tome desprevenido(a) si la persona desiste. Además, no se desmorone. Desistir no significa que se acabó el viaje. Significa que se perdió algunas salidas de la carretera, pero sin duda sigue en el camino.

Todos los cambios que ha hecho hasta ahora siguen ahí. Usted mejoró su calidad de vida al ampliar su círculo social, incluyó recompensas en sus interacciones y se quitó de encima los hábitos nocivos de encubrir y solucionar. Incluso tuvo éxito al lograr que su ser querido admitiera que el tratamiento era una necesidad. Si lo hizo una vez, puede volver a hacerlo. Todo lo que hizo esta vez volverá a funcionar (con modificaciones basadas en la experiencia). De eso no hay duda. La pregunta que queda es si usted quiere continuar. Piense cuidadosamente en esto antes de decidir. A veces, su instinto le dice que desista porque está cansado(a) y desanimado(a), pero realmente no está listo(a) para *renunciar* a su ser querido. En otras ocasiones, realmente llegó la hora de desistir.

Mantenerse motivado(a)

La motivación fluctúa. Una serie de eventos confluyen para motivarlo(a) a hacer cambios (usted siente que puede escalar cualquier montaña) y, luego, otra serie de eventos hacen que sienta que un solo paso más es demasiado. A veces, la motivación simplemente se desvanece porque el trabajo es duro y los resultados son mínimos.

Los cambios que ya realizó son apenas el inicio de un largo proceso continuo. En algunas ocasiones, será emocionante y estimulante, y en otras será desalentador. Puede ser especialmente difícil mantener la motivación si siente que es el(la) único(a) que hace todo el trabajo, mientras que su ser querido no ayuda en nada. Cuando empieza a pensar así, es fácil perder el interés. Sin embargo, hay cosas que puede hacer para ayudarse a seguir motivado(a).

No pierda de vista la meta

Cuando los aventureros que escalan las altas montañas nevadas se arrastran en medio del hielo y el frío, se mantienen motivados y con vida mirando con un ojo el pico elevado y con el otro los detalles necesarios para mantenerse vivos y seguir avanzando. Usted sabe qué espera lograr con todo este trabajo y ya decidió que vale la pena el esfuerzo. Recuerde todos los días (y cada hora, si es necesario) adónde trata de llegar. Revise las notas que tomó en las actividades iniciales y sueñe un poco. No pierda de vista la meta para que el esfuerzo de llegar a ella sea menos intenso.

No pierda de vista los detalles

Puede pasar mucho tiempo antes de que su vida se parezca realmente a lo que quiere lograr con su meta. Sin embargo, cada día que haga cambios pequeños, se acerca más a ese sueño. Deles seguimiento a todos los planes, intentos y resultados, y recompense cada uno de sus esfuerzos. Esos son los detalles que generan el éxito. ¡Considérelos!

Piense en su inversión

Cuando esté harto(a) y sienta que quiere desistir, tome un minuto para revisar cuánto ha invertido en esta relación. El tiempo, la energía y el amor que ha puesto eventualmente pueden dar resultado. Pero requiere tiempo y, por lo general, inversiones continuas. Si se retira de forma prematura, no solo perderá la posibilidad de conquistar sus metas, sino también todo lo que haya invertido. Mientras su meta sea valiosa para usted, la inversión no será tan grande.

Salga adelante con la ayuda de sus amigos

No olvide que usted cuenta con gente que puede ayudarlo(a). Las personas a las que les haya confiado su situación pueden ofrecerle un gran apoyo. Desde ensayar los escenarios con usted, hasta motivarlo con charlas o apenas compartir una taza de café en silencio: pueden brindarle la tranquilidad y la atención necesarias para aliviar su desánimo y volver a elevar su motivación. No se sabotee asumiendo que nadie querrá ayudarlo(a). A la mayoría de la gente le gusta ayudar a los demás, así que piense en su solicitud de ayuda como algo bonito que le está brindando a un amigo. Le está proporcionando a esa persona la oportunidad de hacer algo que la haga sentirse bien.

Confíe en su comunidad

Si necesita más apoyo del que su círculo social puede brindar, busque a los grupos de apoyo de la comunidad para las personas que están en su situación. Casi todas las comunidades del país tienen reuniones grupales de los Doce Pasos a las que puede asistir para compartir su carga con otras personas que llevan un peso similar sobre sus hombros. Si llama a organizaciones religiosas, el YMCA, el centro local de veteranos o clínicas comunitarias también podrá descubrir grupos de su interés que puedan ayudarlo(a) en este periodo. Como ya hemos repetido: usted no está solo(a). El consumo excesivo de alcohol es casi un pasatiempo nacional, así que hay muchas otras personas en su misma situación: con un ser querido que bebe y el deseo de una vida mejor. Esas personas pueden ser una fuente espectacular de coomprensión, soporte y motivación.

Cuándo desistir

Todas las personas que aprenden las *Alternativas* ganan. Usted gana al ver a su ser querido librarse del alcohol o gana la satisfacción de haber hecho todo lo posible y garantizar su derecho a vivir como usted elija. Entonces, la pregunta es: ¿cuándo decidir que ha hecho todo lo posible? Para ayudarlo(a) a decidir, hágase las siguientes preguntas:

- En la medida de mis posibilidades, ¿pude de forma constante trazar el mapa de las situaciones problemáticas y planear conductas más eficaces y sin enfrentamientos para mí?
- ¿Practiqué un estilo de comunicación PIUS?
- ¿Les he dado seguimiento a mis planes y los he ajustado a partir de esas experiencias?
- ¿He dejado de actuar como el(la) guardián(a) de mi ser querido y le he permitido experientar las consecuencias reales de la bebida?
- ¿He recompensado a mi ser querido por no beber y le he vuelto tan agradable como es posible estar sobrio conmigo y/o con la familia?

- ¿He agregado actividades placenteras a mi propia vida de modo que no esté totalmente absorto(a) por los problemas de la bebida?
- ¿He descubierto cuáles son las mejores oportunidades para sugerir el tratamiento y he planeado cómo las voy a usar?
- ¿He buscado una opción de tratamiento razonable y se la he puesto a la disposición a mi ser querido?
- ¿Se me ocurrió algo que pensé que podría ayudar y tuve la intención de hacerlo pero al final no lo hice?
- ¿Puedo ver un futuro interesante con esta persona?
- Una vez que supere la falta de mi ser querido, ¿el futuro sin él me dará más paz y felicidad que un futuro con él?

Al responder estas preguntas, recuerde: ***usted merece ser feliz.*** Nadie tiene que ganarse la felicidad a través del sufrimiento. Cuando usted ha hecho todo lo que ha podido para mejorar la vida con su ser querido que bebe y nada ha mejorado, podría ser hora de considerar la vida sin él. Sabemos del dolor que conlleva pensar en renunciar a esta relación que se ha esforzado tanto por preservar, pero también sabemos del dolor que conlleva seguir golpeándose la cabeza contra un muro. Lo hemos visto con mucha frecuencia. Cuando usted ha hecho todo lo posible, se debe a sí mismo concentrarse por completo en usted y en cualquier otro miembro de la familia del que sea responsable. Todos ustedes merecen una vida sin miedo, sin enojo y sin alcohol. Esa vida les pertenecerá, con su ser querido que bebe o no. Su decisión es la correcta.

Resumen de la acción

A medida que siga adelante, recuerde que el camino que recorremos cambia. A veces es plano y a veces está lleno de baches (lapsus). Seguir el rumbo depende de su intención de contornar esos obstáculos. Son una parte natural de este proceso y pueden volverlo(a) más fuerte si los usa para concluir qué salió mal y qué salió bien. Avanzar a su meta final, es decir, a la vida que quiere con su ser amado, es un proceso sinuoso. En muchos casos es posible. Y, cuando resulte demasiado difícil de lograr, usted puede salirse del camino con la tranquilidad de haber hecho todo lo que pudo por mantener la relación juntos. De cualquier modo, puede crear una vida que sienta adecuada para usted... con o sin su ser querido que bebe. Usted se la merece.

Repaso

- Los lapsus o errores son una parte natural de la vida. Por eso, se esperan en cualquier proceso de cambio.
- Las situaciones de alto riesgo son las circunstancias en las que es más probable que ocurran lapsus.
- Al analizar las circunstancias en las que los lapsus ocurren y los nuevos medios para manejar esas circunstancias, usted puede usar los periodos de lapsus frecuentes para fortalecer su capacidad de avanzar hacia sus metas.

Kathy y Jim: mirar al futuro

Kathy estaba con los nervios de punta al pensar en cómo sería su consulta con Jim y la psicóloga. Temía que la terapeuta presionara demasiado a Jim y lo hiciera enojar o que él apareciera con su malhumor típico. Cuando llegaron al consultorio, a Kathy le sudaban las manos de la angustia. "¿Qué te pasa?" le preguntó Jim. Kathy respondió que ella realmente quería que las cosas se arreglaran entre ellos y estaba muy nerviosa por la cita. Agregó que no quería molestarlo. Jim le tomó la mano y le recordó que si no le gustaba, él sabía que no tenía que volver, así que no había problema.

En la consulta, la psicóloga le preguntó a Jim por su relación con Kathy y lo que le gustaba y lo que no de su vida juntos. También le preguntó si alguna vez le preocupaba su consumo de alcohol y cómo creía que sería su vida si bebiera menos. Al principio, Jim se sentía un poco inseguro para hablar pero pronto ganó confianza y empezó a explorar los temas con la terapeuta. Al final de la sesión, aceptó regresar la semana siguiente para seguir ayudando en la terapia "de Kathy".

Esa noche, cuando Jim y Kathy se encontraron en casa después del trabajo, ella le agradeció de nuevo por haber ido y le dijo cuánto su participación significaba para ella. Jim se sintió muy bien con la situación; hacía mucho tiempo que no sentía que podía contribuir con la felicidad de Kathy. Ella estaba eufórica. Sabía que el camino por delante aún tenía muchos baches, pero por fin, sabía que estaban en la ruta correcta.

Referencias

Ellis, B. H., I. McCan, G. Price y C. M. Sewell. 1992. "The New Mexico treatment outcome study: Evaluating the utility of existing information systems". *Journal of Health Care for the Poor and Underserved* 3, N°. 1:138-50.

Johnson, V. E. 1986. *"Intervention: How to help those who don't want help"*. Minneapolis, Minn.: Johnson Institute.

Meyers, R. J. y J. E. Smith. 1995. *"Clinical guide to alcohol treatment: The community reinforcement approach"*. Nueva York: Guilford Press.

Meyers, R. J., W. R. Miller, D. E. Hill y J. S. Tonigan. 1999. "Community reinforcement and family training (CRAFT): Engaging unmotivated drug users in treatment". *Journal of Substance Abuse* 10, N°. 3:291-308.

Meyers, R. J., W. R. Miller, J. E. Smith y J. S. Tonigan. 2002. "A randomized trial of two methods for engaging treatment-refusing drug users through concerned significant others". *Journal of Consulting and Clinical Psychology* 70, N°. 5:1182-85.

Miller, W. R. y R. K. Hester. 1986. "Inpatient alcoholism treatment: Who benefits?". *American Psychologist* 41:794 805.

Miller, W. R., R. J. Meyers y J. S. Tonigan. 1999. "Engaging the unmotivated in treatment for alcohol problems: A comparison of three intervention strategies". *Journal of Consulting and Clinical Psychology* 67, N°. 5:688-97.

Nowinski, J. K. 1998. *"Family recovery and substance abuse: A twelve-step guide for treatment"*. Thousand Oaks, Calif.: Sage Publications.

Índice

V

Acerca de los autores

El Dr. Robert J. Meyers es profesor asociado de investigación en psicología de la Universidad de Nuevo México. También es director asociado del LifeLink Training Institute en Sante Fe, Nuevo México. El Dr. Meyers ha trabajado en el campo del consumo de drogas durante más de veintisiete años y ha publicado varios libros y docenas de artículos al respecto. Es reconocido por sus capacitaciones y talleres carismáticos acerca de temas diversos. Es uno de los padres del Community Reinforcement Approach (CRA, Enfoque de refuerzo comunitario) para el tratamiento ambulatorio de pacientes y el creador de la Community Reinforcement and Family Training (CRAFT, Refuerzo comunitario y capacitación familiar).

La Dra. Brenda L. Wolfe es piscóloga clínica. Además de su consultorio privado, la Dra. Wolfe participa en investigación colaborativa en la Universidad de Nuevo México, se desempeña como consultora corporativa para el desarrollo de servicios basados en la psicología y forma parte de varias organizaciones profesionales. Sus libros y artículos han aparecido tanto en medios de consumo popular como profesionales.

Acerca de Hazelden Publishing

Como parte de la Hazelden Betty Ford Foundation, Hazelden Publishing ofrece recursos educativos de punta y libros inspiracionales. Nuestros trabajos impresos y digitales ayudan a guiar a las personas en tratamiento y recuperación, así como a sus seres queridos. Los profesionales que trabajan para prevenir y tratar las adicciones también encuentran en Hazelden Publishing programas escolares basados en evidencia, soluciones de contenido digital y videos para el uso en escuelas, programas de tratamiento, programas correccionales y sistemas de registros médicos electrónicos. También ofrecemos capacitación para la implementación de nuestros programas escolares.

Mediante sus trabajos publicados y digitales, Hazelden Publishing extiende la sanación y la esperanza a las personas, las familias y las comunidades afectadas por la adicción y los problemas relacionados con ella.